EARLY PENNSYLVANIA
ARTS AND CRAFTS

OTHER BOOKS BY JOHN JOSEPH STOUDT

*Consider the Lilies, How They Grow—An Interpretation of the Symbolism
   of Pennsylvania German Art*
Jacob Boehme's "The Way to Christ" in Modern Translation
Pennsylvania Folk Art—An Interpretation
Pennsylvania German Poetry: 1685–1830
Private Devotions for Home and Church
Sunrise to Eternity—A Study in Jacob Boehme's Life and Thought
Devotions and Prayers of Johann Arndt
*Caspar Schwenkfeld von Ossig's "Passional and Prayerbook" in Modern
   Translation*
Ephrata—A History (With James Ernst)
Ordeal at Valley Forge

EARLY PENNSYLVANIA
ARTS AND CRAFTS

By

John Joseph Stoudt

With a Foreword by
S. K. Stevens
Executive Director
Pennsylvania Historical and Museum Commission

SOUTH BRUNSWICK
NEW YORK: A.S. BARNES and COMPANY, INC.
LONDON: THOMAS YOSELOFF LTD

Library of Congress Catalogue Card Number: 64-21360

A.S. Barnes and Company, Inc.
Cranbury, New Jersey 08512

Thomas Yoseloff Ltd
108 New Bond Street
London W1Y OQX, England

SBN: 498 06061 6
Printed in the United States of America

To
The Theological Faculty,
Phillips University, Marburg,
With Deep Admiration and Gratitude.

FOREWORD

Pennsylvania's cultural heritage is a magnificently rich one, but it is only within this century that we have rediscovered and grown to revere its splendid diversity. Early historians loudly proclaimed the "flowering of New England," forgetting that while that region's writers were defining culture in their own terms, Pennsylvania's artists and craftsmen were quietly at work developing a tradition strongly reflecting their own prosperous colony and state.

Pennsylvania's traditions are polygonal, representing a collage of many national groupings—English, Scots, Swedes, and Germans are just a few of those represented. Set against a typically American background, their old world cultures have been fused and edited to create our Pennsylvania inheritance.

The "plain people," especially the Amish, are the group most Americans first associate with the phrase "Pennsylvania culture," but these sects represent only one aspect of our state's distinctive character.

Our artists and craftsmen working in the eighteenth and early nineteenth centuries created a tradition of beauty representing every level of cultural taste from the most earthy primitive to the starchiest academic. Pennsylvania has given life to scores of anonymous folk painters whose strongly patterned work helped satisfy the average person's craving for beauty; we nurtured the Moravian artist Valentine Haidt, and one of our colonial citizens, Benjamin West, was elevated to the presidency of England's exclusive Royal Academy.

Country cabinet makers produced utilitarian but brightly painted German-influenced furniture at the same time that the Bachmans of Lancaster and the Saverys and Afflects of Philadelphia were creating their great masterpieces of Chippendale design. Craftsmen-builders constructed prosaic cottages, like the Morton house, reproduced old world interiors as represented by the Mueller rooms now in the Philadelphia Museum of Art, and created sophisticated examples of eighteenth- and nineteenth-century design typified by Hope Lodge and the Second Bank of the United States. Pennsylvania's potters produced redware and common salt glaze pottery, but they could also rise to the excellence of Tucker porcelain.

This diversity, which is the keystone of the uniqueness that is Pennsylvania, can be pointed up in discussing any category among our artifacts.

In *Early Pennsylvania Arts and Crafts,* John Joseph Stoudt emphasizes the broad base

7

of our culture by bringing to focus the knowledge and talents he has acquired from a lifetime of studying and writing about Pennsylvania.

Not a catalog of Pennsylvania's artifact tradition, this volume is an interpretive work that examines our artisans' productions not as mere objects but as expressions of our over-all culture. Unique in its completeness, *Early Pennsylvania Arts and Crafts* does not limit itself to one or two categories, say glass or wood craft, as do most works, but it attempts to include the entire spectrum of our artistic heritage and give the reader a new respect for the quality and massiveness of the production of generations of Pennsylvania artisans.

S. K. Stevens, Executive Director
Pennsylvania Historical and Museum Commission

PREFACE

The purpose of this book is to explain the cultural and historical meaning of the arts and crafts made in Pennsylvania from its founding in the 1680s to the coming of the industrial revolution. We shall of course picture these pieces, but our ultimate purpose is to suggest that these tangible things were products of the human imagination and so illuminate the spirit of the people who made them.

Culture is a form of spirit. As the philosopher Heidegger has said: what a man seeks he makes and what a man makes shows what he thinks and believes. A portrait reveals not only an artist's style but also the subject's self-consciousness; a pewter chalice bears both form and faith; and a birth certificate has symbolic designs as well as record of belief. The objects which we collect, and which are so admired, are then more than lovely bits of decoration; they are keys which unlock the spirit of those who made them and of those who have used them.

However, those of us who, living in a time when man is straining to fly to the moon, share this enthusiasm for early American culture need no longer apologize for this interest. Now we know that early America was neither drab nor empty of charm, nor void of the comforting pleasures of eye more often associated with older cultures. Although the frontier was then still quite evident, eighteenth-century Pennsylvania knew a somewhat plain graciousness which lifted this province above the level of humdrum awkardness.

During the seventeenth century, American culture belonged to New England and to the southern lands; in the eighteenth century the focus was upon Pennsylvania. Here much meaningful history unfolded; and here too, due to the peculiar conditions of its founding, much creative work was done. In the broadest sense we may perhaps say that here western man found both freedom of spirit and vast fertile lands, twin needs in his search for cultural self-expression. It was not accident that Philadelphia became capital of a new nation; the cultural forms made in "the city"—as Philadelphia still is known to the people of the hinterland—were creative and they were early subjects of study. Her architecture, art, and history have attracted much attention and her cultural achievements often have been described. Now that the crust of years is being pealed off, "the city" is having a new birth, a movement which is spreading to provincial towns as well.

We propose to describe the culture of all of Pennsylvania, city and hinterland, for while

Philadelphia has been known for her culture the up-country areas only lately have come to be appreciated. We can remember when the Pennsylvania Germans were the "dumb Dutch" without a golden touch, before exploiters and promoters had distorted the popular image. Now the Pennsylvania Dutch are somewhat better known although more often through misconceptions like "hex signs," Amish "blue gates," the outlandish distelfink and the silly "button wont bell, please bump."

The first collectors of up-country things were lonely souls. Among these was Samuel W. Pennypacker, former governor of the Commonwealth, whose enthusiasm was so broad and eclectic that many of the pieces now exhibited in museums were first seen in his collection. Henry Chapman Mercer put together his comprehensive collections of tools, and at the turn of the century he was already writing about iron stove-plates which projected the Bible in iron. Edwin Atlee Barber discovered up-country ceramics and his work, which he called *Tulipware,* published in 1903, is still standard. In 1914 Frederick W. Hunter brought out the work on Stiegel glass which called attention to this craft. Several early articles in the *Saturday Evening Post* by Edwin LeFevre and the discovery by Esther Stevens Brazer of the Jonestown school of chest painters called attention to the newly-exhibited deForrest collection in the Metropolitan Museum of Art in New York.

The first representative showing of up-country arts and crafts was in 1926 in the Pennsylvania building at the Sesqui-Centennial Exposition in Philadelphia. This was gathered together by John Baer Stoudt. He felt that this exposition was even more significant than his gathering of the "liberty bells" of interior Pennsylvania. Many of the pieces now being exhibited in the museums were first displayed there.

By 1930, perhaps because of this stimulus, interest in up-country pieces began to match that shown in the work of the brilliant Philadelphia craftsmen. In 1937 the Pennsylvania German Folklore Society published my *Consider the Lilies, How they Grow—An Interpretation of the Symbolism of Pennsylvania German Art.* Here I tried to show that the meaning of this art was to be found in the religious literature of the Pennsylvania German people. In this same year the Pennsylvania German Society brought out Henry Borneman's *Illuminated Manuscripts,* a lavishly printed work in which brilliant color reproductions showed the color-richness of these pieces. During this period two public exhibitions drew further attention—the rooms in the Metropolitan Museum and the rooms from the Mühlbach house in the Philadelphia Museum of Art. Other scattered exhibitions were also on display.

Meanwhile a second generation of enthusiasts for up-country pieces was beginning to assemble the great collections which now are for the most part in the public domain. The Schwenkfelder Library quietly gathered what is unquestionably the finest collection of illuminated writings. Henry Francis duPont was making his magnificent Winterthur Museum and Titus Geesey was collecting avidly. George and Henry Landis were putting together much of the exhibition which now comprises the Pennsylvania Farm Museum at Landis Valley. J. Stodgell Stokes, George Horace Lorimer, Mrs. Ralph Beaver Strassburger, Levi Yoder, and Arthur Sussell, among others, were assembling pieces; and Henry Borneman's collection, now in the Free Library of Philadelphia, was growing. The German Government ordered a comprehensive collection made, and New York merchants catered to a sophisticated interest in "primitives" which stimulated some students.

Interest in Pennsylvania folk art now is international. The opening of the American Museum in Britain at Claverton Manor, Bath, with its fine collections of Philadelphia pewter, Stiegel glass, painted tin and the two stunning rooms of Pennsylvania Dutch stuff—not to mention the fine Philadelphia high-boy which Henry duPont gave—is a piece of historical justice. Here at this famous eighteenth-century spa, where the aristocracy of Georgian Britain lolled away their leisure hours, the arts and crafts of the crude Colonials—Philadelphia provincials and up-country "boors"—are now the center of attention.

These many fine collections on public display, magnificent replicas like Pennsbury, restorations like Hope Lodge, Ephrata, Harmony and Graeme Park go to show that the cultural objects of early Pennsylvania have made deep impact on the popular consciousness. Indeed, interest in our arts and crafts now is high in Germany too, and while American Museums vie with each other to get representative pieces, slips of gaudily-decorated paper have become treasures of metropolitan libraries. The popular interest is thus becoming ever more expansive, and while Pennsylvania craft art is certainly not America's only folk art it is surely the best known.

So in a short quarter of a century the arts and crafts of early Pennsylvania, city as well as country, have established the creativity of this Commonwealth. No other American region did better work, for the brilliant Philadelphia cabinetmakers and silversmiths were joined by their up-country neighbors to make cultural forms as fine as anything in the new world. One distinguished British art historian has said that he adores Pennsylvania folk art and a learned folklorist in Germany has asserted that our art bears international rather than provincial significance.

Greater than this widening interest in the objects has been the deepening of the understanding of what they mean. Years ago the common floral motif was simply a tulip, and the student was referred to the tulpo-mania of seventeenth-century Holland. My books tried to show that up-country designs came from the religious culture of the Pennsylvania German sects and that they took inspiration, if not actual imagery, from our religious poetry.

These books evoked controversy. Many persons refuse to believe that Pennsylvania folk art is symbolic. However, several European authorities, including the director of the *Institut für Mitteleuropäische Volksforschung* at Marburg, see Pennsylvania illuminated manuscripts as the link between European folk art and the religious poetry of the baroque.

May I here re-state the two presuppositions on which my point of view rests. First, these designs take meaning from the culture which surrounded them, and they are related to other cultural forms like religious poetry, folklore and religious literature. Secondly, these designs are not representational copies of natural objects nor do they try to show us what natural flowers look like. As with the popular arts of the orient they show designs, taken from nature, which express a meaning deeply grounded in the human spirit.

Donald A. Shelley has defined folk art as "representing a group tradition, rather than individual accomplishment." How true! However, we shall not spend energy tracking down the identity of individual artists but we shall try to relate the meaning of this folk art to his group tradition. The phrase "group tradition" is vague. The shared culture of the Pennsylvania Germans, however, is not; it is a well-known historical phenomenon which was expressed in folk art as well as in other cultural media. All Pennsylvania art was an expression of the spirit of the people who made it for style is really an order of thought which is expressed in culture because it is the movement, rhythm, symmetry and *Geist* which makes pieces flow together, giving them unity and lithe vitality. And, as far as folk art is concerned, style is a shared spirit which expresses itself in similar forms.

Just as interest in collecting Pennsylvania arts and crafts has grown so too has awareness of what they mean. Although the general lines of meaning now are becoming clear, we have to say that not all answers nor all designs are known. For example, the celebrated *Vorschrift* made in 1801 by the Reverend George Geistweite, which is a thesaurus of motifs, has several designs on it which are not yet clear as to meaning. However, we do believe that the point of view which sees traditional Christian symbols expressed in both Pennsylvania sectarian hymnody and in Pennsylvania folk art will in the end prove correct, and the folk arts and crafts of piedmont Pennsylvania will come to be recognized as a sincere expression of the people who made them.

John Joseph Stoudt

ACKNOWLEDGMENTS

Among the many individuals who have helped us to understand Pennsylvania arts and crafts none has been more generous and sympathetic than the dean of collectors of American decorative arts, Henry Francis duPont. Likewise, Titus Geesey, snapper-up of the best pieces of Pennsylvania craft decoration, has been most kind. Andrew Berky, Director of the Schwenkfelder Library and custodian of its fine collection of illuminated writings, has been helpful. Gerhard Heilfurth, Eric de Jonge and August Closs have aided in interpretation. The following persons have allowed use of their pieces: Joe Kindig, Jr., Philip F. Cowan, John Y. Kohl, George Horace Lorimer, Daniel M. Yost II, Robert L. Schaeffer, Robert L. Schaffer, Jr., William W. Swallow, A. K. Hostetter, Mrs. Vernon K. Melhado, Arthur J. Sussel, J. Stodgell Stokes, Mrs. Ralph Beaver Strassburger, Gertrude Rittenhouse, Paul J. deLong, Elizabeth deLong Stoudt, Kirke Bryan, Howard J. Fretz, Helen S. Johnson, Edward W. Schlechter, Oliver Lewis Christman, P. M. Vogt. The drawing which Eleanor Barba made of the Stauffer *Webkämme* was used for a color plate. Others who have been helpful have been: Stuart Bolger, Arthur D. Graeff, Kenneth J. Hamilton, Frank J. Schmidt.

The following organizations have cooperated in supplying information or in allowing their pieces to be illustrated: The Pennsylvania Historical and Museum Commission, which has supplied photographs of its many properties herein illustrated; the Board of Elders of the Northern Diocese of the Church of the United Brethren in the United States of America, which through Bishop Kenneth J. Hamilton has granted permission to reproduce the copyrighted paintings of Johann Valentin Haidt; Universal Atlas Cement, a Division of United States Steel Corporation, which has supplied a photograph of the Wilson Block House still standing on its property; the Whitman Chocolate Company, which has allowed several of its samplers to be illustrated; Independence National Historical Park, a branch of the Department of the Interior which has allowed use of its collection of photographs; and the Index of American Design in the National Gallery, Washington.

The following museums and their kind directors have been helpful: The Philadelphia Museum of Art, and Henri Marceau who allowed the photograph files to be rifled and their collections reproduced without limit; the Henry Francis duPont Winterthur Museum and John Sweeney, The Yale University Art Gallery, especially the Lelia A. and John Hill Morgan Collection; the Fogg Museum of Harvard University; the American Museum in

Great Britain, and Dallas Pratt; the Music Division of the Library of Congress, where the two great Ephrata manuscripts are housed; the Landis Valley Farm Museum; the Barnes Foundation in Merion; the Metropolitan Museum of Art in New York; the Kemmerer Museum in Bethlehem; the Rare Book Room of the Free Library of Philadelphia; and the Frick Art Reference Library in New York.

The following historical societies and libraries are to be thanked: The Pennsylvania State Library, the Historical Society of Pennsylvania, the New-York Historical Society in New York City, the Historical Society of the Reformed Church in the United States, the Historical Society of Berks County, the Historical Society of Bucks County, the Historical Society of Montgomery County, the Historical Society of York County, the Historical and Geneological Society of Northampton County, the Franklin and Marshall College Library, the Library of the American Philosophical Society, the Library of the German Society of Pennsylvania, and the Carl Schurz Memorial Foundation.

Photographic help has come from: John Kubil, Karl F. Lutz, Guy Reinert, Relix Reichmann, Titus Geesey, Larry Burns, Carl Rath, Owen C. Stout, J. Richard Thorne, Mel Horst, and Stuart Dewson. A. J. Wyatt, staff photographer for the Philadelphia Museum of Art, has allowed free use of his prints. Some of the photographs were in my father's notes from older photographers like Henry Chapman Mercer, W. W. Dietrich and some were his own shots. However, my college classmate, William B. Daub, has been most considerate in his help, taking great pains and time to photograph difficult pieces.

Special thanks are due to the Directors of the Pennsylvania German Society and to the Publication Committee of the Pennsylvania German Folklore Society for permission to use color plates which they own.

Then my publisher, Thomas Yoseloff, has been more than helpful; he has been enthusiastic and willing to back enthusiasm with more tangible evidences of his interest.

To my father, John Baer Stoudt, I am in increasing obligation. It was his vision, his imagination, which saw the significance of Pennsylvania arts and crafts. At a time when no one else shared that vision he communicated to me the meaning of our art. From him I learned to appreciate the culture of my own people and to see what it means for American history.

And then there is my wife. What a bore I must be to her. This book is, in a sense a token both of her patience and love. And to Johnny, my deep apologies. You need your father too, and this book has robbed you of attention you should have had.

CONTENTS

Vorschrift: "**For the Best Singer in the Second Class.**"
(Courtesy the Rare Book Room, Philadelphia Free Library, and the Pennsylvania German Society.)

Decorated Lehigh County Barn.

Portrait of George Washington by Andrew Schultz.
(Courtesy Schwenkfelder Library: Photo by William B. Daub.)

Drawing Room, Mayor Powel's House, Philadelphia. This room, now restored, saw George Washington and other notables of Colonial and Federal Philadelphia gather in the great days of the Eighteenth Century.
(Courtesy Philadelphia Society for the Preservation of Landmarks.)

Decorated Clock Case, Nineteenth Century, painted in the Mahantongo Valley.
(Courtesy The Philadelphia Museum of Art, Geesey Collection.)

The Waynesboro Teapot.
(Courtesy Mr. Wayne Kindig, Jr.)

Corner of Mary Ott's Coverlet. These pieces were woven on looms which itinerant weavers carted from farm to farm.
(Courtesy of the Historical Society of Montgomery County.)

Painted Tinware. This craft was plied throughout the Eastern States in early and mid-Nineteenth Century.

Pennsylvania Pottery. Ceramic ware came in many forms and colors. Only the unusual piece was decorated or otherwise molded.

(Courtesy Mr. Titus Geesey.)

Ceramic Toys. Among the rarest pieces of the potter's art are toys, mostly bird whistles.

(Courtesy Mr. Titus Geesey.)

American Glass Group. (left to right) Sugar Bowl, late Eighteenth Century, attributed to Wistarberg, N. J.; Goblet, by John Frederick Amelung, New Bremen, Md., 1793; Sugar Bowl, attributed to glassworks of Henry William Stiegel, Manheim, Pa., ca. 1765-1774; Pitcher with "lily pad" decoration, ca. 1840-1860.
(Courtesy the Corning Museum of Glass.)

Collection of Stiegel Glass.
(Courtesy of Hershey Museum, Hershey, Pa.)

Self-Portrait of John Meng, Germantown.
(Courtesy the Historical Society of Pennsylvania.)

Carolina Elisabeth Baum's Birth Certificate. From Dauphin County.
(Courtesy the Rare Book Room, Philadelphia Free Library, and the Pennsylvania German Society.)

Esther Bechtel's Book Plate.
*(Courtesy the Rare Book Room, Philadelphia Free Library, and
the Pennsylvania German Society.)*

Anna Stauffer's Book Plate.
*(Courtesy the Rare Book Room, Philadelphia Free Library, and
the Pennsylvania German Society.)*

Catherine Guth's Book Plate.
(Courtesy the Rare Book Room, Philadelphia Free Library, and the Pennsylvania German Society.)

Vorschrift: Susanna Hübner.
(Courtesy the Rare Book Room, Philadelphia Free Library, and the Pennsylvania German Society.)

Book Mark.
(Courtesy Rare Book Room, Philadelphia Free Library, and the Pennsylvania German Society.)

Jacob Bick's House Blessing.
(Courtesy the Rare Book Room, Philadelphia Free Library, and the Pennsylvania German Society.)

INTRODUCTION

1.

Early Pennsylvania art was as diversified as its inhabitants. Variety of geography, people, and tradition made for cultural heterogeneity which moved from log cabin to Georgian mansion, from elegantly classical Philadelphia furniture to awkward back-country pieces, from mystical calligraphy at Ephrata to naturalistic realism with John James Audubon, from Chinese Chippendale to Germanic *schank,* from paintings by a Quaker who became president of the Royal Academy in London to anonymous folk portraits, from exquisitely wrought silver to earthenware pottery, and from the most delicately cut-out valentines to crude scribblings—a rich, varied expression of human creativity.

In early Pennsylvania, as in Europe, this was a time of rich contradiction. The age of reason was reflected in the conversation of Philadelphia coffee houses also visited by red men of the forests. Cultured dandies like Sir William Keith dressed in latest London fashions, with powdered periwigs and frilly laces, while plain Quakers and Mennonites mingled with buckskin-wearing frontiersmen. Philadelphia knew both the religious fanaticism of a man like Matthias Baumann of Oley, who offered to walk across the Delaware to prove his doctrine true, and the deist liberalism of Thomas Jefferson. Philistine and revolutionary, tory and patriot, anglophile and anglophobe rubbed elbows in a land inhabited by Swedes, Dutch, English, Welsh, Germans, French Huguenots, Scotch-Irish, Delawares, and Susquehannocks. Moreover, this was the age of liberation: of the middle classes from feudalism, of philosophy from theology, of America from Britain and of the American worker from the restrictions of European guilds. This was a time when the handicrafts reached their zenith; for the industrial revolution was advancing and soon it would overwhelm human creativity with the monotony of repetitive acts.

Like other American colonies, Pennsylvania stood between old world and new. Here too was the invigorating challenge of the American frontier. Here European man faced the cultural forces which were making the transition from feudalism to democracy, from serfdom to middle-class society. Under the pressures of this new land—and surely in the hope of its rich new promise—the cultural revolution which the eighteenth century was producing moved to its inevitable conclusion. When the century opened, Philadelphia was a small tidewater village more closely linked to the old world than to the vast new continent before it. When the century closed, Philadelphia was capital of a new nation where accredited ambassadors from old world empires mingled with frontiersmen. Fertile, vast, and blessedly free, Pennsylvania was destined to become keystone in the arch of American states; and her long valleys, pointing deep into interior America, became highways to the frontier.

When their colonial containment had been broken, New England Yankees took to the sea, setting out in speedy clippers for China's silks and South sea whales. Meanwhile, Pennsylvania farmers were casting hungry glances down the long Appalachian valleys to rich new acres waiting for their ploughs. While Yankees sailed their clippers to China, Pennsylvanians drove their Conestogas—"ships of inland commerce," Dr. Benjamin Rush called them—deep into the American interior, and wheat harvested as far as Winchester, Virginia, was milled in Pennsylvania and shipped to the West Indies.

Although hinterland and port areas were thus joined, there was still cultural cleavage. While the distinction between frontier and stable tidewater cultures is well known, little seems to be understood about the cultural differences which separated tidewater from piedmont. Geographically the tidewater area in Pennsylvania is quite small, limited to the area below the fall line of the Delaware at Trenton. No great bays stab deep into the interior, highways by which European ships might bring old world things close to the heart of the new. The broad Susquehanna, which traverses the commonwealth and penetrates deep into the hinterland, is navigable nowhere within its borders. Like the rivers, roads to the hinterland were also poor. So carriage of bulky articles from tidewater ports to piedmont interior was difficult.

Geography thus divided early Pennsylvania into three areas: tidewater, the piedmont which extended from this fall line to the first range of the Appalachians, and the transmountain frontier. Before the American Revolution the Blue Mountains, which arch across the south-eastern third of the commonwealth, were the wall of civilization, separating piedmont from frontier. Now we are beginning to understand the equally significant line which separated piedmont from tidewater.

Ever since Frederick Jackson Turner advanced his views on the significance of the frontier in American life, they have evoked controversy. He suggested that the frontier absorbed rebellious non-conforming persons, allowing escape from restricting social conditions into an area where freer, deeper passions could be expressed. Turner's orientation was to the midwestern nineteenth-century frontier.

May we suggest that, at least during the eighteenth century, there was in Pennsylvania, and perhaps also in the other colonies, an equally significant cultural division, paralleling the geographical, between tidewater and piedmont. For in between port and mountainous areas lay a region which, at least in Pennsylvania, was a culturally significant melting-pot where new values were emerging and where new forms were being made.

This is no new idea. Rather it was first broached by an astute observer of the American scene, Crèvecoeur, who, in an illuminating passage from the famous third chapter of *Letters From an American Farmer,* noted that piedmont farmers were another breed different from both tidewater merchant and frontiersmen. His words bear quotation:

Those who live near the sea . . . [are] more bold and enterprising; this leads them to neglect the confined occupations of the land. They see and converse with a variety of people, their intercourse with mankind becomes extensive. The sea inspires them with a love of traffic, a desire of transporting produce from one place to another; and leads them to a variety of resources which supply the place of labour. Those who inhabit the middle settlements, by far the most numerous, must be very different; the simple cultivation of the earth purifies them, but the indulgences of the government, the soft remonstrances of religion, the rank of independent freeholders, must necessarily inspire them with sentiments, very little known in Europe among people of the same class. . . Europe has no such class of men; the early knowledge they acquire, the early bargains they make, give them a great deal of sagacity. As freemen they will be litigious; pride and obstinacy are often the cause of law suits. . . As citizens . . . they will carefully read the newspapers, enter into every political discussion, freely blame or censure governors or others. As farmers they will be careful and anxious to get as much as they can, because what they get is their own. . . As Christians, religion curbs them not in their opinions; the general indulgence leaves everyone to think for themselves in spiritual matters. . . Industry, good living, selfishness, litigiousness, country politics, the pride of freemen, religious indifference, are the characterstics. If you recede still farther from the sea, you will come into more modern settlements; they exhibit the same strong lineaments, in ruder appearance.

These words, rich in insight, from a competent contemporary observer suggest that the "middle settlements" in the Pennsylvania piedmont were the place where new cultural forms were emerging.

So we may perhaps say that an indigenous culture was coming forth in the Pennsylvania piedmont where values and forms were appearing which were new creations. Moreover, the Pennsylvania piedmont was chiefly settled by Germans. Germanic settlement had of course started in Germantown under Francis Daniel Pastorius and had moved from thence to Skippack and even to Falckner Swamp. The Swedes had settled far up the Schuylkill.

However, it is historically inaccurate to assume that the Pennsylvania piedmont was settled by immigrants overflowing through the port of Philadelphia. This was not the case. The fertile interior valleys were first settled by Germans who had entered America through New York where they had lived in the Schoharie region. From there they came down to Oley, Maxatawney, Pequea and Tulpehocken. These settlers, sometimes called "Kocherthal Colonists" after their leader, formed a rich resevoir of fresh settlers who, despairing of life in New York, came to the fertile limestone bottoms of Pennsylvania. As early as 1712 Jacob Stauber (forbear of President Eisenhower's mother, now spelled Stover) was in Oley, Berks, and in 1729 he was in Virginia. By 1720 the main interior valleys were settled, not by Germans overflowing from the City, but by rugged pioneers who had come down from New York, attracted by the fertility of Pennsylvania. These people, German and Huguenot, formed an independent self-reliant group in interior Pennsylvania and as early as 1720 were petitioning for roads to join their settlements to tidewater. At this time settlement in Lancaster was just beginning to become firm.

Between Philadelphia and the mountains lay the great piedmont valleys which curve down across eastern America from New England to Georgia; and by 1720 these valleys were already settled by a land-hungry people. The area was a "fertile crescent" which was to become the highway to interior America. These settlers soon were joined by wave after wave of immigrants who entered America through the port of Philadelphia. By 1750 settlement of the piedmont was almost complete.

Thus Pennsylvania settlement came to be regionalized. Germans were original settlers in a land area just about as large as the Colonies of Massachusetts, Connecticut, and Rhode Island together, even spilling over into the western areas of some southern Colonies. These Pennsylvania piedmont settlers spoke their own language, preferred certain types of soil, and worshipped in their own ways. The line which Marcus Lambert drew defining the areas where the Pennsylvania Dutch dialect is spoken can be superimposed on the area where limestone soil is to be found; thus we see the truth of the saying that if you are standing on limestone soil and speak Pennsylvania Dutch you will be answered in the same dialect. Not only did Germans choose these soils for settlement; they brought their own languages, customs and religions—the area which William J. Hinke defined as containing German Reformed Congregations before 1750 is approximately the same as the limestone area.

Examination of the American population as recorded in the 1790 Census, by means of linguistic techniques, shows that of a total Caucasian population 60.9 per cent were English, 14.3 per cent Scotch-Irish and Ulsterites, 8.7 per cent German, 5.4 per cent French and Swedish, 3.7 per cent southern Irish and 7 per cent unassignable. At the height of the German and the start of the Scotch-Irish migration the Reverend William Smith estimated that there were 220,000 persons in Pennsylvania of whom about one-third (73,000) were Germans, two-fifths (88,000) Quakers and one-fifth (44,000) Scotch-Irish. Linguistic methods of analysis do not recognize the Jaegers who became Hunters, Schmidts who became Smiths, Hochs who became Highs, Tonelliers who became Coopers, Vaudrins who became Woodrings, and Staubers who became Stovers. Nor does this method count the large Huguenot element that spoke German, was partly of Alsatian origin, and was submerged within the Pennsylvania German population.

Most estimates, divide the Pennsylvania population around 1770 into thirds: one-third Quaker and English living chiefly in Philadelphia; one-third German living mainly in the piedmont; and one-third Scotch-Irish living in the main beyond the mountains. Isaac Sharpless estimated the Quaker element in both Pennsylvania and Maryland at the outbreak of the Revolution to be no more than 20,000, leaving over 50,000 non-Quaker Anglo-Saxons. Germans were variously estimated at from 100,000 to 130,000, perhaps higher, and Scotch-Irish in an equal if not slightly larger number. German-speaking inhabitants of Pennsylvania were therefore outnumbered two-to-one.

Not all Quakers lived in tidewater nor did all Germans dwell in the piedmont. However, Philadelphia Germans soon became part of the metropolitain culture; the German Society of Pennsylvania was predominately a city organization whose aim was to help newly-arrived settlers. So too Quakers who lived far from the City, like those in the Exeter and Maiden Creek Meetings, soon acquired the cultural traits of their neighbors with whom they sometimes intermarried, contrary to prevailing Quaker practice.

Now, if early Pennsylvania was thus cut up by geography into three regions, settled by three different ethnic groups, then it is clear that each region would produce a different cultural pattern.

So, as Crèvecoeur saw, three cultural patterns were evolving in early Pennsylvania. During the first half-century the plain mood dominated the city itself and there was curious mixing of Quaker plainness with European elegance. After 1750, however, this changed. More and more the elegance of Europe was reflected in what was being made in the city and plain Quaker merchant was becoming a rich business man through continuing—and highly profitable—trade with Europe. After the Revolution this plain mood dominated the piedmont region from whence it was carried into interior America. Here in the piedmont true American styles were being made, hybrid mixtures of elegant and plain out of which new forms were to come.

The elegant cultural mode came to brilliant expression in the merchant-craftsmen of Philadelphia after 1750, especially in the cabinetmakers; although surely the elegance of the silversmiths was clear from the start. These workmen looked to Europe—to London, Paris, Greece, Rome, and even to China—rather than to Lancaster and Bethlehem. Theirs was an international taste, a world of high fashion in which the overwhelming influence of the era of Louis XIV on politics, society, literature, and culture was obvious. The Italian baroque had been frenchified by LeBrun and LePoutre to make the style known as Louis Quatorze, sometimes also called rococo, which was to melt into Louis Seize and eventually into Regency and Empire. In American tidewater furniture this meant expensive imported woods, slavish imitation of Chippendale and other European style-setters, superficial and even rococo decoration, and magnificent symmetry—on the whole a style more imitative of Europe than America.

The "plain" cultural mode was an American creation. It was, to some degree at least, conscious reaction against the effete elegance of the rococo; for especially among our plain sects there was reaction against the elegant as worldly and linked to corrupt culture. It also was heir of German peasant culture. Yet it was far from primitive, and, in the field of furniture, it showed good form and symmetry, and excellent workmanship, employing mostly native woods. So in early Pennsylvania we must distinguish among elegant, plain and primitive, for the plain was a style with its own roots and rationale.

Common to all regions, the primitive mode was ephemeral. It was simply the first stage in cultural adjustment to the frontier, and so it was soon outgrown as the environment matured and expanded. As the frontier receded and as piedmont culture developed, new stability was won which showed itself as something different from European ways. A new synthesis had come which joined what had been brought from the old world with what was needed to live in the new; and so, like the American himself, whom Crevecoeur described, the American style took basically European stuff and changed it for use in the new world.

Tidewater America, then, where old world styles were being imitated, was not the place where American culture was made. Rather it was the piedmont where inherited imported cultural modes faced the frontier and cultural gestation took place. The frontier was itself accultural for culture needs some stability for forms to be created. It was in truth the piedmont craftsmen who, facing the interior of the continent, began to make those styles which were to develop into the American plain.

Surely new cultural values emerged in piedmont areas, new freedoms, new forms. We should not isolate these piedmont settlements, as H. B. Parkes does in *The American Experience*, by saying that for generations these German communities remained almost isolated from American life around them. Far from being isolated, the Pennsylvania piedmont was the highway to the West, leading down the Shenandoah and over the hills into Kentucky, a trail which a son of the Pennsylvania piedmont, Daniel Boone, blazed. Just as the Scotch-Irish, passing through the German settlements, took the log cabin with them, making it the mark of the frontier, so other cultural forms escaped into the expanding American West to become the things out of which our American culture was to evolve.

2.

By thus saying that the Pennsylvania piedmont was not only different from tidewater in culture and spirit, by thus implying that different cultural modes arose, we are led to assert that the Quaker mood of early Philadelphia and the Pietism of the German piedmont were influential aesthetic forms.

The mood which Quakerism and Pietism created has been called "plain." This was a consciously chosen way of life in rebellion against the artificial world of elegant fashion then coming from feudal society. Both Quaker and Pietist rejected "the world," meaning high society. The gray garb of Quaker, the broad-brimmed and undoffed hat, Moravian bonnets, and Amish buttonless cloaks were outer evidences of inner revolt against a world of laces, periwigs, and decadent morals. During the first half of the eighteenth century this mood prevailed in Quaker-dominated Philadelphia, and the way of life it created was similar to that of the German Pietists.

This mood was anti-worldly in the sense that it rejected the fashions coming from the corrupt court at Versailles. It did not reject the natural world—the world which faced Quaker and Pietist in the American wilderness. The intense interest in natural science among Quakers like William Bartram and Pietists like George deBenneville, the deep seriousness about agriculture and above all the enthusiasm for the day-by-day tasks of conquering the natural environment, produced an interest in temporal matters which was different from traditional other-worldliness. For both Quaker and Pietist had gained new religious hope which separated their faith from the orthodox. Where traditional religion was seeking to win a place for man in a Kingdom in Heaven, the Pennsylvania sectarian was trying to build this kingdom on earth. New Englanders had been concerned about a safe life after death, as their vast sermonic literature on the subject shows; the Pennsylvania Quaker-Pietist was seeking to bring down the New Jerusalem to earth and to live out the full thousand years in peace. Puritans may have been building a theocratic order, but their final hope was to escape mortal existence in a safe and secure immortality.

This transformation of religious hope from the next world to this world, which marks both Quaker and Pietist, was the prerequisite for the tremendous development of arts and crafts in Pennsylvania as well as determinative for their style. For only when man devoutly seeks to build the new order on earth will he take pains to create serious cultural forms.

From this plain mood the future American spirit was to issue, a spirit which showed itself in Pennsylvania a full century before it appeared in New England transcendentalism. The American revolt against Calvinism had begun in Pennsylvania early in the eighteenth century, and although some historians may argue that the American renaissance first showed with Emerson and his circle, Parrington's judgment in *Main Currents in American Thought,* that the years between 1720 and 1763 were crucial for the forming of the American spirit, has to be considered. These decades, even in Europe, separated two worlds—before the middle of the eighteenth century the dominant mood had been aristocratic, looking backward to feudalism and medievalism. Tempered by a severe classicism, which took values from Greece and Rome, this mood was reflected in architecture, furniture, Wedgewood pottery, and other fashionable forms. After the middle of the century a new spirit began to show, one which was to take inspiration from the world around us and which was to look to the new age to come.

Pennsylvania sectarians, Quaker and Pietist, already had broken with that form of orthodoxy which denied, or minimized, the reality of the visible world. Thus Pennsylvania sectarianism distinguished itself from the Great Awakening; Jonathan Edwards had small hope for man in the world; and the Puritan was making his election sure, proving himself to be one of the chosen saints. Pietists were sure that God's kingdom was coming here, the thousand years of peace and plenty, and to support life in this great age they built rugged stone houses, sturdy furniture, and enduring forms to last out the age.

Of all American provinces Pennsylvania was unique in opportunity to build this new world. While Rhode Island was also a land of freedom, she had no vast virginal lands, fertile and lush, where this new age could emerge. Pennsylvania had both freedom and fertility. It was not hemmed in by close-minded Congregationalism on the one hand and by the sea on the other. Rather her broad valleys opened on a wide continent, a vast new wilderness which could be entered from the trails crossing Pennsylvania, highways by which cultural forms made in the piedmont were borne to the burgeoning West. Certain it is that the elegant forms of tidewater America did not penetrate deeply into interior America; rather they were transformed in the piedmont and so brought into the new world.

Moreover, there was no established church. Here all faiths were equal. Here was no Mather dynasty, no planter aristocracy, no group seeking to preserve the *status quo.* New England dissenters were invited to migrate; Puritanism was not for export. In Pennsylvania dissent piled on dissent, for already in 1760 one leader of Pennsylvania sectarianism wrote:

"In Pennsylvania we have many religious opinions, but only one religion—the Pennsylvania religion of 'go a little, give a little, live and let live.' " This did Johann Adam Gruber express the American spirit.

Historians of the spirit—from which, we contend, cultural forms derive—have found difference between the mystical aspirations of British dissent and those of American Pietism. The former had a deeper Quietist mood, and more subjective and more inclined to withdraw from society. During the first half-century of her history, while Quakers were in control of the holy experiment, Pennsylvania was nourished by this vitality for building a new world. The strains of doctrinaire views, especially an unrealistic interpretation of the doctrine of non-resistance and an equally romanticized attitude towards Indians, broke the Quaker hold on provincial affairs.

All this is important for the management of the natural world, for the development of the crafts, and for enjoyment of the arts. Here at the heart of religion those tastes arose which controlled what man made and what he enjoyed. The plain mood, which was expressed in Quakerism and Pietism, was, then, result of deliberate choice. It was, in fact, reaction. In place of pride and search for rank, title, and, nobility of birth the Pennsylvania dissenter wanted a world of egalitarian brotherhood—the familiar "thee," "thou" and *du.* In place of exclusiveness and elected sainthood, the universality of grace and the salvation of all. In place of a feudal society the "philadelphian" world. In place of excess, moderation. In place of laces and periwigs, plain clothes and cut hair. In place of the lewd theatre, Bible study. In place of witty salons, devout conventicles. In place of cathedrals, plain meeting houses. In place of loose morals, marital fidelity, and even the virginal life. In short, the Quaker-Pietist sought to replace the decadent elegant with the moral plain.

So, as tidewater elegance reflected the feudal world of Europe, Quaker and Pietist plain was linked to the egalitarian and philadelphian spirit which was emerging in piedmont America. The hope of a new social order rested in the core of the plain. This was clearly expressed by Daniel Falckner, an early Pietist, who wrote that Pennsylvania was

a country that supports its labors abundantly; there is plenty of food. What pleases me most is that one can be peasant, scholar, priest and nobleman at once without interference, which of all modes of living has been found to be the best and most satisfactory since patriarchial times. To be a peasant and nothing else, is a sort of animal life; to be a scholar, and nothing else, such as in Europe, is a morbid and self-indulgent existence; to be a priest and nothing else, ties life to blunders and responsibilities; to be a nobleman and nothing else, makes godless and riotous.

Ye Europeans . . . consider, unless you put off your soiled garments . . . you cannot enter the philadelphia which the Lord awakens . . . .

Here, indeed, was a new way of life, reflecting a new mood, which showed itself in the projection of simpler tastes and plainer aesthetic values. The strictness of Quakers in early Philadelphia is well-known; when children and servants stole a few apples they were billed as showing licentious liberty. Christmas mumming, horse-racing, and other sports were frowned upon. The fairs held annually after 1679 were avoided.

Already in 1697 the Philadelphia Yearly Meeting advised Friends to keep to plain apparel, to avoid "long-lapped sleeves or coats gathered at the sides or superfluous buttons, or broad ribbons about their hats or long curled periwigs." Excess in furniture and interior appointments was to be shunned. In 1711 the Chester Meeting expected its Overseers to see that there was no excessive drinking, swearing, cursing, lying; to see that there was no superfluity in apparel or furniture in all its branches; and to see that there was only plain scriptural language with the familiar "thee" and "thou."

While Quakers thus formulated opposition to elegance in formal disciplines, Pietists were less formal but equally strong. We dare not make the mistake of assuming that those Pennsylvania Germans who wore no plain clothes were the "gay" Dutch. Among Lutheran and Reformed church people there was also strong rebellion against elegance and while they wore no special garb they preferred plainness. Most denominational leaders, especially Lutheran, were Pietist in spirit and there was still puritan sentiment among the Reformed. Some groups were more strongly opposed to elegance than others, but in general the Germans of the piedmont, sectarian as well as church people, were firmly opposed to elegance in dress, furniture, and even decoration.

This plain tradition, firmly based on religion, has to be distinguished from the primitive which has no rationale. The former was, as we have said, deliberately arrived at and so produced plain forms from choice, made by skilled craftsmen who, had they so chosen, could have produced the elegant pieces of their city neighbors. The primitive mode was not the result of skill but of the lack of it.

Two plain periods emerged in early Pennsylvania: first, the period of the Quaker plain which lasted from the founding of the Commonwealth by Penn until the time when Quaker control ceased; second, the period from about 1760 to 1830 when the plain mood, coming from the sects, dominated the piedmont. Among Germans, with the exception of glass and stove-plates, most crafts were made after the Revolutionary War by the first or second American generations; they were new creations, not just memory arts and crafts or peasant ways transplanted to the new world. On the contrary these crafts were made within a fairly well-established land, products of a pre-industrial economy, based of course on European forms but nourished by the new values which Crèvecoeur saw coming out in the middle settlements.

This difference between elegant and plain was clear also in the arrangement of the houses. The traveller, Dr. Schoepff, who passed through Pennsylvania in 1783, said that the Pennsylvania Germans lived

. . . frugally, often badly. There is wanting among them the simple unaffected neatness of the English settlers, who make it a point, as far as they are able, to live seemly, in a well-furnished house in every way as comports the gentleman. The economy of the German farmer in Pennsylvania is precisely the same as that customary in Germany . . . A great four-cornered stove, a table in the corner with benches fastened to the wall, everything daubed with red, and above a shelf with the universal farmer's library: the Almamack and Song Book, a small German 'Garden of Paradise'. Habermann's and the Bible.

The *Garden of Paradise* was Johann Arndt's great devotional work and Habermann's was also a prayerbook. Note that the German table was not set in the center of the room, as in English houses, nor was the German room generally decorated. The crafted piece—chest, pie-plate, etc—was unusual.

This distinction between the Anglo-Saxon ideal of the gentleman, shared to a degree by Quakers, and the German peasant culture is basic for understanding early Pennsylvania art. The emerging middle-class culture reflected more those values from peasant culture than those issuing from aristocratic ideals like that of the "gentleman."

So we may, then, see that three spiritual points of view showed in early Pennsylvania: first was an orthodox one, a reflection of feudalism, that sought the elegant in art and the tory view in politics; second was a dissenting tradition, related to the emerging middle class view, related to the plain; and third there was primitivism on the frontier that was expressed in revivalism and was but passing substance on an over-receding and westward-moving frontier.

It was not just accident that the Quaker sectarian of early Philadelphia saw his sons enter Episcopal Churches again; nor was it accidental that the frontier was swept again and again by revivalism. The tory merchant of tidewater who lived in the city surrounded by Georgian and Chippendale pieces of imported mahogany and the frontiersman in his cabin living with the barest of axe-hewn appointments, are well-established figures on the American scene.

Less well-known, however, is the dissenter, living chiefly in the piedmont, and who we believe, was progenitor of the vast middle-class plainness that swept interior America. For was it not the piedmont where Europe met the new America and where those forms that were brought from the old world were made into things suitable for use in the new?

3.

If we thus suggest that geographically, culturally and spiritually Pennsylvania knew three modes, then we also shall have to assert that three socio-economic patterns also were apparent in these earlier years.

In tidewater appeared a mercantile-craft economy which was to develop into modern capitalism. In the piedmont appeared an agricultural-craft economy which was founded on the farm-craft villages of Europe. On the frontier, again, were rudiments of a barter economy. The distinction between merchant-craftsman and farmer-craftsman is, we believe, significant.

The socio-economic system which began to show in the Pennsylvania piedmont was neither a subsistence-level New England farm nor a southern slave-worked plantation. It was instead an integrated farm-craft pattern. Speaking of the piedmont Germans, Crèvecoeur said: "They have been a useful acquisition to the Continent, and to Pennsylvania in particular; to them it owes some of its prosperity, to their mechanical knowledge and patience it owes the finest mills in America, the best teams of horses, and many other advantages." By "mills" he means manufactures.

The Pennsylvania piedmont craftsman was first of all a farmer. He lived on his own land and farming was his main business. He also was a craftsman. However, the largest development of crafts was in gristmills for by the time of the American Revolution hundreds of them were flourishing along the Skippack, Perkiomen, Pequea, Conestoga, Codorus and Conewago, exporting flour to West Indian and European markets. By 1751 about 80,000 bushels of wheat were being exported, 100,000 barrels of flour were being milled, and 90,000 bushels of corn were being exported—a total grain export worth then over $1,000,000. Thus the agricultural basis was early established.

By the middle of the eighteenth century the dual agricultural-craft economy of the Pennsylvania piedmont was solidly grounded. This is clear from the advertisements in Christopher Sauer's newspaper offering "plantations" for sale. Jacob Beyerley of Lancaster offered his plantation with attached oil and sawmills for sale on December 16, 1741. Daniel Womelsdorf of Oley offered his plantation with mill and Peter Koch the same on June 1, 1752. Herman Riedt offered plantation and gristmill in June, 1755, and Matthias Heinrich sixty acres with sawmill in September. A Tulpehocken plantation with two dwellings, gristmill and sawmill was offered in April, 1756. Johannes Grothaus offered to sell his plantation with a "long-established tile kiln" in February, 1757.

This farm-craft economy, originally based on the German agricultural village, developed in Pennsylvania into a mode which linked these older ways with Pietist views on one hand and with American needs on the other. Farming and the crafts came to be pursued on individual plantations.

This system needed balanced communities within an area—all farms could not perform the same craft. One was a potter, one a cabinetmaker, one a blacksmith, one a papermaker, etc. Thus regions developed. To this was added the so-called "congregational village" idea. Here the economy was ordered by religious motives. The economic system came to be an expression of piety, especially among the Moravians and at Ephrata.

When Count Nicholas Ludwig von Zinzendorf the Moravian leader was about to leave Pennsylvania after a memorable year he delivered on January 9, 1743, a farewell address in Stephen Benezet's house in Philadelphia. He called it his "Pennsylvania Testament." This is, we believe, one of the great documents in Pennsylvania economic history. Here a brilliant religious leader sketched the relationship between faith and economic life, distinguishing between a religiously-grounded commune and what he called the "single plantation system." Here was, in truth, a novel economic theory which took the old German agricultural village and made it a socio-religious economy where all of life became subservient to religion.

The Moravian Congregational villages which resulted at Bethlehem and elsewhere were based on the motto: *in commune oramus, in commune laboramus, in commune patimus, in commune gaudimus*—together we pray, together we work, together we suffer, together we rejoice. This unified the village and stimulated the crafts. Members of the Bethlehem village were bound only by their word. There were no contracts. They worked for no compensation, only for keep. What more was needed was supplied. All industries were congregational and the individual yielded time and talent to serve it. Under Bishop Spangenberg's wise leadership Bethlehem became almost self-sufficient, producing farm products like grain and vegetables, fruit, flax, and feed, as well as meat, milk, butter, eggs, leather, and wool. These agricultural products were augmented by crafts. There was little outside commerce. Trade was local.

Seventy-two trades were recognized in 1759, seventeen years after the village's founding. Other Moravian communities like Nazareth, Emmaus, and Lititz had similar organizations. Crèvecoeur said that the Moravians never settled singly; the whole colony migrated, carrying social forms, including economic and craft patterns, along with them.

In these communal villages crafts were plied and skills nurtured. Prices were regulated to meet external trade; they were fixed; there was no bartering. The original plans of these villages, that of Emmaus published in P. A. Barba's *They Came to Emmaus*, show how the old German village in Pennsylvania became a religiously controlled system where fields were not tilled for profit nor crafts plied for gain, but where all work was done for the glory and welfare of the congregation. We must indeed admire the bold faith of these Pietists whose courage led them to create, if only for a few short decades, an economic system of dynamic character.

Even more dramatic than these Moravian villages was the farm-craft economy as it developed at Ephrata. Here too a strongly religious motive controlled the economy and up to the year 1745, when Israel Eckerlin was sacked, it was an interesting expression of communal pietism.

Ephrata had three orders: unmarried brothers, unmarried sisters, and married householders. The last group lived on and farmed their own land, and they were joined to the Congregation both religiously and economically. The unmarried orders, living in the Cloisters, performed the crafts.

Israel Eckerlin was a man of bold dreams. Son of a town councillor of Strassburg, Alsace, whose leanings towards Pietism had caused his banishment, Eckerlin, with almost martinet-like zeal, drove towards making Ephrata a strong economy. He took a loose association of religious contemplatives and made it a driving progressive economy. Almost with the zeal of a capitalist entrepreneur, he pushed towards making the Community independent; and it produced more than it could use. A thousand fruit trees were planted. In 1741 the Brethren inherited a gristmill newly built of stone and with two pairs of stones. This was followed by a sawmill, oilmill, papermill and fullery. Also there were many looms and a tannery for making leather to bind books printed by the Brethren. Prior Eckerlin even had agents in Philadelphia; Wilhelm Jung (Young) was one of them. Before his "fall" on September 4, 1745, three pairs of oxen were taking flour, oil, and paper to the city each week.

Eckerlin's social and economic vision was too much for Conrad Beissel with his dream of poverty of spirit. Eckerlin was removed. The Community was returned to frugality and poverty, not wealth, was shared. These later years, though, were culturally productive in poetry, art and music, and many crafts. The Sisters knitted, washed, cooked, preserved food, wove, and wrote musical manuscripts. At least fifty members of the Ephrata Community wrote poetry, some of the deepest verse to appear in Colonial America. The old dream of a driving economy was over.

These systems, while close to the old German agricultural village, were new in their interpretation of religious ideals. Piety gave them purpose. This same principle, but in lesser degree, gave other areas similar integration. Just as the Pietists rebelled against lifeless church and corrupt culture, so they were also looking for an economic pattern without greed. The pattern which resulted, evident in early Pennsylvania for several decades, was soon overwhelmed by the mercantile capitalism which emerged in the city, with Benjamin Franklin as prototype and spokesman.

Professor Wertenbacker has suggested that culture came from East Anglia to New England and from the Rhineland to the Schuylkill with but little change. While New England may have imitated old England, German Pennsylvania used Old World patterns only to develop something new. Land was cheap and fertile; the farmer was now a *Freiherr*, not a peasant, living on his own land and not in villages as in Germany. Secondly, where Pennsylvanians lived in communities—a rarity in early Pennsylvania—a profound religious impulse motivated their economy.

Oley was one of the regions where a somewhat integrated economy began to show. Each farm had its craft. In summer the fields were worked, but in winter crafts were pursued. One plantation was associated with the Oley Furnace for in Oley there was no "iron plantation." The Hochs were blacksmiths, the Yoders cabinetmakers, the Keims clockmakers, the Weidners potters, and so forth. As a region, and not as a village as in Europe, Oley was an economic unit, and this was—at least for the Germans—something new.

So, as far as the crafts were concerned, this community pattern, either as a congregational village or in integrated regions, stimulated the worker's imagination, freeing him from tradition and letting him work in new ways.

The ethos of these farm-craft communities was different from that of the merchant-craft economy of the city, as different as Benjamin Franklin's philosophy was from Zinzendorf's piety. In place of a clever merchant drawing customers to his shop by advertising, the peddler with his pack took wares from the City to the plantations, weavers went from farm to farm and *Lohnschreiber* travelled making *Taufscheine* for their keep.

Moreover, the non-importation policy of the British government encouraged home industry. Why pay the tax if you can make what you need? Furthermore, large-scale industrial enterprises failed. The steel works on Seventh Street in the city were making good wares, but not enough. Bonnin and Morris were making buttons, but not for the Amish, who never wore them. A lottery was held to promote the woolen industry, and it was planned to bring in Scotch and Irish weavers. This failed. The most ambitious scheme for developing American manufacture was the Society for the Cultivation of Silk. Prizes were offered for the most cocoons and Johanna Ettwein of Bethlehem won. "Baron" Stiegel made wonderful glass, but he went bankrupt and his furnaces were shaky financially.

The mercantile-craft economy of the city had to create industries in the modern sense to compete with British manufacturing; the farm-crafts of the piedmont did not have this competition. While some Philadelphia products were sent abroad, notably furniture, so too piedmont grain was exported.

Crafts also were plied in the developing provincial towns. The amount of cloth woven in Lancaster homes between May, 1769, and May, 1770, was 27,793 yards with six or seven thousand more yards on the looms. The following crafts emerged in piedmont: distilling, sugar refineries, chocolate manufacturing, whiskey distilling, potash manufacturing, and broom, brush, and pump manufacturing.

Where tidewater craftsmen imitated international styles, individualism emerged in the piedmont crafts. Where Philadelphia merchants followed the styles set abroad, piedmont workers took what they had known and adapted it to their new environment.

In the final analysis, however, the farm-craft economy was to be overwhelmed by the dynamic capitalism of the industrial revolution, but not before it had produced the cultural forms which now attract us, expressing a spirit which even today pulses with extraordinary vigor and verve.

4.

This tension between aristocratic, fashionable, elegant tidewater and peasant, traditional, and plain piedmont accentuated the usual polarity of city and province—the polarity on which the distinction between fine arts and folk arts rests.

In Europe, as Herder had observed, *Volkskunst* was the crafts of agricultural villages as contrasted with the cosmopolitan art of cities. In addition to being farmers' art, European *Volkskunst* also included handiwork of fishermen, miners, and shepherds. The foundation of European *Volkskunst* was its constancy in custom, life-forms and traditions. This is why, once a type has been made, individual pieces may be far younger than the first form. Dating European folk art is risky business.

The arts and crafts of piedmont Pennsylvania were much more than German peasant art and craft forms transplanted to the new world. While in general Pennsylvania folk art stood in contrast to highly fashionable Philadelphia pieces, tension between city and provinces tended to weaken as the years went on and especially in furniture English forms were adopted.

However, Pennsylvania folk arts and crafts differ from European *Volkskunst* in two significant respects:

First, Pennsylvania craftsmen were facing a new environment. This was no primitive art. Skilled workers, arriving in the new land with few tools were faced with an untamed environment. They had to start all over again, repeating the craft history of the race, and becoming unwilling primitives in order to bring civilization to this new land. Those crafts like painting, iron-making, and glass-making—plied with European tools and in European manner—were as fine as anything done in Europe. So, workers capable of more sophisticated work were doing things in primitive ways. While their cousins made Meissen and Dresden china Pennsylvanians were making earthenware pottery. In the manufacture of musical instruments, especially organs, Pennsylvanians were far from unsophisticated, and they even improved on European ways. On the whole, however, this enforced primitivism gave Pennsylvania crafts greater sophistication than in the usual forms of European *Volkskunst*, allowing our pieces to show an imaginative realization beyond that which the pieces themselves imply. Moreover, it made a swift transition to more culturally-developed forms, allowing workmen, once the first period had passed, to more quickly to more sophisticated ways.

Secondly—and equally significant—Pennsylvania piedmont craftsman shared a special religious point of view which gave fresh emphasis to old motifs. The folk art of piedmont Pennsylvania was in large measure influenced by the sectarian ideas of our religious groups. These were religious radicals who had moved beyond the Reformation synthesis, beyond the puritanical iconoclasm of Protestant churches. Like the counter-reformation Catholics they were reacting against impoverishment of spiritual imagination within orthodox Protestantism and their hymnals are full of the richly imaginative poetry of the baroque. This poetry, which was their everyday companion, filled their minds with figures and images capable of being used as artistic motifs. Unlike the baroque architecture of the Bavarian hills, heaven did not come down to our plain meeting-houses; rather the fulness of religious imagery spilled over on paper, wood, and the substances of daily work.

The Pennsylvania sectarian hymnals, then, afford the poetical keys which, when transposed into graphic symbols, are the designs of piedmont folk art. Generally speaking, the baroque religious poets revived medieval imagery and their symbols are those of medieval art; but new phases do appear and these sometimes are new interpretations of old themes. These "flowry" hymns of the Pennsylvania sects, like the Bethlehem Moravians and Ephrata, were outgrowths from the main traditions of Christian imagery.

The images used in Pennsylvania sectarian hymnals fit into known literary traditions. It is the genius of the Pennsylvania illuminated manuscript, especially the *Vorschrift* made in the sectarian school, that it unlocks not only the meaning of Pennsylvania designs but also serves as a key to open the treaures of European *Volkskunst*.

Can we be sure that our Pennsylvania designs are these literary images? It is the author's belief that the many pieces of Pennsylvania folk art from the great Ephrata manuscripts to sgraffito pie-plates on which both words and designs are joined are adequate proof that artistic and literary traditions went hand in hand. For certain it is that many pieces of Pennsylvania folk art link these two traditions and we can now say that any point of view which denies their connection will have to explain away why they are so joined.

Thus we come to the basic principle for determining the meaning of Pennsylvania folk art. We do not just look at designs and then try to figure out what they are. No! We examine designs and then search old sectarian hymnals for the literary expression which fits. In humility, it is not what *we* say designs look like to us; rather it is what the designs meant to the artists who made them.

Being a symbolic and not a representational art these designs mean more than what they say. This is what symbols do. They uncover meanings deeper than what the surface reveals. Falling leaves, for example, *symbolize* death. Why? What joins falling leaves and death?

A symbol links the familiar, often a natural object like falling leaves, with something more abstract. This link becomes "true" for us, persuades us of a connection between object and idea. This link also shows as something mysterious because it gives depth to designs which on the surface seem to resemble natural objects. These symbols are not arbitrary. We do not choose them, saying that this means that; rather, symbols grow. They come into being because mysterious links join them with meanings which are more than literal. Unlike signs, which merely stand for something else, pointing towards it, symbols link something obvious with deeper meaning. Their roots go down into man's subconscious where object and meaning are joined in a way which is mysterious to the rational mind.

Almost every phase of Pennsylvania folk art from barns to buttermolds and from birth certificates to tombstones shows an unusual power of symbolic reference. So when we say that Pennsylvania folk art is symbolic we declare that it does more than just show us natural objects. Were this the case, were our artists meaning to show what the natural world looks like, our roses would look like roses, our birds would be identifiable, and there would be no controversy over calling the dominant floral motif a lily. Pennsylvania folk art is ambiguous.

Several meanings can be given to each design. However, this ambiguity shows that our artists were not meaning to portray nature. So to compare these designs with nature is to miss their meaning.

Being ambiguous, we need verbal clues to join meaning with designs. Distant as we are in time and spirit from the mood of the artists, we can only know what they were thinking if we find words along with designs. Thus the flowers which Margaretha Thomme of Ephrata drew on paper were the roses and lilies which Conrad Beissel was writing about in his poetry, and the birds were the turtledoves.

Now for a deeper problem. Both designs and words—symbols and images—come from the same human consciousness wherein design and meaning are joined. The link which binds them arises deep in man's subconscious mind, and modern psychologists—probing these depths—have found that beneath the conscious and rational level lies a well of meaning which comes to formed expression either as design or as poetic image, that both are not merely linked but expressions of one subconscious pattern. These deep-grounded patterns have been called "archetypes" by Carl Jung because they are, he believed, the patterned meaning-forms which come to expression when and as man becomes a person. They are the forms of personal integration. So art, which uses designs, and poetry, which uses images, are both projections of deep inner patterns by which man's creative spirit finds form. It is not a question of whether Pennsylvania folk artists "knew" what their designs meant; they were making them, and this already was meaningful.

As symbols these archetypes are universal. Much craft art the world over exhibits these motifs—modes of abstraction which have arisen with surprising spontaneity among all peoples. This is why much Pennsylvania folk art resembles that of other peoples. Early nineteenth-century Pennsylvania pottery is similar to that made in Somerset, England, during the eighteenth century or even that of tenth-century China. Some of the carving is close to that of Norway and New Zealand. There is no fundamental difference between German and English samplers in Pennsylvania, or between those of Bulgaria and Greece. Pennsylvania embroidered wool could have been found in Egyptian burial grounds or in Victorian cottages. Over and over again Pennsylvania folk art shows its kinship with the decorative arts of all peoples and insofar as our art shares these universal "archetypes" it is graphic representation of deeply-rooted human thought-forms. It is, above all, a human art.

5.

The Pennsylvania piedmont, however, beginning at the first escarpment north of the city, was where old world met new. The road through Trappe, where the Speaker of the First and Third American Congresses was raised, led into the interior, through fertile Oley to Harris' Ferry and then to who knows where?

During the eighteenth century, Conestoga wagons travelled this road, hauling grain raised and milled in Pennsylvania to Philadelphia for shipment abroad. At the close of the century the wagons began to go the other way, driving westward over the Cumberland trail and southward down the Shenandoah. The same vehicle, made in the Pennsylvania piedmont as an American adaptation of a European form, which during the Colonial period had carried grain to dockside in the city, during the nineteenth century carried America to the Pacific. The piedmont was the link.

But it was more than a link. It was the place where new cultural forms, and the values they implied, were being made.

In 1815 when British General Packenham landed at New Orleans he was met by a force of frontiersmen. Andrew Jackson threw up three lines of defense. First were eight hundred regulars and two thousand frontiersmen, armed with a product of the Pennsylvania piedmont —the long rifle. They stopped twelve thousand British regulars. The first casualties were the officers. Two thousand British fell—finally commanded by a major, every other higher officer having been lost including General Packenham. What was the difference? Two things: the new individualism and the Pennsylvania long rifle.

Pennsylvania, then, was a land of cultural synthesis. More than any other American region it showed the deep-rooted cultural conflict between a decaying feudal order and the new society emerging in the American hinterland. This difference was dramatically figured by two celebrations held in Pennsylvania in May, 1778. The first was the pageant produced at Valley Forge by Colonel Morgan's Corps of sharpshooters who acted out a story treating of the brotherhood of all men—red and white. The second was the celebrated *Mischianza* produced by the British troops in occupied Philadelphia in which plumed knights, pages, squires, ladies—the whole caboodle of feudal foolishness—paraded in the streets of William Penn's town. Thus two worlds faced each other across the line dividing tidewater from piedmont.

The cultural forms created in early Pennsylvania betray the phases of this struggle. Modes came, bloomed, and died. During the period in which they were in bloom, they were an astonishing expression of the human spirit, possible only in the tolerant land of William Penn where, for the first time, western man was free to make values and to create forms in and through which his spirit might be expressed.

ARCHITECTURE

The universal cultural form which appeared in early Pennsylvania as an expression of spiritual creativity was domestic architecture. From magnificent manor houses erected in imitation of feudal baronies to the log cabin which was to symbolize the western frontier, the Pennsylvania structures showed wide diversity, hybridization and cultural eclecticism. Here traditional and even classical forms of building came in touch with the incipient romanticism of the frontier, and from this clash a new blend arose, issuing in an American form.

At first, of course, there were no structures, just river caves. A pit was dug about three feet deep by the river bank, well up from the water. Walls were carried up from the ground to the height of a tall man standing erect. These then were enclosed by interlocking saplings. The roof was of the same. The floor was earth.

The next step was the erection of primitive dwellings for there was little elegance during these earlier years. Primitive conditions and simple Quaker tastes made life less than comfortably plain. During these earlier years, before the building crafts were established, Pennsylvania was dependent upon Europe for much that made life bearable. The meager store of things which the settlers had brought along was augmented by imported pewter, china, silver, books, paintings, carpets, and furniture—things which could be displayed in the "wainscotted palaces" of the still strongly Quaker colony.

With the passing years plain tastes quietly grew more elegant. Houses that had been stately when William Penn walked the streets of his country town became homely and uncomfortably tight for later generations. The pent roof and gallery slowly gave way to brick and marble belts, the hood to classical pediments, the simple cornice to molded wood, and plain doorways to recessed entrances. Also the plain mood which had dominated the first half century of the city passed out into the piedmont where Welsh Quaker and German Pietist came to express this spirit. So the classical elegance of the aristocratic Colonial gave way before the developing plain of the emerging middle classes.

One structure stood out in early Pennsylvania from the mass of plain and even primitive dwellings and that was the Proprietor's great estate along the Delaware River twenty miles above the city. (Fig. 2) William Penn had sent out letters from England to his American

Fig. 1. Independence Hall.

agents, containing detailed descriptions of the kind of structure he wanted built. It was to be a great mansion erected in the style of other estates in tidewater America, the one seat in Colonial Pennsylvania comparable to the mansions of southern planters. Although it was somewhat elegant for a simple Quaker, which Penn was not, it still was not as elaborate as the great manor houses of Britain.

Pennsbury was a two-and-a-half story structure, sixty feet wide, facing the Delaware, oriented towards the old world, with a large hall extending the width of the first floor into which three parlors communicated. As with most later Pennsylvania farms, Pennsbury had a so-called "summer kitchen" detached to one side; and unlike other farms it had a brew house, laundry, and large stable for twelve carriage horses. Unlike Mount Vernon, all outbuildings were in line with the main house. The grounds were terraced between the house and river, poplars shaded the path thereto, and the river itself was the avenue of communication—suggesting the intimacy of Pennsbury with the old world. The gardens were formally developed and English trees—walnuts, hawthorns, hazels, fruits—were set out and planted.

The Penns lived at Pennsbury during the spring and summer of 1701. They returned to England after their second American visit. Deborah Logan spoke of Mistress Penn as a "delicate and pretty woman, sitting beside the cradle of her infant," known as the American John.

When William Penn entertained at Pennsbury it was as the prince of a vast American domain; he was only partly the simple Quaker. His courtier's mood also was well-rooted in his spirit, and when he passed down the Delaware on an eight-oared barge he was in fact the governor on his way to attend affairs of state.

Unfortunately the original buildings at Pennsbury decayed, but the letters which Penn had written to his American agents survived. So under careful and expert guidance Pennsbury was rebuilt and now it looks much as it did when the province was young. The restoration is authentic; the only lack is the mood of mellowness which only time gives. Even the plants in the garden are as Penn ordered. Walking these prim paths we can share the serenity

Fig. 2. William Penn's mansion at Pennsbury (restored), seen from the river side.

of an earlier age, for we may imagine the yard filled with nervous horses and perhaps, in our mind's eye, we can see the immobile Delaware chiefs, Lapawinzo and Tischohan, posing to be painted by the artist Hesselius.

Pennsbury though was not typical of early Pennsylvania architecture. It was the Proprietor's mansion and it had cost five thousand pounds sterling, far more than ordinary people could afford. It was classical, aristocratic, European, taking inspiration from English baronial estates and it was not of a piece with the plainness of the emerging middle classes. William Penn—sometimes Quaker, sometimes courtier—expressed his aristocratic mood when he ordered his seat built by the tranquil Delaware.

Primitive Tidewater Architecture

The first dwellings in Pennsylvania—then but a small area surrounding Philadelphia— took inspiration from European patterns. They were of course temporary, put together as passing shelter until new structures could be built. Few of these early structures have survived, but there is some historical evidence to show how these structures were made.

The *Journal* of the Labadist Jasper Danckert suggests that the first buildings in Pennsylvania were imitations of the half-timbered construction of northern Europe. Jacob Hendrick's house, the *Journal* says, was built in the Swedish manner, a block house that was nothing more than whole trees split through the middle or else, in other instances, squared from rough logs and then laid in the form of a rectangle, one upon the other, as high as the house was desired. The ends of the timbers were let into one another about a foot from the ends, half of one into half of another. The ceiling and roof did not show good workmanship except among the most careful people who sometimes painted ceilings and put in glass windows. Doors generally were wide and low; one had to stoop on entering. Generally these homes were tight and warm, heat coming from a fireplace and chimney. This type of structure, called *Blockwerk* in German, was known in all northern Europe—Scandinavia, Northern Russia, Carpathia, the Alps—but not in Britain. The log cabin thus began its new world life with the Swedes who preceded the Quakers to Pennsylvania.

Among Anglo-Saxons another form of timbered construction appeared. This was the clapboard-covered timbered house. First a wooden frame was made, such as is customary in Westphalia and in Altona near Hamburg, but not as strongly made. Boards then were split like roofer's staves, but not bent. These were shaved so that the thickest was about a "pinck" thick, that is like a little finger. The other edge was sharpened to knife-like thinness. These boards, five or six feet long, were nailed to the outside of the frame, with ends overlapping. The better of these houses were plastered with clay, thus resembling half-timbering or *Fachwerk*.

Still another primitive architectural form may be deduced from historical accounts and it is the frame house which William Penn described in his promotional pamphlet *Information and Direction to Such Persons as are Inclined to America*. Whether this describes an actual building or whether it was meant merely to help prospective settlers for their coming, is not quite clear although the probability is that there were a few such structures in the province. He wrote:

To build a House of thirty foot long and eighteen foot broad with a partition near the middle, and another to divide one end of the House into two small rooms, there must be eight trees of about fifteen foot long, which the House must stand upon, and four pieces, two of thirty foot long and two of eighteen foot long, for Plates, which must be upon the top of these Posts, the whole length and breadth of the House for the Gists to rest upon. There must be ten Gists of Twenty

Fig. 3. The Morton cabin, an example of Swedish timbered construction.

foot long to be upon the ends of the Gists for Rafters to be fixed upon, twelve pare of Rafters about twenty foot to bear the Roof of the House, with several other small pieces, or Windbeams, Braces, Studs, &c, which are made out of waste Timber. For covering the House, ends and sides, and for the loft we use Clapboard, which is rived feather-edged of five foot and a half long, that, well-drawn, lyes close and smooth. The Lodging Room may be lined with the same, and filled up in between, which is very warm. These Houses usually endure for ten years without repairs.

There were no provisions for doors, windows or chimneys. Doors were fashioned from riven stuff with leather hinges and wooden latch bars. Windows were closed by clapboard shutters. Most of these houses had but one chimney, usually outside the gable end of the sitting room, made of clay or stone, but sometimes of wood. The floor generally was earth.

Fig. 4. The Brinton 1704 house, an example of English-type stone construction in early Pennsylvania.

Fig. 5. The William Rittenhouse paper mill, an example of Germanic stone construction.

Early Pennsylvania Swedes also built of stone. John Bartram's house was a large stone house which had been built around an earlier stone cabin erected as early as 1650.

Germans also built in stone, like the Germanic-spirited Rittenhouse house and paper-mill which was built in Germantown sometime around 1707.

These, then, were the primitive structures in tidewater Pennsylvania during the earliest period: the Swedish log cabin, a variant of the half-timbered house, the clapboard house, and the small stone cabin. In the piedmont these three structures were to reappear in somewhat more sophisticated form, reflecting a more basic Germanic type of construction which already was somewhat advanced beyond the primitive forms.

The Greene Country Town

The primitive structures of early Pennsylvania were prelude to the development of more permanent buildings, forms which took shape from a combination of European tradition and American need. William Penn wrote in the often quoted fifteenth article of his pamphlet: "Let every House be placed, if the Person Pleases, in ye middle of its plot, as to the breadth by way of it, that so there may be ground on each side for Gardens and Orchards, or fields, y'it may be a greene Country Town, wch will never be burnt, and always wholesome." *Never be burnt!*—the great London fire of 1666 was surely in his mind.

So, at first, brick houses were built in the city, at first quite small then larger in the new London mode. Old London, maze of half-timbered structures and winding crooked streets and lanes, had been replaced by a more orderly plan. The London Rebuilding Act of 1667 had allowed four kinds of brick houses and these set the patterns not only for the British capital but also for early Philadelphia and, with adaptations, for the later provincial towns. By 1690, Philadelphia had almost a thousand homes, mostly brick, two stories high, built in this London manner.

Fig. 6. The Letitia House, typical of early architecture in Philadelphia.

However, there was a second, and minor, influence upon Philadelphia which came out of Germantown, settled only a few years later than the city itself. Here the land was not cut up into plantations of miniscule size. Francis Daniel Pastorius wrote to Penn in 1701 that this village was cut up into lots "and more compacted settlements" because he said that his German countrymen followed this method. Evidently there was a difference between these two areas.

In 1683 Holme's map shows that Philadelphia was indeed a rectangular city. In 1698 Gabriel Thomas called it a "noble and beautiful" city of about two thousand homes which were stately and inhabited, made of brick and "generally three stories high." Characteristic features of these early city homes was the penthouse, the roofed projection between upper and lower windows. The pent roof was not Germanic, as some would suggest, but it can be traced back to the restored London after the great fire. Also, almost every house had its balcony. The business streets were closely built-up with rectangular brick-front houses, shops with small panes, swinging signboards and wrought-iron balconies with roofs sloping steeply down. Everywhere were chimney pots in the English mode.

In 1687 the British architect, James Porteus, built for Samuel Carpenter the house variously known as the Slate Roof House and the Letitia House (Fig. 6). Originally it stood near the Delaware River, but now it has been moved to Fairmount Park. This charming little structure was typical of the smaller merchant houses in the early city, and it reflects simpler

Fig. 7. Eltreth's Alley, surviving example of the city streets in the early period.

Fig. 8. The Betsy Ross House, Philadelphia.

ways of living and an unobtrusive plain mood. The solid brick walls, white windows, door frames, simple cornices, and pent roof betray this spirit. Indeed, this house was owned and lived in by William Penn himself and was for a time the seat of the colonial government. It is similar to the Benezet house in Germantown, which is made of dressed stone instead of brick. Washington's Headquarters at Valley Forge is a translation of the Letitia House into undressed stone.

The houses in Elfreth's Alley (Fig. 7) also retain this simple mood of the early city. Brick paving in sidewalk and alleyway, the small dormers and square windows of the houses with no pent roofs, give an even simpler mood of the closely gathered town snuggling by a mighty river, far from the centers of the old world. Here is a town that does not yet have roots in the new world and is closer to London in spirit than it is to the limestone bottoms of interior Pennsylvania.

This same simple Quaker plainness is likewise evident in one of the more famous shrines of American history, the Betsy Ross House. (Fig. 8). Smaller than the Letitia House and more cluttered by pent roof and massive shutters, this house communicates the lack of ostentation in plain and Quaker Philadelphia.

In these and similar structures the plain Quakers of early Philadelphia began life in the Pennsylvania Colony, expressing in their architecture their religious distrust of formal elegance which then was coming into the fashionable world from French modes. For when it was founded, and for a half century, Pennsylvania was plain in mood and in spirit.

Primitive Piedmont Architecture

As with the early Pennsylvania Swedes the log cabin also appeared among the Germans, apparently independent of Swedish influence and based upon indigenous Germanic forms. These piedmont log cabins show the influences of timbered construction of the forested German regions like Schwarzwald and Odenwald, especially in the matter of notching the logs. Four methods of notching, all Germanic, have been found in the surviving log cabins of the Pennsylvania piedmont, the most interesting of which is the *Schwalbenschwanz* or swallow-tail notching, which demanded skilled hatchet work. The surfaces drained outwards, protecting the inner walls. The style of notching was usually used with dressed and squared logs prepared with the broadaxe. At times simpler methods of setting logs on each other alternatingly, as in the Hunter's cabin near Allentown, were used. (Fig. 9). And at other times more familiar undressed logs were used, the style later made popular in the West. Professor Wertenbacker has found regional patterns in the notching of eastern Pennsylvania sabins, an interesting and suggestive point because of regional diversity in other cultural forms as well as ethnic differences.

Log houses of several types have been found at Landis Valley, Emmaus, Landis' store, along the Perkiomen and Skippack. The first house in Bethlehem also was of logs and one also survives in Lititz. German settlers in the Shenandoah in Virginia took these forms into the developing frontier from when they spread into Kentucky and other trans-Appalachian areas.

The most famous of all log-cabin communities during the eighteenth century was Valley Forge where in a few weeks the Continental Army housed itself snugly, showing how versatile a form the log cabin was, capable of being erected quickly and thus adaptable to volatile frontier conditions. The pattern for these huts, including those used for field hospitals, was set by General Washington's general orders, thus demonstrating that the log cabin had become an established American form capable of being employed under the most trying conditions. German methods of notching already were standard among other ethnic groups as we learn from this versified description of a Valley Forge hospital hut written by Surgeon Albigence Waldo, a New Englander, for whom log cabins were somewhat novel. The structure was

> . . . of ponderous logs
> Whose bulk disdains the winds or fogs
> The sides and ends are fitly raised
> And by dove-tail each corner's brac'd;
> Which fire and smoke has now made dry—
> Next, straw wraps o'er the tender pole,

Fig. 9. Hunter's cabin near Allentown, example of Germanic-style timbered construction.

Next, earth, then splints o'erlay the whole,
Although it leaks when show'rs are o'er,
It did not leak two hours before.
Two chimneys plac'd at op'site angles
Keep smoke from causing oaths and wrangles.

Three windows, plac'd all in sight,
Through oiled paper give us light.
One door on wooden hinges hung,
Lets in the friends.

The second type of primitive dwelling in the Pennsylvania piedmont, which also was evident in a simpler form in tidewater areas, was the half-timbered structure (*Fachwerkbau*). This was imitative of a cultural form found in Normandy, the Netherlands, Germany as far east as Poland, and parts of the Balkans and parts of Great Britain.

The most celebrated example of half-timbering in piedmont Pennsylvania, still standing although now clapboarded against the weather, is the *Gemeinhaus* in Moravian Bethlehem. For more than two centuries this structure has served as home, hospice, manse, church, administrative offices, academy, dispensary, town hall, etc. Its foundations were laid September 29, 1742, and it was built with the help of limeburners, quarrymen, masons, board-cutters, and teamsters from Goshenhoppen, Whitemarsh, Maxatawney, and Lower Saucon. Probably the most celebrated group of half-timbered buildings still standing are the several Ephrata buildings. Further examples of this form, which survived to the beginning of the twentieth century are the Moravian schoolhouse (Fig. 10) in Oley built by Samuel Hoch and the Sawbuck house in Landis Valley. The sketches of Lewis Miller of York show the buildings of his time, and they also reveal how widespread this form was at the start of the nineteenth century. Some of these York structures now are being restored.

The third primitive form of structure in piedmont Pennsylvania was the stone cabin, (Fig. 11), which was found here in many forms reflecting its diverse European background; it is found in Britain, France, Spain, and the whole Mediterranean region. This became an unusually versatile structure. Several features of our Pennsylvania stone cabins take us back to medieval Germany. On the older and larger plantations this structure was put to several uses: spring house, bake house, summer kitchen, and so forth. The spring house on the Johannes Hoch farm in Oley (Fig. 12)—the Hochs were of Swiss origin—is a good example of the adaptation of the high-pitched roof cabin to uses other than housing. The use of this structure for housing is shown in the Paul Grosscup cabin (Fig. 13), illustrated from an old photograph as it is now demolished. When it was used as a dwelling the structure was somewhat larger and it had a fireplace and chimney, usually placed in the middle. Casement style windows were sometimes set in starkly solid walls of masonry. A fine example of this

Fig. 10. Moravian schoolhouse in Oley built by Samuel Hoch, an example of half-timbered construction.

Fig. · 11. The Herr cabin in Lancaster, an example of Germanic stone
construction.

dwelling still stands in upper Bucks County along the road from Richlandtown to Heller-
town. With its inwardly opening casements and huge central fireplace it is one of the finest
examples of this old stone cabin. The Bertolet cabin in Oley likewise betrays similar development, and the deTurk house in the same valley is a later variant.

Taken together, the primitive phase of Pennsylvania architecture in the piedmont repeated the phases of European building: wooden (*Holzbau*), half-timbering (*Fachwerkbau*),
earthen structures (*Erdbaüten*) and stone structures (*Steinbau*). As half-timbering dominated Germany so it came also to dominate the early Pennsylvania landscape.

We must not romanticize about eighteenth-century Pennsylvania and assume that the
countryside was made up of large stone mansions in Georgian style. These great stone houses
were rare and during the first half of the century non-existent outside of the tidewater area.
For the greater part of the century the Pennsylvania piedmont was dominated by half-
timbered constructions of mortar and stone and these primitive stone cabins. The more

Fig. 12. This springhouse on the Johannes Hoch plantation in Oley is one of the oldest structures surviving in piedmont Pennsylvania. The tiles on the roof, which take us back to Europe, were made by George Adam Weidner, potter, who was the neighbor to the Hochs.

Fig. 13. A 1905 photograph showing the Paul Grosscup cabin, Rockland township, Berks, showing the primitive stone cabin, with the step Germanic roof. The first part of the structure is the left portion.

affluent farmers boarded their houses on the outside and sometimes even painted these boards to look like brick. When masonry construction did come to the towns and villages it was of brick and this was towards the end of the eighteenth century. After the American Revolution, Reading, for example, began to have brick houses with white steps, like those in Philadelphia.

The traveller Cazenove said that when he visited Hummelstown near the end of the century it still had fifty houses of logs and mortar with small English windows. Harrisburg, founded in 1785, two years later had 300 houses of brick and mortar, again with English-style windows. When this traveller got beyond Carlisle he says that he found wretched houses of logs without windows and with chimneys of sticks and clay. Shippensburg had 30 two-story houses of stone and about 140 "wretched huts of wood, logs and clay." York, even at this late period, had about 400 dwellings of which about 60 were of brick "newly built" and the remainder were log huts. Lancaster, then the largest inland town in America, had only a few brick houses and a large number of log houses. In Chester County, nearer the tidewater area, Cazenove reported that the houses and barns were of limestone and very few of brick.

There can be no question then that these primitive types of structures dominated the Pennsylvania piedmont during the eighteenth century, augmented after the middle of the century by the appearance of plain farmhouses.

Elegant Tidewater Mansions

By 1720 the Province was established. It was growing fast. Fresh streams of immigrants, English, German and Swiss, were pouring into the Colony and Philadelphia was becoming both prosperous and active.

In 1724, due to this pressure of expansion, a major step in the development of Pennsylvania architecture took place with the founding of the Carpenter's Company with headquarters in Carpenter's Hall, which was built in the same year. Here was the organization in Pennsylvania of a guild which created—or perhaps which merely transplanted from Europe —those styles which were to dominate Pennsylvania Colonial: the Doric doorway, the Palladian window, the distinctive mantle and the graceful dormer. The *Manual* of the Carpenter's Company was in the pocket of every craftsman from New Castle (the Read House) to Maxatawney (the Merkle House). Not only was domestic architecture thus influenced by the classic revival then sweeping Britain, but even public buildings from Carpenter's Hall to the old capitol at Trenton and the court houses in York, Lancaster, and Reading show this influence. Around 1750-1760 these workmen began to erect structures in the older piedmont settlements such as Oley, Maxatawney, and Tulpehocken where this style became distinctly a Pennsylvania form.

However, while early Philadelphia still was plain and while the city was taking form— patterned after the London which had arisen from the ashes of the great fire—the tidewater countryside was becoming the place where large homes, somewhat imitative of British landed estates, were being built. In 1698 Richard Ellis of Bryn Mawr wrote that "they begin now to build houses with stone, & many with brick, whc may be made any place here." In 1704 he created his own place, later to be known as Harriton after its subsequent owner, Richard Harrison. Here Charles Thompson, Secretary of the Continental Congress, lived between 1774 and the year of his death, 1824.

From then on elegant country estates, patterned after the seats of landed British nobility, began to appear in and around the city. Some of these no longer survive. When in 1717, Fair Hill, residence of James Norris, Sr. in Northern Liberties, was completed it was the loveliest place yet built in Pennsylvania, with the exception of Pennsbury. It was a reflection

Fig. 14. Cedar Grove, Philadelphia.

of the old world for it imitated Dolobran, the Lloyd family estate in Wales, and its windows and sashes were imported from England. Its entrance hall was large and magnificently paved with black and white marble. Two large parlors flanked an imposing staircase. The courts and gardens were in the mood of the placid country seats described in Addison and Steele's *Spectator*. With gravel walks an porterres, it was British to the core. Isaac Norris, Jr.—"Speaker Isaac"—succeeded his father as owner of Fair Hill, and he added his wonderful library, a suitable retreat from a busy political life.

Now preserved in Fairmont Park, Cedar Grove, which originally stood in Frankford (Fig. 14) was erected piece by piece—the oldest part dating from 1721, but with later additions creating an imposing structure. Of native stone—one of the first to employ this material—and with its handsome panelling, this home was in the Paschall and Morris families.

In 1722 the place now known as Graeme Park (Fig. 15), first called Fountain Low, was erected in Horsham, the country seat of Sir William Keith, Lieutenant Governor of Pennsylvania from 1717 to 1726. Here distinctly American features began to show, although they still were superficial, laid over a definitely European structure. The panelling was simple, and here we feel that the owner was still struggling mightily with a Quaker conscience; yet even at this mansion, built for the foppish governor who wore laces and periwigs, things dared not be too elegant. After 1737 it passed into the hands of Dr. Thomas Graeme, from whom it got its name.

Moore Hall in Chester County, a few miles northwest of Valley Forge, was also erected in

Fig. 15. Graeme Park, Horsham.

1722 and it has the same general character of the other country seats of this period. Here lived one of Pennsylvania's celebrated torys, the Honorable William Moore, Judge of the Orphans' Court of Chester, who carried on with a baronial air, attended by slaves and redemptioners. He was a lordly and lively aristocrat. Here at Moore Hall officers of the Continental Army were billeted, against the owner's desire, during the Valley Forge period. Here too the Committee of Continental Congress met to investigate the conditions of the army.

In 1722 Hope Lodge (Fig. 16) was built in Whitemarsh by Edward Farmer. It is said to have been erected from plans drawn by a pupil of Sir Christopher Wren. In 1746 Samuel Morris purchased it for a bride who never came, and it served also as a hospital after the battle of Germantown. Here too, like so many Pennsylvania seats, Washington was entertained. Hope Lodge, with its broad hall, generous rooms, Delft tiles, Scottish marble, and British arrangement suggests a mood not Pennsylvanian in spirit although the kitchen does breathe native air. The interior vistas are classical and not in true harmony with the plain mood.

In 1724 Waynesborough was created, similar enough in style to Moore Hall to lead to the conclusion that the same builder erected both. Here lived Captain Anthony Wayne who arrived here in 1722 and who died in 1739; and here his famous grandson was born who became a general in the Continental Army and eventually its commander.

In 1728 Stenton (Fig. 17), home of James Logan who was William Penn's business agent, was built four miles from the city. Here, however, a Quaker note of simplicity was evident in the plain panelling on the parlor walls, wooden pegs in place of closets, and the general lack of ostentation. Logan, who managed Penn's affairs for a half century, was a brilliant and accomplished man—scholar, scientist, statesman, jurist, farmer, and merchant—and his house was graced by Washington's presence as well as serving as headquarters for the British during the battle of Germantown.

These early country seats, and a few others, while exhibiting a grandeur more solid than the plain houses of the city, were not as elegant as contemporary European manors. Here in this province there still was something plain, controlled by a prim Quaker conscience. Nor can we say that these early tidewater mansions were indigenous, expressing a Pennsylvania mood. There were far too imitative of British country seats for that. Then too they seem to be enveloped by the quaintness of the Quaker "thee" and "thou" for the time of untrammelled elegance had not yet come to a province still heavily under the Quaker spirit.

If we draw a line from a place on the Delaware a few miles above Trenton, somewhere around Washington's Crossing, to a point where the Pennsylvania border joins Maryland and Delaware following generally the line of the escarpment which begins the piedmont area, we shall enclose on the seaward side structures of brick and on the mountain side structures of stone. This, generally conceived, is the brick line which separates tidewater and piedmont architecture in this period. Washington's headquarters at Valley Forge, the Potts home, is simply a stone version of the Letitia Street House in the city. Although never hard and fast, this line was apparent. Germantown, an exception, was within the line, and the construction generally was of stone. The Hiester House in Sumneytown was of brick. However, in a general way we may say that this line separates brick dwellings like those in New Castle, Delaware, and in Salem County, New Jersey, from stone dwellings in Maxatawney and Tulpehocken.

These brick and stone mansions of tidewater followed the patterns of the British architects Webb and Wren, although modified by Quaker plainness. On the whole, though, they were not yet indigenous to the soil of Pennsylvania for they took style and spirit from the old world.

Fig. 16. Hope Lodge, Whitemarsh, said to have been built from plans drawn up by students of Christopher Wren.

Fig. 17. Stenton, home of James Logan.

Plain Farmhouses and Plain Meetinghouses

Interior Pennsylvania was the land of both the plain farmhouse and the plain meeting-house for the greater part of the eighteenth century. Although a great deal of timbered construction—both log cabins and half-timbered buildings—survived until as late as 1800, survivals of the primitive structures that had characterized the earliest period were rare. There also was evident a pattern of stone structures, partly coming from the Germantown influence, and around 1740 stone structures began to appear in the piedmont.

These stone houses—they were no longer cabins—were American adaptations from primitive forms in the piedmont that took their patterns from structures in the Rhineland. There was little stone building in Great Britain like it, and they seem to be related to the stone house in the villages of Alsace and the Palatinate where there was less timbered construction than in other German areas. If one disregards the barn sections of the stone structures in the Kusel area of the Palatinate, such as are illustrated in Theodor Zink's *Deutsche Volkskunst, Band XII, Die Pfalz* (plates 5, 7, 8), it is easy to see the prototype of these plain farmhouses in eastern Pennsylvania. There was indeed a German prototype of the simpler stone structures for the Georgian influence had not yet conquered the countryside, however strong an influence it may have been in the city.

So we must conclude that there were three types of stone structures in interior Pennsylvania that arose without help from the Carpenters' Company: first was the stone cabin, like the Grosscup cabin in Berks or the Herr Cabin in Lancaster, which was a steep-roofed and simple stone structure; second came the plain farmhouses without Georgian or classical influences in the earlier years and whose ancestry goes back to Germany; and third, after 1760, classical features begin to show as added decorative features and not as part of the structure itself. Finally, around 1800, Georgian mansions almost as fine as those of tidewater were being built.

This second group of structures, the plain farmhouses, came to be widespread in interior Pennsylvania between 1740 and 1790. An experienced eye can soon pick them out. We here illustrate three of these plain farmhouses in the order of their erection.

The first (Fig. 18) is the Lorenz Guth home in Lehigh, which has a datestone dated

Fig. 18. The Lorenz Guth House in Lehigh, an example of the plain farmhouse that developed from the Germanic stone cabin.

Fig. 19. Basement tiles in the Guth homestead, Lehigh, showing decorations.

1745. Here we find a structure with a chimney in the middle of the house, not at the ends. Three small shutterless windows and one door break the stark stone facade. The roof is no longer quite as steep as on the primitive stone cabin, but it still has considerable pitch. This Guth homestead has several interesting features. In the front wall, beneath the chimney, is an iron fireback which was cast in Zinsweiler, Alsace, and which was brought along from Europe. Also the basement of this house was tiled with squares, probably baked in Pennsylvania, and which were molded and incised with designs—a forgotten phase of Pennsylvania craft art (Fig. 19).

The second plain farmhouse (Fig. 20), dated 1754 and no longer standing, is here reproduced from a photograph taken on March 26, 1887. This shows an extremely interesting structure with roof only partly pitched and sloping away in the rear to a kitchen. Here too is found undressed stone with irregularly spaced windows—the shutters are later—and the chimneys now have been moved to the gable ends of the house.

The third farmhouse pictured (Fig. 21) is no longer just another plain house. This is Johann Michael Staudt's house at Stoudt's Ferry, dating from around 1760. Here we are not quite in the Georgian style yet, but we are getting mighty close to it, indeed. Regularity of spacing has come along with good proportion, two front doors. There are no dormers yet, but there are two massive chimneys of brick at the gable ends and the most notable feature,. coming from the City, is a porch with classical columns. The roof has become flatter, too, and here we are in truth near to the Georgian style.

Early Pennsylvania, land of the plain farmhouse, also was the land of plain meeting-houses. The dissenting religious groups who settled the Province were the first to build houses for worship. These were of logs, but stone and brick soon followed. In 1695 the Friends Meeting of Merion replaced their log structure with a stone one in which William Penn himself preached. In 1697 the Abington Friends Meeting, in existence since 1683 and using a log house, erected a stone one where Benjamin Lay, early abolitionist, worshipped. A year later

Fig. 20. An 1887 photograph of a Germanic stone house in Chester County.

Fig. 21. The John Michael Staudt home, Stoudt's Ferry, Berks.

the Norriton Presbyterian church, which had grown out of an originally Dutch Calvinist congregation, erected a stone building in which many distinguished persons including Washington, Franklin and David Rittenhouse attended worship. Here too the forebears of Mary Todd, wife of Abraham Lincoln, worshipped.

The beginning of the eighteenth century saw many buildings for worship constructed— the Plymouth Friends, Gwynedd Friends, Falckner Swamp Luthern, St. James Episcopal in Evansburg, St. Thomas Episcopal in Whitemarsh, and St. Davids in Radnor. These early structures were small and plain, well-suited to uncomplicated provincial living.

Most of these meetinghouses were of unadorned stone, and they were crude in appearance, expressive of the desire for simplicity. The Dunker Meetinghouse near Pricetown,

Fig. 22. Church of the Brethren (Dunkard) Meetinghouse, Pricetown, Berks.

Fig. 23. Quaker Meetinghouse, Exeter Township, Berks, one of the meetings outside the tidewater area. To this meeting Squire Boone, father of Daniel, belonged, and from this meeting he was expelled for allowing his son Israel to marry out of meeting.

Fig. 24. Restored interior of Augustus Lutheran Church, Trappe, 1743.

Fig. 25. A 1905 photograph of the Lutheran Church, Kutztown, Berks.

Berks (Fig. 22), erected around 1722 with central chimney and walls of undressed stone, is entirely typical of this mood. Likewise the Exeter Friends Meeting—"ye Quaker Meeting House near George Boone's mill in Oley"—expressed a stolid spirit of dissenting honesty (Fig. 23). Like so many other Meetings the first structure was of logs and around 1730, or just afterwards, the present structure was erected for Quakers who had come to Oley from Gwynedd and Abington. This Exeter Meeting during its older years was the spiritual home of many families later to become famous in American history. Here worshipped Squire Boone and his son Daniel, and here too worshipped Anthony Lee who descendents went to Virginia.

The simple unadorned interiors of these early structures matched the exterior, as is seen in the Augustus Lutheran Church, Trappe (Fig. 24), oldest Lutheran sanctuary in America. Here labored the patriarch, Heinrich Melchior Muhlenburg, father of Revolutionary General Peter Muhlenburg and of Friedrich Augustus Muhlenburg, speaker of the First American Congress.

Gradually however as the classical tastes of the age of reason came to be known in the interior, the decorative details common to that style were laid over basically plain structures. So when the old wooden church for the Lutherans in Kutztown was erected it was adorned by classical columns and pediments, as in the picture taken in 1905 before it was demolished (Fig. 25). The interior of these older churches was arranged around an altar in the center of the sanctuary, and preaching was done from a "wine glass pulpit" placed at the side of the room, like the one illustrated from the old Brickerville Church in Lancaster (Fig. 26).

Farmhouses in the piedmont, and meetinghouses from the city to the mountains, expressed the mood of the young and growing colony—honest Quaker simplicity and Pietist plainness.

Fig. 26. Wine-glass pulpit in the Brickerville Church, Lancaster.

Ephrata and Moravian Architecture

Surely the epitome of the plain mood in early Pennsylvania was achieved at Ephrata in Lancaster County. Here arose a religious society under the leadership of the enigmatic Conrad Beissel in which rules and disciplines were so formulated as to oppose elegance in all its forms. The Ephrata Societies, believing that European culture was dying, awaited the coming of the new world in the Conestoga wilderness.

The buildings (Figs. 27, 28, 29), now being restored by the Pennsylvania Historical and Museum Commission, were not the first buildings that were erected at Ephrata; nor are they, architecturally speaking, the most interesting. There is however little accurate information about early Ephrata structures and the best that we can do is to piece together a chronology of these structures. From the best available information we can, perhaps, put together a tolerably correct account.

We know that the third cabin erected at the place called Ephrata was built in 1732 and that a common bakehouse was also in existence at this time.

Fig. 27. Springtime at Ephrata.

Fig. 28. Rear of the Ephrata buildings.

In 1733 the first community structure called the *Berghaus*, was erected on the hill west of the creek. This structure was used for meetings, love feasts, and also as a residence for the Brethren who were to form the inner circle of the male members of Ephrata.

In July, 1735, the first common house, called Kedar, was built. This was a structure three stories high, wholly constructed of wood, even to the pins, hinges and latches. It was half-timbered in traditional fashion and patched with clay and grass. It contained a large hall for worship and one for love feasts. Its upper floor had cells, and there was a small tower housing the clock which had been made by Dr. Christopher deWitt of Germantown, the first tower-clock in the colony.

In 1738 a convent called Zion was begun, stimulated by the financial help of a young Swiss named Yüchley. It was erected on a cleared spot on the *Berghaus* hill near the limits of the Ephrata Camp. Three stories high, the first held a large room, refrectory and food pantrys, the second a large circular room without windows, and on the top was a tower with another clock that had been given to the Ephrata Societies by Peter Miller's father in Germany. This clock had only an hour hand.

In October, 1738, ground was broken for the first church, called the *Bethaus,* which was completed in six weeks but which stood for only three years. It stood near Kedar.

In October, 1741, a new *Bethaus* called Penial was begun in the meadow near Kedar. It was so named because at this spot Conrad Beissel "had unrested his spirit, prayed and had had a vision." It served as a chapel for the Householders, or the married brethren who formed the third order. In size it was forty feet by forty feet, two stories high, light and airy, and its worship hall had a high ceiling with heavy beams. Broad galleries on the north and south sides were supported by posts. No iron was used in its construction. This building survives as part of the present complex of Ephrata buildings.

Fig. 29. Interior of the Chapel at Ephrata.

Fig. 30. The *Gemein Haus*, Bethlehem.

In 1742, under the rule of Israel Eckerlin who was trying to make Ephrata a self-sustaining commune, a flour mill, paper mill, oil mill and saw mill were added. In 1743 a print shop was built.

Late in 1743 the second major building which still stands, called Hebron, was begun, its gable placed at right angles to Penial. It was seventy by thirty feet and had two entrances, one for each sex. The highpitched roof was to ward off the heavy snows. It had equally spaced windows, doors five feet high with wooden latches, cells ten feet by five feet each with a small window, a bench for sleeping with wood block pillows. The stairway was dark and narrow leading to the upper floors, which have sleeping cells grouped about a common room. The cells were unheated, but each common room had an iron stove.

Knowledge of the Moravian architecture coming from the center of the church at Bethlehem is not yet complete. The first house which stood where Bethlehem now is was the small log house, now restored, where on Sunday, December 24, 1741, the Christmas vigils were celebrated and the place named. During the next summer other smallish log houses were built, one having a hospital room. A primitive log tavern also was built.

In September, 1742, the chief building of early Bethlehem was begun, the *Gemein Haus* (Fig. 30), a log structure originally forty-five feet by thirty feet with a roof ridge truncated at the gables. Intended for many purposes this building was the traditional *Sbor* or *Dun*, church house, of Bohemia and Moravia which was more than a manse but also served as hospice, office, academy, etc. This Bethlehem structure still stands, although its logs now are concealed by sheaths.

Early in 1743 a grist mill was built in Bethlehem, and other buildings for the crafts begun. Meanwhile a stone structure was erected in the Moravian village of Nazareth which was planned to be a part of an interracial experiment where a Negro school and cabins for Indians were envisaged.

Another important structure in Bethlehem was *das Gasthaus zur Krone,* the Crown Inn, which was started in 1744. There soon followed the middle section of the old Seminary locally known as the "bell house" which contained a refectory for the single brothers, a general dining room, and apartments for private living. More stone structures soon followed.

Several early Bethlehem Moravians were trained architects. The original plans for the Sun Inn, built in 1758 to replace the Crown, survive (Fig. 31), and they show that architects of professional competence were working in Bethlehem at this early date, making this village equal to Philadelphia in architectual importance. The extent of building in Bethlehem at this

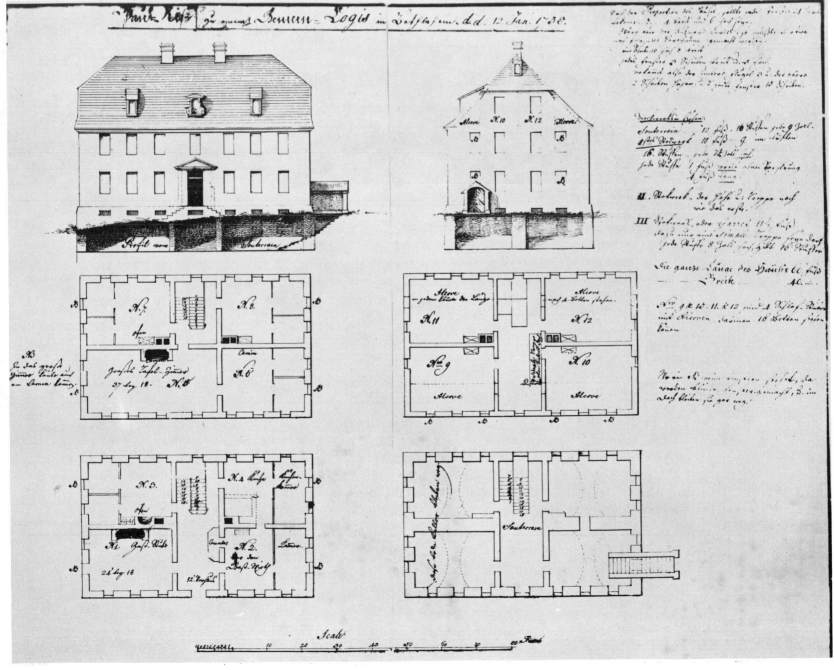

Fig. 31. Original plans of the Sun Hotel, Bethlehem.

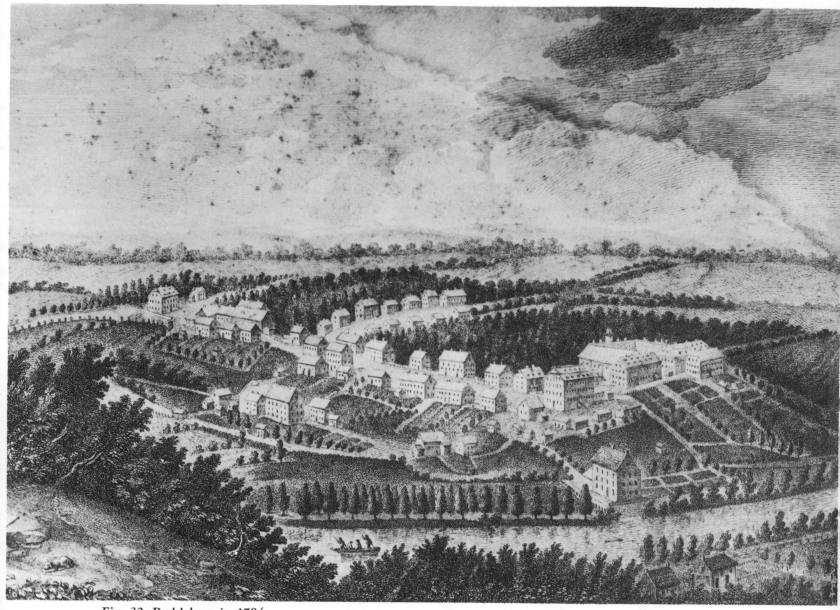

Fig. 32. Bethlehem in 1784.

time was such that many mills and workshops were built by these trained men; in 1746 a linen-bleaching establishment was erected and in 1747 two sawmills.

By the end of the century, as old engravings show (Fig. 32), Bethlehem was a Pennsylvania community with an atmosphere of its own, typically Continental in architecture which made travellers from the old world remember with nostalgia the cities they had left behind. Indeed, even today, walking in the old section of the city, one easily imagines himself in the cities of eighteenth-century Saxony.

Coming of the Georgian

The so-called Georgian style of architecture, in which the classicism of eighteenth-century Europe came to elegant provincial expression, first appeared in Pennsylvania. Slow to come to New England because it was hard to express its finely classical spirit in wood, the stone and brick structures of Pennsylvania—as well as later ones in Virginia and South Carolina—served to bring to the American countryside, especially the banks of the Schuylkill in Philadelphia, a mood almost elegantly European.

However, already in Hope Lodge in Whitemarsh the classicism of Wren and his school had produced a structure in brick which was Georgian in style. Then too, the basically Germanic stone structure, as shown by Johann Michael Staudt's farmhouse at Stoudt's Ferry, had already evolved to the point where by the simple addition of a few classical decorative features a Georgian mood could be gained. Thus the so-called Pastorius House from Germantown, which dates from about 1760, marks the transition from the plain stone farmhouse to the developing Georgian (Fig. 33). This same mood was also carried to other buildings in the country, especially some of the stone houses in the Coventry region of Chester County and Pottsgrove, which was built for the iron master John Potts in 1752 (Fig. 34). This home, which was used by General Washington as headquarters in September, 1777, marks the high point of development in the stone house which appears to have entered Pennsylvania through Germantown.

The traditional Georgian facade was generally a rectangular expression of the classical golden mean proportion—three measures wide and two measures high. It was usually set high on its foundation and showed impressive panelled doorways with classical pilasters, multi-

Fig. 33. The "Pastorius House" in Germantown.

Fig. 34. Pottsgrove, Pottstown, showing the influence of Germantown architecture.

paned windows, and narrow dormers. Inside, the house was classical in spirit with woodwork rich in finish and craftsmanship, handsome staircases with sweeping polished handrails, panelled rooms with hardwood floors, and small fireplaces with either marble or tiled facades. The Pennsylvania Georgian mansion was a fit structure to house the magnificent classical furniture then being made by the Philadelphia craftsmen.

One of the earliest of these Georgian mansions was Laurel Hill, in Northern Liberties, Fairmont Park. Here is a striking example of the early Philadelphia Georgian, a structure two stories high, with hipped roof and brick walls painted yellow. The woodwork is white, and its classical doorway is flanked by semi-engaged columns supported by a pediment which is repeated in another pediment above. The original inhabitants were a family friendly to the proprietor, Francis Rawle.

Grumblethrope, the Wister house in Germantown, was built as early as 1744 by John Wister who had come from Heidelberg. This house had many historic associations, for here Franklin erected the first lightning rod in America; and here too Count Zinzendorf visited, and the chairs known as the "Zinzendorf chairs" long were cherished. As it now stands the structure has been considerably modified. Originally it had a plain stone front with no dormers above and with a pent roof between the stories. It was much like the Pastorius house and Pottsgrove, probably a later expression of the Germanic stone house. In 1908 it underwent modernization when the front facade was redone and the classical columns were added to the doorway. However, this historic Pennsylvania structure still expresses the mood of the Georgian style in its well-proportioned lines and almost classical symmetry of line. The date of the original structure is about 1755.

One of the most interesting of the distinctly Philadelphia Georgian houses is Woodford, also standing in Northern Liberties, Fairmont Park, where Isaac Wharton once lived. This structure dates from before 1756, when extensive enlargements were added. Its central hall runs the full depth of the house, and inside are lovely carved chimney pieces and woodwork. Here lived William Coleman, Franklin's friend, who was member of the famous "Junto"—scholar, jurist and merchant of note (Fig. 35).

Surely the most historic of all Pennsylvania Georgian structures is Clivenden, home of the Chew family in Germantown. (Fig. 36) Judge Benjamin Chew was one of Philadelphia's most distinguished citizens. His house, two and a half stories high, with stone steps, fluted

Fig. 35. Woodford, Philadelphia.

Fig. 36. Clivenden, the Chew House in Germantown. The Battle of German-town was fought around the house.

columns of Doric style, is entirely typical of Philadelphia Georgian and an excellent example of the austere, scholarly phase of the Georgian before "prettiness" appeared. With massive panelled chimneys and classic doorways, the walls are topped by urns. This house was the scene of many historic events and filled with important personages such as Lafayette who visited in 1825. Its builder was Judge Chew, Virginia born but with a Quaker grandmother, a man who could not keep away from conflict with the Monthly Meeting of the Quakers. Dittys were written about this tension:

> Immortal Chew first set our Quakers right
> He made it plain they might resist and fight;
> And the gravest Dons agreed to what he said,
> And freely gave their coat for the King's aid,
> For war successful, and for peace and trade.

Clivenden was the scene of the chief incident in the Battle of Germantown, October 4, 1777. British soldiers of the Fortieth Regiment entered the house and used it as a fortress, barring the doors and shutters. This resistance slowed the American advance and upset Washington's plan for the battle, and the house showed its effects. Plaster was pitted and a six pound ball had entered a window, passed through four partitions, and out the back. Here too lived Peggy Chew, one of the Judge's romantic daughters, who was involved with the British Major André.

One of the most beautiful structures in all America, an exquisite example of the Philadelphia Georgian, is Mount Pleasant, also in Fairmont Park. This noble eighteenth-century structure, which John Adams called the most elegant seat in Pennsylvania, dates from around 1760 (Fig. 37). It is built of cut stone with heavy brick groins, great quadruple chimney stacks, a broad flight of stone steps leading to a pedimented Doric dorway, and a hipped roof. Inside are hand-tooled cornices, pilasters, pediments, recessed cupboards, arched chimneys—a magnificent structure. Originally it was built by Captain John MacPherson, a Scotch sailor from Edinburgh, who called it Clunie. General Benedict Arnold, military governor of the city, bought it for his bride, Peggy Shippen, March 22, 1779. It was later leased to Baron von Steuben and was owned for a time by Jonathan Williams, the first Superintendent of West Point.

The Philadelphia Georgian came to brilliant expression in the city itself in the Powel House (Fig. 39), built by Charles Stedman in 1765 and purchased by Samuel Powel four years later. On the outside this was a city dwelling in the plain London style, typical of the row house. Inside, however, it was the epitome of eighteenth-century elegance. Here dined and danced the great and near great, gracing the magnificent interior with its impressive pannelling, solid mahogany doors, carved mantles, expansive fireplaces, many-paned windows,

Fig. 37. Mount Pleasant, Philadelphia. Restored in 1925, this is the finest piece of domestic architecture of the early Pennsylvania period.

Fig. 38. Vernon Park, the John Wister home in Germantown.

ornately plastered ceilings, and ballustraded stairways. In the garden stood elegant statuary imported from Europe. On the whole this was the masterpiece of city architecture and its upstairs drawing room was the ball room for great social occasions. Its exquisite, carved fireplace represents a hunting scene and on the ceiling above are armorial bearings with decorative plaster.

The Georgian style of architecture, then, took three forms: a basically Wren-like building like Hope Lodge and the Fisher House of Oley (Fig. 40), which was a development of the classical style in brick and stone; the structure whose facade was broken by classical pediments, and this style was confined almost wholly to the suburbs surrounding the city; and the style that was the modification of the Powel house, Georgian adapted to the city.

By the end of the eighteenth century architecture and carpentry were standardized. To the books already available for young architects and carpenters, many were being written by American authors. Philadelphia builders added to this list. Among these works was William Pain's *The Practical House Carpenter; or Youth's Instructor, Containing a Great Variety of Useful Designs in Carpentry and Architecture*, published in 1797. Another work, obviously designed for apprentices but still embodying the best designs, was Owen Biddle's *The Young Carpenter's Assistant; or a System of Architecture Adapted to the Style of Building in the United States*, published in 1810.

Fig. 39. The Powel House, Philadelphia, finest Georgian structure in the city.

Fig. 40. The Fisher House, Oley. Of undressed stone.

Some Public Buildings

Unquestionably the most important public building which stood in early Philadelphia was the Old Court House, or Town Hall, which was begun in 1707. It stood on Market Street west of Second Street, and it was the first venture of the young city in public architecture. Patterned after the town halls of England it also served as the center of the city's market system. Built of brick it had casements glazed with small diamond-shaped panes set in lead. In the front was a balcony set over an arched doorway, with stairs on each side. From this balcony elections were held. The provincial voters from city as well as country ascended the flight of stairs on the north, gave in their votes at the door, and then descended the south flight of stairs. From this balcony monarchs were proclaimed, newly-appointed governors addressed the people, and public proclamations were made. Under the arch the public auctions and vendues of the city were made. Behind this court house (Fig. 41) were market stalls for farmers from Pennsylvania and New Jersey, protected by a roof which was supported by brick piers and had a broad aisle down the middle. The illustration of this important early Philadelphia structure is taken from a broadside caricature of one of the most famous elections in our Colonial history—the time when the Germans switched their allegiance from the Quakers and voted with the Franklin party, and the tide of provincial affairs turned.

While the city was still doing its municipal and legal business in the Old Court House a second public structure, the Pennsylvania State House, was started about the year 1732 at Fifth and Chestnut Streets. By 1736 the first meeting of the Pennsylvania General Assembly was held in this structure. Originally the large central building lacked its center tower; not until 1791 was the tower finished. The entire complex of buildings, which became the center of memorable events—the signing of the Declaration of Independence and the ratification of the Constitution of the United States—was neither early Quaker nor Philadelphia Georgian. The buildings lacked the pent roof and door hood of the former and the classical ornateness

Fig. 41. Rare contemporary view of the Court House or Town Hall of Philadelphia, 1707. From a broadside ballad printed about 1765.

of the latter. The tower, added later, is however typical of Philadelphia Georgian, and it had the usual Doric doorway, Palladian windows, and Ionic and Corinthian pilasters which are reminiscent of Robert Smith and his school. The State House was the center of a group of buildings all in similar style which included the Episcopal Academy, Philosophical Hall, and the Philadelphia Library and Carpenter's Hall. An idea of how it looked near the end of the eighteenth century can be gotten from a corner of Charles Willson Peale's portrait of Gerard (Fig. 42). During most of the eighteenth century, up to the end of the Revolution, the State House yard was merely a fenced-in lot and did not have serpentine walks with gravelled paths.

Other significant public structures were being erected in the city. In 1747 the German Reformed Congregation built a six-cornered church in a style which was popular in the interior regions of the province. In 1756 the eastern block of the Pennsylvania Hospital was finished, and the next year the Bettering House in Spruce Street, above Ninth, was completed.

After the drab years of the American Revolution, when there was very little building of any kind, the city entered into what has been called the golden age of its architecture. In

Fig. 42. Independence Hall as it was. Detail from the Charles Willson Peale portrait of Gerard.

Fig. 43. The Bank of the United States on Third Street.

1790 the Library Company erected its home at Fifth and Library Streets. A new court house replaced the historic old one which had served for so many years. In 1791 a new theater was erected on Chestnut Street near Sixth, much to the chagrin of the Quakers. In 1792 the federal government began a presidential mansion, which was finished in 1797 but neither George Washington nor John Adams lived in it. In 1796 the west wing of the Pennsylvania Hospital, an example of Philadelphia Georgian, was erected.

The Georgian style, which had found so wide an acceptance in early Pennsylvania, and whose decorative details were usually laid over other forms, was not the only style which came to influence early Pennsylvania. In 1797 the First Bank of the United States was completed and the bank, which had formerly used Carpenter's Hall, moved into the new building on Third Street between Chestnut and Walnut Streets. Here a new mood began. Here classical architecture took its own form, and the so-called Greek Revival, which began in America here, was the use of forms which were more than merely decorative but which were soundly classical in pattern and design.

There followed in the city the Academy of Fine Arts in 1806 and the second Bank of the United States on Chestnut Street above Fourth Street in 1819, now known as the Old Custom House. With these structures the Greek Revival was soundly rooted in the city, and the public architecture reflected the classical temples of Greece.

Meanwhile, in the provincial towns, the public buildings also were being erected but with fewer classical influences. The court houses in the county seats of York, Lancaster, Reading, Allentown and to the east were expressions, not of the old Town Hall in old Philadelphia, but of the new marrrage of Georgian and classical styles. Lewis Miller's drawing of the York County Court House, with the hay scale erected in 1835 (Fig. 44), gives interesting glimpses into the life of the town.

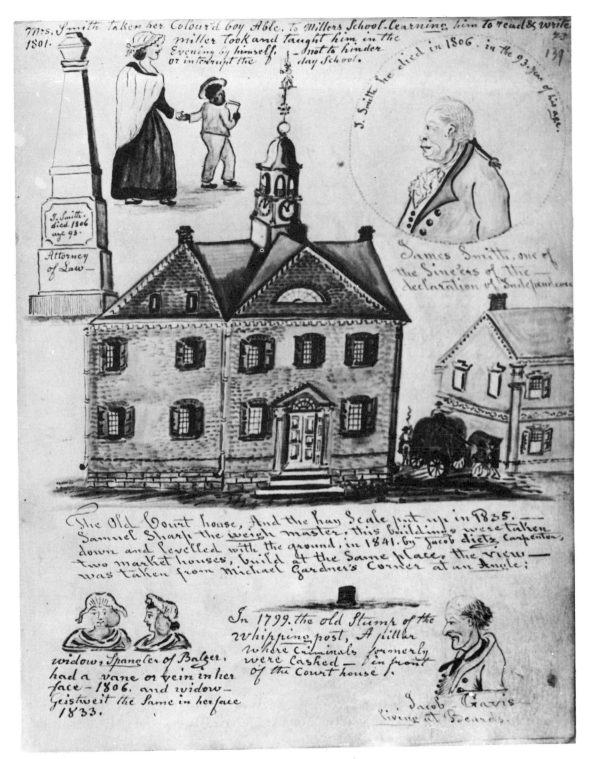

Fig. 44. Lewis Miller's sketch of the court house in York.

In the piedmont the German stone cabin had become the pattern out of which grew the plain meetinghouse. And from this plain meeting house the plain schoolhouse emerged, sometimes acquiring a classical doorway and hood, giving it a soundly Georgian mood. Thus the "Wolf Academy" (Fig. 45), near Bath, where George Wolfe who later became governor of the Commonwealth taught school, was adorned with pediment and columns which were severely classical in style. Built about 1815 this structure, now demolished but here shown in a photograph taken in 1914, reveals how the classical revival was early evident in the Pennsylvania piedmont.

Fig. 45. A 1914 photograph of the Wolff Academy, Bath, showing the lovely classical doorway.

A Fort in the Land of Peace

During the earlier years Pennsylvania was governed by men skilled in the peaceful arts although here and there along the rugged frontier forts were erected to protect the settlers from marauding savages. These were of course no European-type bastions, impervious to seige, but far plainer structures more suited to a quieter way of life. The enemy was no drilled legion from European princes but the restless savages across the mountains.

When these Indians—incited by the French, infuriated by white chicanery, and emboldened by whiskey—broke through frontier settlements into the developing piedmont the whole colony was excited and Philadelphia, long protected by the layer of German farms encircling it, became alarmed. This precipitated the one great political crisis of pre-Revolutionary Pennsylvania.

One of the forts erected against this menace was the Wilson Block House, a structure still standing at Northampton (Fig. 46). In January, 1756, when "Colonel" Benjamin Franklin, at the head of hastily-raised provincial troops, approached Bethlehem he found all in confusion. Families had loaded their belongings on sturdy German wagons and had decamped from their settlements. When Franklin's small force, hardly more than a patrol, arrived at Gnadenhütten, scene of a massacre, they began to build a fort named in honor of Franklin's friend William Allen. Other block houses were built at strategic points from the Delaware Water Gap to beyond Sunbury.

One of these forts was erected near the mill of Jost Dreisbach at Howersville. It is a small eight-cornered stone structure with walls two feet thick. It has no windows, but seven portholes, with a door on the south side. It has been preserved from weathering by the addition of stucco coating, a slate roof and a retaining wall behind it to protect it from the flooding creek nearby.

Fig. 46. The Wilson Block House, Northampton, erected by Benjamin Franklin.

The Pennsylvania Barn

Hot summers and long cold winters made for both good crops of hay and many months during which the domestic animals had to be fed. And so, from the demands of the new American environment, came a new structure, the massive Pennsylvania barn, an enduring and rugged symbol of the prosperous farm-craft economy of the Pennsylvania piedmont.

Already in the eighteenth century the Pennsylvania barn, then not yet at the zenith of its development, attracted comment from visitors who remarked about its size. Like the long

Fig. 47. Decorated barn near the Chestnut Hill Church, Lehigh.

rifle, the Pennsylvania barn was an adaptation of European forms. No other American colony developed an architectural form as unique as this one: a place to store grain, a stable, and sometimes the first temporary shelter for human beings.

The earliest structure was the unsheathed log barn. Few, if any, of these survive. From old photographs we can see what the eighteenth-century countryside must have looked like with split-rail fences and timbered structures. Stone barns did not appear until about 1740 or 1750. The first structures were wood, reminiscent of the timbered buildings of northern Europe.

There was then threefold evolution from these primitive structures to the modern massive barn of today. First, as stated, was the log barn, often with dwelling attached, built in traditional European timbered construction. Next came the small stone barn, often with some wood, already an adaptation to meet American conditions. Finally, about the middle of the nineteenth century, came the large stone barn which now dominates our present landscape. Each structure was part-traditional and part-adaptation to American conditions in the same way that the frontiersman took the European axe and made it into the curve-handled balanced American tool.

The second stage brought the small structure which is reminiscent of the cantilever or over-hanging forebay barn of parts of the Palatinate and Alpine heights. An interesting feature of some of these barns is the cluster of loopholes or ballustrades in the walls with widened inner spaces for discharging small arms. Straw thatch or hand-split wooden shingles were used for the roof. Although this second phase of the Pennsylvania barn recalls European forms, it was not a blind imitation of old world modes but showed imaginative adaptation.

The third phase of Pennsylvania barn construction, from about 1840 to 1860 and beyond, was that of the large massive barn we see today. Here we are well beyond the period of migration; the builders of these barns were the third or fourth American generation; therefore it seems needless to try to trace these barns back to Europe.

This three-fold development shows the dynamic movement from frontier to stable settlement. The log structures were, as always, symbols of the frontier. After 1740, as the piedmont

Fig. 48. Rear of a decorated barn.

Fig. 49. Decorated barn, Berks County, circa 1865.

Fig. 50. The six-lobed star (*Sechsstern*) and the traditional heart, Berks County.

Fig. 51. Barn near Steinsberg, Lehigh, decorated by Noah Weiss, the woodcarver.

Fig. 52. Barn near New Smithville, Berks.

Fig. 53. Decorated *Vorschuss* near Allentown.

came to be developed and as some sense of stability came, the smaller stone-wood barns appeared. Finally, after 1840, the huge barn came.

If we study the second stage structures and ignore the larger nineteenth-century barns, we can see that the line which separates piedmont and tidewater again is reflected in these barns of the 1740-1840 period and which appear above the escarpment which runs just below Trappe, along the "Lambert line" that also separates the English-speaking from the dialect-speaking people.

Very few of these 1740-1840 structures were decorated. Most early barns were unpainted, for painting of barns did not begin until about 1850. The dating of these barns shows when the painting was done, not when the barn was built.

The question of the meaning of the six-lobed and other geometrical designs painted on the barns after 1850 is highly controversial. Some claim that these designs were put on the barns to scare the witches away. This theory has many fallacies. In the first place, it is human beings, not cattle or domestic animals, who are bewitched. The little dickens who assaults cattle is not a witch but Puck, Robin Goodfellow, or, as we say in Germanic Pennsylvania, "Bucklich Männli." To protect cattle and other animals against this michievous sprite, the Pennsylvania Germans made small charms and nailed them to the barn rafters. Then butter would churn, milk would come, and the garden would grow. The hex or witch was active against human beings and so no sign ought to be painted on a barn.

The second reason why it is difficult to believe that barn signs are hex signs is simply because the Pennsylvania German people themselves do not believe it. This theory has been made outside of Pennsylvania. Over four hundred people, whose barns have these signs on them, were interviewed, many vehemently deny belief in witches, and some argue that this theory comes from "outsiders" and then they tell them where they may proceed to. None willingly confesses to this belief.

The third reason why the hex sign theory is not acceptable is because, in Europe, these designs have religious association. The distinguished German architect, Dr. Karl Rumpf, has published an article in *Rheinisches Jahrbuch Für Volkskunde* entitled "Geometrische Ornamentik an südtiroler Stadeltoren" in which he traces these six-lobed designs back to South Tirol. Dr. Rumpf pictures one of these barn-doors with designs and the letters I H S and a cross. Now, if this be a hex sign no one—no one in his right mind—would use these holy symbols in association with it! While there is some talismanic meaning linked with it, and while it is a good-luck symbol, surely it has nothing to do with *hexen* or other demonic characters.

To admit that these designs are talismanic, however, is not to say that they do not bring good luck. This, though, is true of any religious symbol, even of the crucifixes, medals, and the images of holy persons. They are employed to bring good fortune rather than to ward off the witches.

FURNITURE

L ike architecture, which it expresses, furniture was dependent upon cultural modes too. In Pennsylvania three phases were apparent—elegant, primitive, and plain—and we have to distinguish between them.

Originally furniture was not movable. The English *furniture*, the German *Möbel*, and the French *meuble* imply mobility—the idea that these pieces can be moved from place to place. Here already the distinction between primitive and developed furniture is implied for in the earliest period, furniture was built in and was the work of the house carpenter. The German word *Zimmermann*, meaning carpenter, suggests that his task was to build the furniture into a room.

Freely movable furniture did not appear in rural Britain or Germany until the end of the fourteenth century and even afterwards. Until well into the eighteenth century in Pennsylvania, much interior appointment was built in. In those days carpenters were easily recognizable, as they went from place to place, by their characteristic garb—wide trousers, cut-out vests, gnarled walking sticks and tool chests. It was these workmen who made the beds, tables, benches, and wardrobes in the earliest period, and with the passing of primitive buildings most of their work has disappeared.

So the primitive Pennsylvania cabin was furnished—if this be the correct word—with tables of hewn stuff which often rested on ponderous puncheons driven into the ground. Blocks of wood, stools, and benches served for sitting, and crude wooden bedsteads or berths were contrived along the walls, sometimes in tiers to accomodate the large families. There were, many times, no beds at all and the people slept on pallets, wrapped in bedding of zealously hoarded material brought from the old world.

So primitive furniture was really not cabinetmaker's work but was either built in as part of the room or made by carpenters as mobile pieces. Very little of this primitive furniture has come down, and our great museums seem to have been made not to show the history of furnishings but to show off the finest examples. Evidence of this furniture does, however, show up, such as the interesting picture—molded into an iron stove plate dated 1746—that shows a Pennsylvania Dutch maiden dancing to a fiddler and a primitive sawbuck table with a glass and mug of beer (Fig. 55).

Fig. 54. Painted arrowback Pennsylvania settee.

Moreover, there also is little evidence regarding the source of the plain tradition among the early Pennsylvania Quakers. We may perhaps deduce what this view was by evidence from Ireland gathered by the Quaker historian, Frederick Tolles, who found that Irish Friends drew up a paper decrying elegance in furniture, saying,

As to chest of drawers, they ought to be plain and of one color, without swelling works.

As to tables and chairs, they ought to be all made plain, without carving, keeping out all new fashions as they come up, and to keep to the fashion that is serviceable.

And as to making great mouldings one above the other, about press-beds and clock-cases, [they] ought to be avoided, only what is decent according to truth.

So that all furniture should be plain and of one color.

In the *Friends Library* for 1838, a periodical which gathered many early Quaker Journals and Diaries, there is printed *Some Account of the Life of Joseph Pike* who has this to say about Quaker views on furniture during this early period:

Our fine veneered and garnished cases of drawers, tables, stands, cabinets, scrutoires, &c, we put away [upon becoming Quakers], or exchanged for decent plain ones of solid wood without superfluous garnishing or ornamental work; our wainscoats or wood-work we had painted of one plain color, our large mouldings or finishings of panelling, &c, our swelling chimney-pieces, curiously turned banisters, we took down and replaced with useful plain wood-work, &c; our curtains,

Fig. 55. Stove plate with fiddler, German dancing woman and sawbuck table,
dated 1746.

with valances, drapery, and fringes that we thought too fine, we put away and cut off; our large looking glasses with decorated frames we sold, or made them into smaller ones; and our [china] closets that were laid out with many little curios or nice things were done away.

Thus on becoming a member of the Society of Friends the new convert was expected to renounce elegance in interior appointments, and he sought to express his simpler tastes by avoiding all unnecessary vanities in dress, speech, manners, architecture, and house furnishings.

So early Pennsylvania had a well-established furniture industry. Cabinet-makers were making plain furniture for the city people. Penn brought a Dutch joiner with him and by 1715 at least sixty furniture makers were working in Pennsylvania, although some of these may have been joiners for a short time, moving quickly to other trades.

It is easy to exaggerate the amount of material imported. The cost of transatlantic freight was so high that only the wealthy could bring in bulky pieces. About 1700 the cost of importing a ton of freight was thirty pounds sterling and for this sum the immigrant could purchase a city block or over six hundred acres of virgin forest with wood enough for many tons of furniture.

This plain spirit was a product of religious dissent. Some would say that the plain tradition is Protestant. This is only partly true. The Reformers were of course iconoclasts, rejecting medieval images; but this plain mood was reflected among sixteenth-century Anabaptists whose descendents also came to Pennsylvania. It became strong during the seventeenth century where a similar spirit was reflected in literature when the euphuistic style of the Elizabethan period was rejected for a simpler mode of writing.

Fig. 56. Pennsylvania pine sawbuck table, circa 1730.

Fig. 57. Pennsylvania pine stretcher table, circa 1750.

Colonial Philadelphia was not all Quaker. Nevertheless the Quakers dominated the trades of joiner, turner, clockmaker, carver, potter, glassmaker, pewterer, and silversmith. They made and sold elegant wares even thought they were reluctant to use them themselves. How they reconciled their own rejection of elegance in private with public manufacture of elegant furniture is not known.

The greatest cabinetmakers of the city in the period of its flourishing were Quakers: Savery, Affleck, Letchworth, Daniel Evans, the Claypooles, and silversmiths Richardsons and Wistars. Not only did these craftsmen sell elegant wares to non-Quakers; they sold to wealthy Quakers too who lived in the comfortable homes on Front and Chestnut Streets. Many of the finest and most elegant pieces of Colonial Pennsylvania furniture came out of old Quaker families, and by the middle of the eighteenth century the pieces made for Friends were no less ornate than those made for non-Quakers. Quakers were in truth plain but they admitted good workmanship and symmetry.

In the piedmont however the plain tradition lasted far longer. Here the plain pieces were sometimes fashioned in pine, in styles that remind us of seventeenth-century Europe.

Pennsylvania Furniture Before Queen Anne

Soon after Pennsylvania was founded William and Mary ascended the British throne and it was not long before the French influences of the Restoration began to give way to a heavier Dutch style. This change was reflected, albeit a bit later, in the earliest furniture made in Pennsylvania.

However, in this first period of Pennsylvania furniture differences were already evident. Post-Restoration English furniture was either of oak or of English walnut. British walnut was paler and easily preyed on by worms, and, at this period, American black walnut, so characteristically Pennsylvania, was not yet being exported in bulk, and the hardwoods later furnished in quantity to Europe were not yet widely used.

This early Pennsylvania furniture then shows the characteristic decorative features of knob, twisted spiral, and modelled turnings. Chairs were high-backed, sometimes with cane panels enclosed by scroll carvings or hand-cut moldings. In addition there were embossed low chests, panelled cupboards, and gateleg tables in walnut, oak, and fruit woods—all in characteristic Dutch-inspired styles.

Ornamentation, much simpler in Pennsylvania than in Britain or Holland, was added by four methods. Veneering was widespread during this period. Next was turning which, while not always graceful, was at least employed for the embellishment of uprights, arm posts, and balusters. The main pattern was the trumpet. Third some Philadelphia furniture of this period is known to have been japanned or lacquered. However, far less Pennsylvania furniture was thus decorated, compared with New England and New York; for where New England joiners used soft porous woods and then covered their imperfections with paint the Pennsylvania craftsmen from the beginning were reluctant to cover the exquisite black walnut with paint. However we do know that some japanning was done around 1700 by Charles Plumley and as late as 1727 japanned furniture of local manufacture was known. The last means of ornamenting was by carving in styles and designs directly imported from foreign originals—shells, straps, and scrolls. In the carving of this period there was precious little that was original and all ornamentation was scratchy and fibrous. At this period the flourishing craftsmen were far more than pioneers with only hatchet and saw, but they were not yet specialized craftsmen; for there was as yet no specialization, and all phases of the craft were performed by one person.

Rare as it is, this early Pennsylvania furniture, made for the wainscoated houses of the young province, was heavy and stiff. Nor was all of it city made; some was manufactured in the sparsely settled outlying areas. However, on the whole the furniture of this period of Pennsylvania history is hard to distinguish from European styles except that our American ornamentation is cruder and somewhat later in period and already a bit old fashioned.

This early period was indeed the age of the table, which came in assorted sizes and shapes, and which was used in every room of the house. Around 1723 Governor Keith had six large folding tables of mahogany and walnut, eight smaller tables, one mahogany tea table, twelve assorted tables, and five assorted tea tables. The gate-leg table was characteristic of this age and long tables were used both as dining tables and as sideboards.

Although these early houses were full of tables, we cannot say the same of bedsteads. Most early inventories mention no bedsteads although there is mention, in listing contents of bedrooms, of bed curtains. We do know that Pennsbury had no bedsteads. This suggests that at this period the bed was still a built-in piece and that most of these early rooms had an alcove or closet bed concealed by drapes. The truth is that moveable bedsteads did not show in quantity in early Pennsylvania until about 1725.

Also during this period the chest of drawers was evolving and had not yet reached the

Fig. 58. Restored dining room at Pennsbury, example of the William and Mary style.

height of its development. First was the plain hinged-top chest. Characteristically seventeenth century this chest next became a box with drawers at the bottom, then a chest of drawers on stump feet, and finally a chest of drawers on legs with stretchers. In early Philadelphia a highboy began to appear, and by 1725 it was almost mandatory for a Colonial gentleman to have a high chest of drawers in his dining room or drawing room.

So by about 1720 Pennsylvania furniture had passed through its imitative stage and was ready to begin its course as an embellishment for the great mansions which were also being erected at this time in Penn's new world land.

Early Plain Chairs

Two kinds of chairs appeared in early Philadelphia as expression of the plain taste which dominated the Quaker town and which rejected the luxury of upholstered furniture. Fewer wing chairs and other upholstered pieces were made in early Philadelphia than in either New England or New York because of the dissenting antagonism to elegant comfort. Both of these chair forms were adaptations of European styles.

The first style was the cane-seated chair, sometimes also called the ladder-back which was almost universal in the city and surrounding regions. It derived from the thin-legged chair popular in Stuart England and it can be traced back to the Yorkshire ladder-back and to some Derbyshire chair forms. However, it was already an adaptation rather than a copy. After the Restoration these Yorkshire chairs had become highly ornate, with finely carved slats. Philadelphia plain traditions rejected these carvings, as well as those of balusters; the slats of Philadelphia chairs were plain and slightly incurved.

So the Philadelphia ladder-back chair became a chair with plainly incurved slats which separated well-turned maple balusters. These balusters were only rarely twisted or shaped like vases. Also the stretchers were relatively simple although in some instances carved heads and arched tops are known to have been made. Moreover, American woods were used; where Yorkshire chairs had been chiefly of oak, the Philadelphia ladder-backs were of maple and sometimes hickory. Sometimes the slats were painted with floral designs.

Three years after the founding of the province, William Stanley and James Claypoole were making these adaptations of Yorkshire ladder-backs in the city. The portrait of the mystic Johannes Kelpius shows him seated on one of these chairs. From 1710 on, this style of chair was widespread in Philadelphia homes, and they were even then considered to be quite fashionable so that craftsmen like William Savery and Caleb Emlen did not disdain to make them.

Of course the Quaker prejudice against upholstered furniture could be kept if one put a cushion on the seat!

The second plain style of chair which became so popular in Philadelphia that it carries the name was the Windsor, known also as the Philadelphia Windsor chair. There can be no question that this originally British style appealed to simpler Quaker tastes. Many of the joiners who made these Windsors were themselves Quakers: Thomas Ackley was a Friend and John Letchworth was a minister among Friends.

The Windsor chair caught on fast in early Philadelphia. Although we cannot say with certainty that Philadelphia was its birthplace, we do know that these chairs were being made here as early as 1708, and that by 1760 the Philadelphia Windsor had outstripped all other chairs in popularity. Thirty of these chairs graced Mount Vernon, and Thomas Jefferson was well-enough acquainted with them to call them "stick chairs."

The Windsor consists of a wooden plank seat, somewhat shaped, which supports both legs and spindles. This related it to the German plank chair. It was fundamentally a peasant style and it also allowed for much individuality which in turn resulted in forceful turnings, graceful legs, varied shapes, and sometimes even an oriental "bamboo" style. The proportions of these chairs were nearly perfect.

While there is no justification for the attempt to periodize the Windsor chair by shape, we may assert that in general those chairs with rectangular backs were made later than those with round backs. Moreover, sometime around 1738, the Windsor chair was made into the rocking chair, first called a "nursing chair." It has not been proven that Benjamin Franklin invented this chair form.

Fig. 59. Windsor chairs in the restored Assembly Room, Independence Hall.

Fig. 60. Restored kitchen, Landis Valley Farm Museum.

So Windsor chairs were being manufactured in Philadelphia after 1715, and from there they were being shipped all over Colonial America. Among the earlier makers were Robert Barton, Joseph Saul, James Cresson and Caleb Emlen. The last of these is known to have made "white chairs, children's chairs and red chairs" before his death in 1748.

The Philadelphia Windsor chair was a fashionable parlor piece. John Penn had a set of Windsors made by John Ware. Stephen Girard also had a set. From Philadelphia these chairs spread all over the Colonies. An advertisement in a Charleston newspaper carried a notice by Messers. Sheed and White offering Philadelphia-made chairs as follows: "well-painted, high-back'd, low back'd, sack-back'd and setees or double seated, fit for piaza or garden, childrens' chairs and low chairs." New York newspapers also mentioned Philadelphia-made chairs for sale and just before the Revolution and immediately thereafter large numbers of these Windsors were being shipped to the other colonies, to the West Indies and even to Europe.

These later Philadelphia Windsors were simplified still more and the pierced slat which was sometimes used on British chairs and which relates it to the European plank chair, was little used in American Windsors. Among later Philadelphia makers were John Gilbert, Samuel Austin, Joseph Arnutt, Francis Trumble, John Briggard, Benjamin Trotter, Samuel Williams, and Jedidiah Snowden. Piedmont craftsmen also were making them.

After 1750 the export of these chairs to Barbados, Salem in New England, St. Christophers, and New Providence became large. As many as sixty chairs were being shipped in one lot, along with book cases, clock cases and other furniture. In 1789 and 1790 shipments in lots from a dozen to a gross were being made. During these years 454 Windsors were shipped to Virginia, 178 to Georgia, 280 to North Carolina, 1790 to Charleston, 450 to Barbados, and 698 to the West Indies—almost four thousand chairs. Many were carried along the back roads into the interior parts of America.

Windsor chairs were solid and durable, well-suited for use in public institutions. The Pennsylvania Hospital and Carpenter's Hall had sets, and Francis Trumble, Joseph Henzer and John Letchworth supplied seventy-eight for the Pennsylvania State House. From tavern to fine mansions, like that of Jonathan Dickinson Sergeant, the Philadelphia Windsor was unquestionably the most successful and popular creation of the plain taste of early Pennsylvania.

The Style of the "Good Queen Anne"

After the first vigorous period of Philadelphia cabinetmaking, which had begun with the founding of the colony and which lasted until about 1720, a noticeable decline in the quality of Pennsylvania furniture set in. The first flush of creativity was over. Buildings, which had been erected in the fresh vigor of the earlier years, decayed. New ones were needed, and about 1720 the large mansions of the tidewater region were beginning to be built.

Although the good Queen Anne—we call her the "good queen" because of her generous help in settling the Germans in Pennsylvania—had ruled from 1702 to 1714, the style which was fashionable in Great Britain during her reign was belated in appearing in Philadelphia. British furniture then still was in the later phases of the age of walnut (1690-1720) which had emerged as an expression of the politer ways of living succeeding the periods of Revolution and Restoration. Queen Anne furniture lost the stiffness of the more formal earlier style and gained marked ease and comfort. A clear elegance and lightness began to show: ponderous gate-legged tables disappeared; chairs no longer had narrow backs; tapestry replaced panelling on the walls; wainscoating replaced larger panels; and finally there was a marked expansion of furniture forms for tea tables, sideboard tables and even card tables—horror to good Quakers—began to show.

Fig. 61. A room of Philadelphia Queen Anne furniture.

While Great Britain thus was moving towards new graciousness, provincial Pennsylvania followed—but more slowly. No true Queen Anne furniture is known to have been made here before 1714, the year the good queen died. In Pennsylvania the William and Mary style died slowly and these new fashions were likewise slow to root; but, once rooted, they too were slow to die, for Queen Anne furniture continued to be made in Pennsylvania well down into the Chippendale period. Thus a piece of Philadelphia Queen Anne furniture may date anywhere from 1715 to 1750 and it dare not be credited to the time when the good queen reigned.

Moreover, in addition to being later in period, Philadelphia Queen Anne furniture also was simpler in style than its British counterpart. Where English Queen Anne furniture depended on carving, gilding, veneering and similar techniques for its decoration, our Pennsylvania furniture was marked by good symmetry and proportion, and it betrayed a delicate grace unequaled by the old world pieces. Our cabinetmakers produced no grotesque birds, no fanciful beasts' heads, no gilding or heavily carved slats. These extravagant motifs, inherited from the furniture of the Stuart period, were definitely out of place in a city whose houses had plain walls, small rooms, whose early architecture was austere, and many of whose citizens wore plain gray clothes.

Philadelphia Queen Anne furniture was none-the-less creative. Our cabinetmakers, possessing few printed patterns, were free to follow their fancies and they developed their own graceful contours without the awkwardness common to British pieces. A few guide books were around but their details seem not to have been imitated; instead, a simpler sincerer symmetry showed in which an American spirit already was evident.

These opening decades of the eighteenth century were still the age of classicism, a time when Latin and Greek were widely read, and when not only literature but all the arts were influenced by classical culture. This influence was, however, direct. Even ordinary craftsmen knew classical forms. They were capable of lifting elements from classical architecture and using them in their work: egg and dart moldings, acanthus leaves, dentils, and astragal beading, all derived from the corinthian column. Such elements were the common property of craftsmen long before Chippendale included them in his book. James Logan of Stenton had in his library a copy of the Latin work on architecture by Vitruvius in which such details were shown.

This was in truth the age of walnut—and more walnut! Our wonderful American native wood, black walnut, was far superior to English wood, so much so that in 1720 the South Sea Company formed a subsidiary to bring it to England. In 1731 walnut worth fifteen thousands pounds sterling was shipped, and by 1770 this had grown to one hundred fifty thousand pounds sterling—a tenfold increase. Logs were rafted down the Pennsylvania rivers and sawed in tidewater, there being forty sawmills in Philadelphia County alone. Why should Pennsylvania craftsmen ignore this magnificent wood that, because of its bitter taste, was not attacked by worms, that did not splinter easily and that took a fine finish, especially when burled?

Other American woods also were used, especially maple, hard and rich-looking, which became so popular that almost every mansion had a room full of maple furniture. Both Stenton and Hope Lodge boasted such rooms. Fruit woods were also popular, but spasmodically, although the straight-grained wild cherry seems to have had a steady vogue because it wore well and became lovelier as it grew older.

Genuine mahogany continued to be imported from Jamaica although it was already becoming scarce and the lighter, straighter-grained, tropical cedar, so often confused with genuine mahogany, was beginning to be used instead. 1708 marks the beginning of the American use of genuine mahogany, but as the years passed, the Cuban and Canary Island red cedar supplanted it.

This age saw the coming of the two-parlor house: one parlor was more formal, the company parlor, and contained chairs, tea tables, corner cupboard (usually built-in), mirror, several walnut tables, and perhaps a desk; the other parlor, less formal, was used for family living and contained a couch bed, chairs, a pine table, cradle, and general family furniture. The formal parlor was genteel in mood, the family parlor homey.

Another innovation during this period was the increased popularity of several furniture forms. There were many more bookcases in use, as well as books. Daybeds or "couch chairs" were in the best family parlors. Side-boards and side tables appeared, some with walnut frames and marble slabs. Knife cases grew more elaborate. Gaming tables of all kinds appeared in spite of the Quaker objection to "vain and evil sports and games." Highboys with matching lowboys stood in almost every well-equipped bedroom, although there was as yet little variety in these pieces. And during this period bedsteads began to appear as separate pieces and no longer as built-in alcoves, especially with hanging curtains; the bed-posts still were hidden by the ever-present drapes. Underneath, however, was the trundle bed with no posts extending above the rails.

So the furniture of the good queen Anne served as the style of transition, linking the forms inherited from the Renaissance with those forms which were to come to glory in the golden age of Philadelphia furniture.

Fig. 62. Philadelphia Georgian furniture.

Philadelphia Georgian Furniture

Was there a Philadelphia Georgian style of furniture, one which is as sharply defined as the earlier Queen Anne or the later Chippendale?

Some students question it and some writers pass directly from Queen Anne to Chippendale. Others however claim to see a specific Georgian style and some even suggest that there were recognizable periods like an earlier Georgian and a later one.

Although in the main, American furniture styles were later than their European prototypes, and also somewhat simpler, there is a question whether all Philadelphia furniture which was made between 1730 and 1750 can be justly classed as Chippendale. Unquestionably there was a period during which Chippendale emerged—that style which was to become so popular—and there can be no doubt that elements of Chippendale were already present in furniture made in Philadelphia during the reign of George II (1727-1760), before the book by Chippendale was published.

The Chippendale style, which appeared full-blown when the book was published in the 1750s, had come to its flowering through a slow process of growth. Transitions were not abrupt. Basically it was a revival of stylistic points which had been current since the beginning of the reign of George II; it was far from an innovation. By the time the *Director* appeared many of the decorative details had been in existence for several decades, and it seems that the British master merely codified practices extant for some time. Thus in dating furniture we study the latest, not the youngest, feature.

However, there is little doubt that between the heavier Queen Anne and the lighter Chippendale there was a style, made by our Philadelphia craftsmen, which was transitional. The solid-backed Queen Anne chairs were carved and lightly shaped until the delicate cut-out and carving of the Chippendale appeared. The room of Georgian furniture illustrated (Fig. 62) shows somewhat less of the delicacy of later Chippendale; it has not yet won grace and a light, airy elegance. The carving here is still hesitant and indistinct and the sweep of the carvings still not quite graceful. Sometimes these pieces with a Georgian "feel" were made after the Chippendale had begun, as in the claw-and-ball chair which dates from about 1765 (Fig. 63).

On the whole, the problem of the furniture made between 1725 and 1750 in Philadelphia is not yet solved.

Fig. 63. Philadelphia claw-and-ball Georgian chair, circa 1760.

Fig. 64. A room of Philadelphia Chippendale furniture.

Philadelphia Chippendale—Triumph of the Elegant

After 1760 Philadelphia furniture, like architecture, was a full expression of the elegant mode then prevailing in Europe. For our provincial cabinetmakers took exquisite European forms and made them even more lovely, lavishing creative imagination in the making of decorative features and forms. The city thus became the undisputed center of American furniture and there arose there, in imitation of European styles, the Philadelphia Chippendale, a fit accompaniment to the Georgian architecture then popular in the colony.

Fig. 65. Philadelphia Chippendale furniture.

The outstanding pieces of Pennsylvania furniture made between 1748 and 1789 were clearly imitative of the English style expressed by Thomas Chippendale who worked as a cabinetmaker in London after 1748. His book, *The Gentleman and Cabinet-Maker's Director,* published in 1754, returned to styles popular in the France of Louis XIV and it revived the elegance of his reign. Scrolls and shellwork returned. Chippendale's book, however influential, was no innovation and many features in it had been current for some time. It brought together many styles, one of which was the Chinese, and the English actor, David Garrick, who was intent upon cutting a figure as a fashionable man, combined Oriental and Gallic styles. Around 1760 this Chinese vogue began to pass; it never really was popular in America.

In adition to Chippendale's book the firm of Ince and John Mayhew also brought out a design book with notes in French and English.

Philadelphia cabinetmakers also had other sources for their forms. There is no longer doubt that the pediment, feature of our highboys, came not from Chippendale but from the many books on architecture then in use in the city. There was in truth close association between architecture and furniture. In England the Adam brothers had been close to Chippendale and in Philadelphia Robert Smith, an early architect, was close friend of Thomas Affleck. David Evans, builder, was cousin of David Evans, cabinetmaker. John Folwell was close to Thomas Nevell. Indeed, books on architecture did influence Philadelphia furniture styles, and they were an unusual source for designs.

So the Philadelphia craftsmen who made these magnificent pieces now known as Philadelphia Chippendale were under the influence of styles made in Europe. Many were themselves European trained. Richard Watson, William Long, William Martin had learned their craft in London and Thomas Affleck, who arrived here in 1763, had a copy of "Shippendale's Designs" to guide him. He was a Quaker who was in love with elegance, a loyalist who associated with the provincial elite, a paramount figure in Philadelphia society, and one of the new breed of genteel Quakers then emerging. Other city craftsmen also were European trained like Hymes Taylor and George Rickey, the latter in Edinburgh.

These masters of the elegant were then imitators of European fashions—to a degree! They also were innovators. They took what they knew and what they had read in books and used it as the basis for a new style of furniture. But they went the books one better! There is no precedent in Chippendale's work for the magnificent highboy such as was made for Col. David Deshler. Our craftsmen became even more elegant workmasters than Europe knew although surely common features are obvious: methods of work, basic design and certain decorative features. Yet our American pieces still stand as independent creations not only because of our native woods, not merely because our pieces were suited to our climate, but because they were freshly conceived.

The magnificence of Philadelphia Chippendale and its unique features lie in the sure artistry of its carving (Fig. 65). Even more than the fine symmetry, which these pieces display, there was an elaboration of the foliage, flowers, and figures which surely were founded in classical culture and in French plastic decoration, but new things were added. Thus one piece shows a magnificent replica in carving of the Aesop fable of the fox and the grapes, an expression of the prevailing classicism, which, joined with Gothic architecture and oriental motifs, made the Chippendale style. The carved skirts of the lowboys, the scalloped and pierced friezes of highboys were unique. Sometimes the carver made bird figures like eagles and cocks, highly ornate; other times the presence of classical urns and acanthus leaves tell of another mood.

There can be no question that Philadelphia Chippendale got its magnificence from its carving, uniquely designed with a fine sense of decorum: not too ornate and not too elaborate, just enough to maintain balance of realization and design. These craftsmen displayed little stiffness but showed rather a light *chinoiserie* and a French *rocaille* spirit which separates their work from the heavier sobriety of English pieces. Philadelphia carving was in truth unique and its leaves, shells and hucks--aided by gadrooning, oriental frets and tassels—were far in advance of anything in the British world of the period.

These carvers who made Philadelphia Chippendale furniture were the finest artisans of early Pennsylvania. While there were degrees of skills, most carvers were so versatile, and indulged in several styles, that the task of comparing pieces with a view to identification by similarity of style is made difficult. John Folwell, Edward James, Jonathan Gastelow, Thomas Tufft, Benjamin Randolph and Thomas Affleck were not just skilled enough to produce many styles of carving, but they also had several ways in which they worked. Then too, carvers moved from shop to shop. While each shop had its carvers and the styles of these artificers can be recognized, these workers were not always employed in the same cabinetmaker's shop and so their styles also moved from shop to shop. William Savery did not do his own carving, and much of the fine work now so admired was done by his workers, now unknown.

Fig. 66. The triumph of Philadelphia cabinetmaking, a highboy, circa 1769.

Fig. 67. Philadelphia lowboy, circa 1760.

To their glory, the Philadelphia cabinetmakers created the highboy. This form, which did not exist in England either in name or in construction, came to be the expression of the spirit of elegant Philadelphia after 1760. As a form this piece remained comparatively stable while its decoration was varied almost infinitely. The magnificent carved Philadelphia highboy (Fig. 66), *circa* 1769, is indeed the triumph of Philadelphia craftsmanship, a blend of all elements—ball-and-claw feet, fluted columns, carved apron, magnificent pediment, and exquisite symmetry. Each creation by a city craftsman differed in detail from other craftsmen and the main features of these pieces was the pediment, richly ornamented and so developed in Pennsylvania that nothing elsewhere in early America can match it.

The lowboy—the name is modern and was unknown in the earlier period when it was called a dressing table or chamber or drawer table—was part of each pretentious city house. (Fig. 67) Here too elaboration of carving was realized and these pieces came to be highly ornate with shells and acanthus leaves and other classical or Gallic motifs. As part of the furnishing of the bedroom they generally were covered by linen cloths and a mirror, a framed Queen Anne walnut piece or scrolled mahogany, either stood on top of them or hung on the wall behind them.

Low and high chests also were made with less carving, for simpler tastes. Many of these pieces were found in the piedmont interior, suggesting that Philadelphia cabinetmakers were making their magnificent Chippendale pieces for the city and these pieces for the plainer people of the interior. The low chest, high chest, chest-on-frame, and chest-on-chest were used in the piedmont more than in the city. The commonest of these low chests had straight fronts, moulded bracket feet, fluted quarter columns and generally four graduated drawers. As a style these forms survived from the Queen Anne period, and these plainer chests were not Pennsylvania creations like the highboy. What the city masters added were serpentine fronts, swelled fronts or bow fronts. Higher chests of six to seven tiers of drawers also were made, and sometimes a chest-on-frame or a chest-on-chest.

Of all Philadelphia Chippendale chairs the most historic is the one Thomas Folwell made for the State House with a carved sunburst to which Benjamin Franklin pointed and asked: "Is it a rising or a setting sun?" (Fig. 68) This chair, the Signer's Chair, was used by John Hancock and the other members of the Continental Congress to subscribe the Declaration of Independence, pledging to each other their lives, their fortunes and their sacred honor. Chippendale chairs of Philadelphia make were rich in their form and variety. They were usually made in sets of six or more, each set differing from the other. The variation of decoration between sets was astonishing—cabriole legs, Marlborough legs, carved with a richness that was rarely overdone. The backs were varied too with a richness which attests to the imaginative creativity of their makers.

Many other noteworthy forms were made by these highly skilled city craftsmen, especially the desk-bookcase or secretary which combined features of the highboy and chest (Fig. 69).

One interesting development was the imitation of Chippendale styles of carving by the Bachman brothers of Lancaster, who worked during and just after the American Revolution. Ignoring Germanic furniture styles, these piedmont craftsmen made pieces almost as fine as those of the city (Fig. 70). Lacking the symmetry of the city pieces, and marked by a touch of ponderousness, the Bachman furniture still was an amazing development by craftsmen who acquired skills that were not native to them. The Bachmans also made Sheraton-style tables with inlaid legs for the more affluent German farmers of the interior, using a technique little employed by early Philadelphia workmen.

On the whole, Philadelphia Chippendale was an exquisite if passing phase of Pennsylvania furniture. It flourished only for a brief time and it did not survive in the plain America

Fig. 68. One of the most famous chairs in America—the "Signers' Chair" from Independence Hall.

Fig. 69. Philadelphia Chippendale secretary-bookcase, circa 1775.

Fig. 70. A secretary-bookcase made by John Bachman, Lancaster, 1775.

which emerged with the end of the Revolution; yet while it lasted it was truly a brilliant expression of Pennsylvania imaginative creativity.

Character of Germanic Furniture

Furniture made by Philadelphia craftsmen and that made in the piedmont areas reflect two differing ways of life. Tidewater elegance, reflecting fashionable Europe, determined not only the styles but even the forms of furniture. Mayor Powel of Philadelphia dined at a table placed in the center of a dining room; he drank tea in an upstairs drawing room from specially made tables; he socialized in a salon. And the furniture he had made to support this way of life differed from that of the piedmont farmer. The latter ate at a kitchen table, sat next to a wallbench, drank coffee from mugs, and socialized in the same all-purpose downstairs room.

The Swedish traveller, Israel Acrelius, wrote that houses in the Pennsylvania tidewater had furniture made mainly from American woods which consisted of dining tables, bureaus, cabinets and chairs—the chairs being of walnut, mahogany, maple, wild-cherry, or sweet gum. Late in the eighteenth century the French traveller, Cazenove, wrote that downstairs in the piedmont farmer's house was a room which contained a farmer's bed and cradle, a stove, a little mirror, a walnut bureau, a table, and sometimes a clock—a reflection of the German peasant's *stube*. Upstairs, he wrote, the house was devoid of furniture, being divided into rooms where the family slept on pallets. Bedsteads were late in coming to the piedmont.

Fig. 71. A display of Pennsylvania German furniture in the Metropolitan Museum of Art, New York.

Further evidence of the difference in furniture forms used in the tidewater and the piedmont comes from comparison of the appraisements of estates and from the sales lists of the cabinetmakers. Comparing the inventory of the estate of Letitia Aubrey who died in 1746 with the inventory of the estate of Johann Phillip Boehm which was exhibited July 13, 1749, we easily see how strong this comparison is, for the differences in furniture forms are marked.

In fact the piedmont farmhouse was arranged for purposes differing from those of the city mansion. In place of the drawing room the farmhouse had its *Spinnstube,* the most important downstairs room in rural houses from Britain to the Himalayas and also early Pennsylvania. The inventory of Boehm's estate includes eleven and three-quarters yards of cloth and seven and three-quarters yards of cloth. In Alsace the spinning room was called the *Kunkelstube,* elsewhere the *Maistube.* In this room the children played while mother and

Fig. 72. Dining room, House of the Mühlbach, showing Pennsylvania German chairs, table, cupboards, and pottery.

Fig. 73. House of the Mühlbach, bedroom.

Fig. 74. Walnut child's rocker.

big sister spun and sewed. Downstairs in the farmer's house was the *Kammer* or master bedroom; upstairs sleeping for the head of the house was unheard of in early years. Where tidewater homes had different tables for breakfast, dining, tea and supper—and in some cases even separate rooms—one table served the farmer for dining, reading the Bible and perusing Christopher Saur's *Geistliche Magazin* which the publisher sent out gratis.

The precise difference between Germanic furniture and Pennsylvania peasant furniture is hard to establish; also the transformation which took place when German furniture was transplanted to America cannot be easily stated. The differences become clear when we study the surviving peasant furniture of Europe and compare it with that of the Pennsylvania piedmont. The Schwenkfelder Museum has set up a Silesian alcove with German furniture imported from the old world. Next to it is an American alcove with Germanic furniture made in Pennsylvania. The contrast is startling. Pennsylvania German furniture has gained a gracefulness and lost its peasant ponderousness. Although there is a obvious Germanic influence there also is no doubt that from the start Pennsylvania piedmont furniture showed a lighter and more delicate mood than that of Germany and also that even at the beginning English influences were at work.

It is important that we study the Pennsylvania piedmont furniture in proper chronology. Then we can see that the piedmont craftsmen were working under a double influence. Not only were they making Germanic forms like the dower chest, *Schank,* and cupboard; they also stood under the influences of the Philadelphia craftsmen; especially the masters whose work they must have admired. So the result was a hybridization. Almost from the start German furniture in the Pennsylvania piedmont was overlaid with non-Germanic features like inlay, fluted corners, ogee moldings and graceful lines.

Apparently, piedmont furniture went through three stages. First furniture was made in forms that were known in Europe—stretchers, plank chairs and generous and awkward cupboards—but already here there was an obvious grace and delicacy of line unknown in European pieces. Next, after the up-country farmer had seen the work of the brilliant Philadelphia craftsmen he went home and put their decorative features on Germanic forms—inlay which came from Hepplewhite, flutted corners, and in a few instances rich carvings. The third phase was when all styles were melted down into a thoroughly American pattern.

Difficulties of fact and interpretation still face the conscientious observer. First of these is the problem of chronology. We must not assume that because Germanic styles appeared in piedmont Pennsylvania they were simply imitations of old world styles. This seemingly reasonable hypothesis does not regard the dates of the similar pieces which survive in German museums. Many German pieces which are most nearly like our Pennsylvania pieces are contemporary with, and sometimes even later than, our pieces. Thus a painted chest from the Bonn region is dated 1793, and many of our Pennsylvania chests antedate it. When we wish to establish dependence we must be sure of our dates.

The second difficulty that faces the conscientious observer is the fact that in the Palatinate, where most Pennsylvania Germans came from, there was little painted furniture. Most was carved. Of course, similar designs were carved on Palatine pieces as were painted on our Pennsylvania pieces—and sometimes even inlaid—but we do have to raise the query why the carving of furniture, a traditional Palatine art, was not much practiced in Pennsylvania. Study of Theodore Zink's Volume XII of *Deutsche Volkskunst* treating of the Palatinate shows that traditional designs were carved there. This is true of chest, *Schank* and cupboards.

So we seem to have to conclude that the decorated furniture of the Pennsylvania piedmont arose in semi-isolation from the painted furniture of eastern and southern Germany. It was no blind copy of German peasant styles. It seems to have arisen in Pennsylvania as a

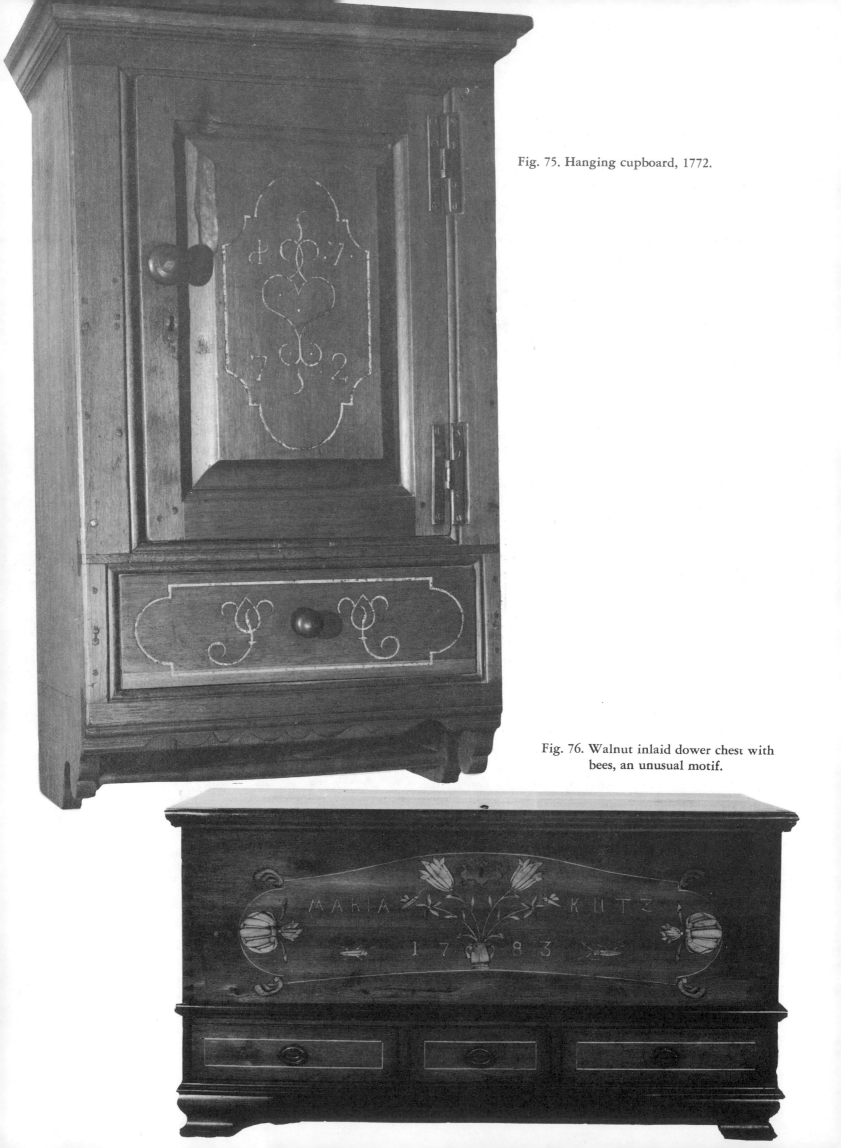

Fig. 75. Hanging cupboard, 1772.

Fig. 76. Walnut inlaid dower chest with
bees, an unusual motif.

semi-independent product, and when we further study the iconography of the decorated furniture of Pennsylvania we find that the motifs were rarely used in European furniture. Then we come face to face with a novel and startling hypothesis that our Germanic furniture in Pennsylvania may have had an independent origin. This seems to be the only conclusion that fits the facts.

Three fundamental furniture forms were introduced into the Pennsylvania piedmont—the dower chest, the wardrobe, and the cupboards in several forms. Each type was already well-established in Europe but upon coming to the New World went through new development.

The Dower Chest

Of all German-derived furniture forms which showed in the Pennsylvania piedmont none is better known—and deservedly—than the dower chest, called in Pennsylvania Dutch the *ausschteier kischt*.

By the time of the Renaissance the chest had become the most important piece of household furniture. It was known in England as early as the middle of the seventeenth century where it was of framed and panelled construction. Many English pieces are of a decayed Renaissance design and have elaborate floral inlay; some were even carved.

The oldest European examples were Romanesque examples and they date from the eleventh century. Some Gothic ones also have been found. North German chests were of carved hardwood, generally oak, while in central and southern Germany—those areas which had been part of the old Roman empire and so were culturally southern in spirit—they were painted and made of soft woods. In the Palatinate designs usually were carved in relief, a technique which did not migrate to Pennsylvania. Painted chests survive from other areas, notably one dated 1661 from Bavaria, one 1793 from Bonn and one 1785 from Upper Austria. In Germany this piece is called a *Truhe*.

The Pennsylvania *ausschteier kischt* had considerable social significance which links it with German folkways. It was part of the young bride's *ausschteier*, or dowry—her collection of clothes, furniture, and household item that she brought with her to her new home and on which she had lavished so much of her girlhood dreams. Ordinary chests were not decorated; only the *aussteier kischt* was.

Many more chests survive from early Pennsylvania than from Germany, and our Pennsylvania chests show a different mood. Most Pennsylvania chests were made of soft wood, painted, although several walnut ones survive like that of Maria Kutz (Fig. 76) which is inlaid with bees and flowers. The earliest known Pennsylvania dower chest is dated 1774. It has no designs, only a name. This seems to suggest that these earlier chests probably had no designs. Generally speaking the dower chest was made in Pennsylvania from just before the American Revolution to about 1815. So our chests are contemporary with, or in some cases a bit older than, similar European pieces.

Many persons claim to be able to recognize regional patterns in the decoration of chests and so categorize them by counties. While variants of style exist and while the work of individuals can be detected, such procedure fails to recognize that many chests were painted by itinerants who worked in several counties. Thus Heinrich Otto's work has been found all over eastern Pennsylvania although he lived in Tulpehocken in western Berks. Both his chests and his *Taufscheine* are found in widely scattered places. The Jonestown school, identified by Esther Stevens Brazer, also worked in a wide area.

Some chests defy all rules. Thus the fine chest in the Barnes Foundation (Fig. 78)—Dr. Barnes placed it beneath a painting by Renoir—has a man's name on it, Michael Fink. Not only is it unusual to find a man's instead of a girl's name on a chest, but here the designs are not feminine but include the traditional *Sechsstern* or barn sign. Can it be that the burly rowdy of the Ohio region, Mike Fink, whose Pennsylvania background is well-known, here put his name on a chest in defiance of tradition?

While Pennsylvania dower chests were Germanic in source, they were not just copies of what was being made in Europe. Thus the magnificent unicorn chest in the Philadelphia Museum of Art appears to be as soundly American as do chests displaying symbols, and the unicorn is certainly an appropriate symbol for a young girl's chest. In the old legend if a virgin entered a forest where a rough unicorn was grazing, as soon as the beast saw her he lost his viciousness and ran to her, nestling in her lap in peaceful sleep. This was certainly appropriate for a dower chest. The Christian application of this legend made Christ the one who slept in the lap of the Virgin. Already in 1579 the unicorn was used in folk art, along with the hart and other creatures. In German dower chests unicorns are rare. Also, the unicorn was thought to be one of the favorite animals of paradise, appearing in this mood on Italian brocades of the fourteenth and fifteenth centuries.

In Pennsylvania the unicorn appeared on both dower chests and *Taufscheine* where it is an appropriate symbol—on the former of chastity and on the latter of innocence. On dower chests it reflects the pagan legend, in *Taufscheine* the Christian.

Fig. 77. Dower chest with recessed panels.

Fig. 78. Michael Finck's chest with *Sechsstern* and hearts.

The dower chest was given to a girl sometime between her eighth and tenth year. Her name was put on it at that time so on the surviving pieces the names are maiden and not married names. Into this chest went all those things which she made, was given, or bought, and she bore it to her new home on her wedding wagon and sometimes the frolickers stood at the end of the lane leading from her home and demanded a "fine" to let the wagon pass. This the groom gladly paid.

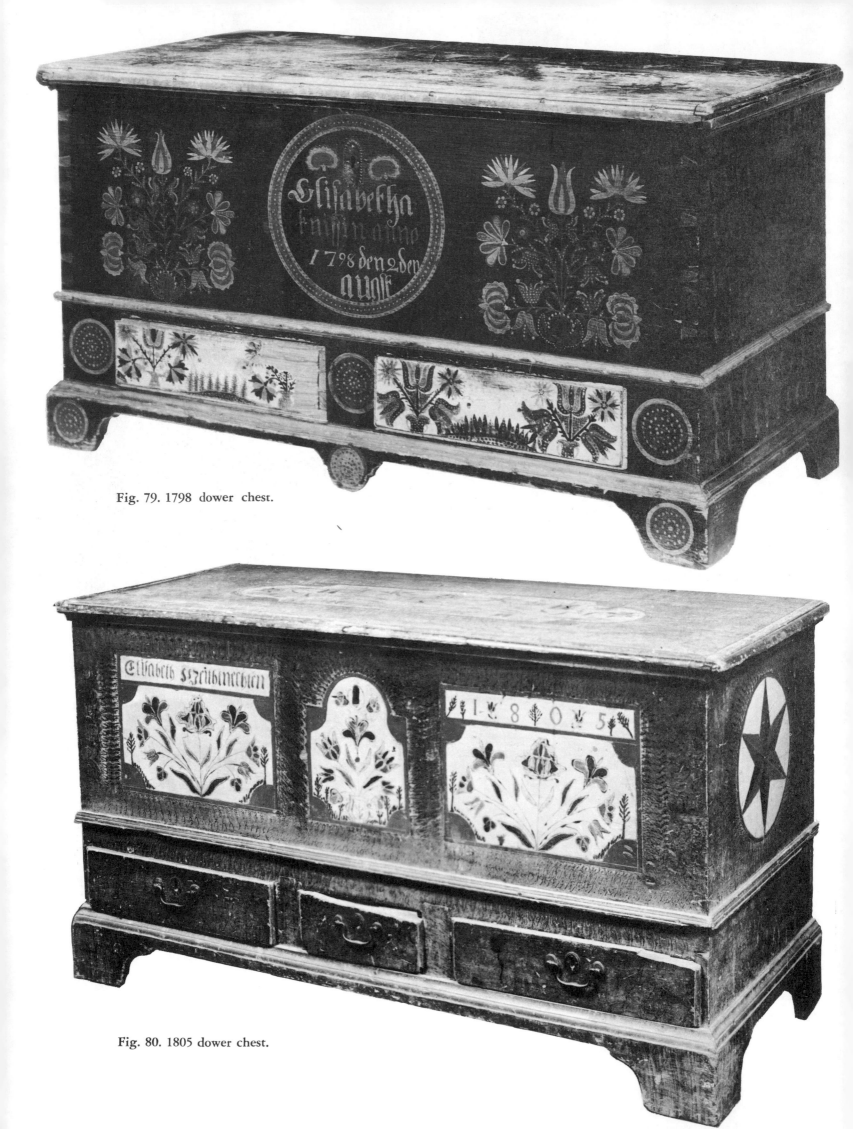

Fig. 79. 1798 dower chest.

Fig. 80. 1805 dower chest.

Fig. 81. Dower chest with two portraits of the maiden. This piece is noteworthy in that it uses the word *"Kist,"* characteristically Pennsylvanian, although the inscription was probably added later.

Fig. 82. Dower chest painted and signed by Christian Seltzer of the "Jonestown school" of chest painters.

The Schank

Another major Germanic furniture form transported to Pennsylvania was the *Schank*, or wardrobe.

In Europe this form had been peculiar to the Rhineland and among the Saxons of Seibenbürgen in Transylvania. Fundamentally Gothic in tone, with two huge doors, swinging from sturdy corner posts, and often with doors laterally divided forming a quadrilateral facade, the *Schank* was essential in early houses where closets, if they existed at all, were far from generous. In Europe this often had been built into the room itself and so was part of the carpenter's work like the one at Steinweiler in the Palatinate. Generally, Rhineland pieces were carved; and the painted ones, baroque in tone, came from southern Germany. In middle German areas the *Schank* began to appear about the middle of the seventeenth century, leaning away from Renaissance forms and starting its individual development. In Holland the piece was called a *kas* and in this form it was brought to New York.

The Pennsylvania German *Schank*, most characteristic of our furniture forms, declares its independence from Germanic forms by a new grace and in some instances by a new light-

Fig. 83. George Huber's *Schank*, probably the finest piece of Pennsylvania German furniture in existence.

ness. Instead of being part of the room, some pieces were even made so they might be dismantled and thus moved from room to room. Moreover, in Pennsylvania inlay replaces carving, giving new delicacy to this somewhat cumbersome piece.

Two significant pieces are in the Geesey collection in the Philadelphia Museum of Art. The earliest of these is the magnificently inlaid Georg Huber *Schank*, probably a Berks County piece, dated 1779. Unquestionably this is the finest piece of Pennsylvania German furniture in existence (Fig. 83). Retaining its Gothic tone in structure, other decorative features are fundamentally baroque in spirit, even classical, and the overall tone of gaudy elaboration is characteristic of the seventeenth century.

Fig. 84. Martin Eisenhauer's *Schank,* 1794. The 1790 census lists Eisenhauer as living in Hereford Township, Berks.

The stylized decoration of the second piece, Martin Eisenhauer's piece (Fig. 89), dated 1794, shows how the painting became subdued and stylized. Eisenhauer lived in Hereford Township, Berks, according to the Census of 1790, but his *Schank* betrays a mood which surely takes us back to the German baroque, especially to the time when gaudy conventionalized designs dominated these massive pieces. The Eisenhauer family of Berks is distantly related to the family of hte same name from Bethel, Lancaster, from which Dwight D. Eisenhower comes.

Although these two magnificent pieces in the Philadelphia Museum of Art show the family names of two Pennsylvania German clans whose sons were in the White House (Huber-Hoover, Eisenhower) no political significance is to be attached to this furniture form.

Germanic Plank Chairs

The Pennsylvania plank chair, which was a popular form of furniture in the early Pennsylvania piedmont and which because of its durability survives in quantity, retained both the anonymity and the variety of its two European prototypes—the peasant *Sessel* and *Stuhl*.

With few exceptions the makers of Pennsylvania plank chairs remain unknown. There were in interior Pennsylvania few chairmakers who specialized in manufacturing plank chairs for an established market. Rather most of these chairs were made for home use by local craftsmen whose chief skills were other than those of the cabinetmaker. This gave them individuality. This craft workmanship, joined with freedom from guild restrictions, made for both variety and development. Ingenuity replaced uniformity, and so many styles of plank chairs were made. Beginning with the forms inherited from the Old World, yet absorbing many new ideas, the final result was a wide range of plain plank chairs which found wide use too. Whether the wooden-seated rocking chair was a Pennsylvania creation has not yet been established; however, old Pennsylvania rockers have come down which point to an early date when these pieces were being made.

The *Sessel*, first of the two inherited Germanic chair forms which lie behind the Pennsylvania development of the plank chair, was an arm-post chair which appeared very early in the Pennsylvania interior. Some of these early arm chairs had upholstered seats while others retained the more traditional seats of rush or wood. However, the *Sessel* was characterized by extended front legs which formed supports for the arms and by extended rear legs which became the posts of the back. Thus they are related to the English ladderback. Three-legged chairs, designed for uneven floors, were rare in early Pennsylvania nor indeed was there much carving of backs. The Kerschner parlor in the Henry Francis duPont Winterthur Museum (Fig. 85) exhibits four types of early Pennsylvania arm chairs.

In Germany the *Stuhl*, second type of inherited wooden chair, had also shown much variety of form. The backs were shaped in S curves, double eights, intertwined serpents, heraldic arms, birds, tulips, *Sechsstern*, and cut-out hearts. Most shaped chairs were from northern Germany while painted chairs came from southern Germany. Both shaped and painted chairs were made in early Pennsylvania, the painted ones coming mostly after the Revolution. Carved and shaped Pennsylvania chairs followed traditional designs in the earlier years, but gradually freedom made for new forms. The plain plank chairs in the Kerschner parlor are still quite traditional. Once it was thoroughly domiciled in Pennsylvania the plank chair "escaped" its traditional patterns and developed many forms. These have been given many modern names: balloon back, arrow back, fiddle back, etc. Moreover, English influences also were at work, and both ladderbacks and Windsors were made in the Pennsylvinia interior. During the nineteenth century these plank chairs, rockers as well as straight ones, began to betray a soundly American mood (Fig. 86).

Fig. 85. An authentic restoration of the Kerschner parlor showing plastered ceiling.

These plank chairs of the piedmont were made chiefly for home use. Sometimes craftsmen whose main work was in other fields took a hand at making plank chairs. John Heckewelder, the famous Moravian missionary to the Indians, made a Philadelphia-style Windsor during his retirement, sometime around 1795 (Fig. 88).

On the whole, plank chairs, both with or without arms, form one of the more interesting phases of early Pennsylvania furniture.

Fig. 86. Several types of Germanic chairs.

Fig. 87. Germanic straight and rocking chairs.

Fig. 89. Painted Pennsylvania chair, mid-nineteenth century.

Later Germanic Furniture

As Pennsylvania developed and as civilization came to be more firmly established here the traditional forms of European peasant furniture began to develop into the style now known as Early American. This was a gradual transition and it took place in other parts of Colonial America. It is of course understandable that the magnificently elegant pieces made by the Philadelphia craftsmen of the eighteenth century would not root themselves in interior America. These pieces were suited for a culture that was European in taste, and they were used mainly in the houses of tidewater America and by those families whose lives reflected European elegance. Surely they were out of step with the plainer tastes which surged up in post Revolutionary America.

The transition from furniture based on European peasant styles to Early American is difficult to trace and document. The most obvious approach is through the continuity of the forms: corner cupboards, the so-called "Dutch cupboard," drop leaf tables, etc. While several of the forms popular in the interior parts were also employed by city craftsmen—the drop-leaf table, for example, was also fashionable in eighteenth-century classical furniture—most of

Fig. 90. Corner cupboard made of walnut in Germantown, circa 1755.

the pieces made in the interior were either imitative of or developments from peasant forms. Thus the movable corner cupboard grew out of the built-in corner cupboard of the peasant's house.

So the Germantown walnut corner cupboard, dating from around 1755 (Fig. 90), is already a transitional piece, having Germanic form and classical moldings, fashionable drawer pulls and other features which link it with the work of the Philadelphia masters. Indeed, many of the craftsmen of the interior soon learned to copy the decorative features of the elegant pieces which were being made in the city, and it is not at all uncommon to find a clock case made in the interior with fluted corners, ogee moldings, and other items of classical decoration. The Bachmans of Lancaster even made pieces of classical elegance. On the whole, however, piedmont craftsmen were not partial, they could make a Dutch cupboard with good Germanic decoration (Fig. 91). Here is little that can be called classical and we note another influence than that which moved the cabinetmakers of the city.

Fig. 91. Rare carved and painted
Dutch cupboard, circa 1760.

Fig. 92. Painted chest of drawers, circa 1780.

Fig. 93. Decorated chest of drawers, late eighteenth century.

Fig. 94. Nineteenth-century furniture.

Other Germanic revivals were also tried. Chests of drawers were made and decorated with designs in the usual peasant style. One such chest, dating from around 1780 (Fig. 92), displays characteristic Germanic panels and designs. Another chest (Fig. 93), dating from about the same period, is even more Germanic in tone and it could have stood in a Rhineland farmhouse.

By the third decade of the nineteenth century the transition from these inherited forms to early American was almost complete in the area on the seaward side of the mountains. Gone were the influences of the classical eighteenth-century furniture and, with one exception, of Germanic peasant styles. An earthy solidness had come, as in the display of American plain in the Berks County Historical Society, which reminds us more of the Pennsylvania

Fig. 95. Painted furniture from the Mahantango Valley, circa 1835.

countryside than of the agricultural villages of Europe. Moreover, this furniture no longer can be distinguished from that of other American provinces. The plain style of the early nineteenth century now had come.

Around the third decade of the nineteenth century, in a small isolated valley northwest of the Blue Mountains, Germanic furniture experienced a modest revival. The furniture of the Mahantango Valley was a throwback to Germanic styles, and it was marked by exceptional elaboration of detail (Fig. 95). Yet American notes intrude. The tall clock case pictures a rattlesnake on the inside of the door, a note surely not European. One of these Mahantango Valley craftsmen was Jacob Maser whose desk (Fig. 96), dating from 1838, was signed by him. This desk was part of the exhibit of Pennsylvania German art in the Pennsylvania building at the Sesquicentennial in Philadelphia in 1926.

On the whole, Germanic style furniture became one of the elements which entered into the making of early American styles.

Fig. 96. A painted desk signed by Jacob Maser and dated 1838. These pieces from the Mahantango Valley were a late manifestation of the painting of furniture. This desk was exhibited at the Sesquicentennial in 1926 and is now in the Henry Francis duPont Winterthur Museum.

The Pendulum Clock

Certainly the pendulum clock was one of the most significant pieces of early Pennsylvania furniture, a necessary piece in colonial homes. The ordinary methods of telling time were by hourglass and sundial, both inconvenient. The clock had been invented by Huyghens in 1682, just as Pennsylvania was being founded, so it was a novelty; and especially the Pietists, for whom time was of special theological meaning, had great interest in clocks.

Many problems are connected with study of early Pennsylvania clocks. The first of these has to do with their manufacture. Many people claim that the person whose name appears on the clockface also made the works. This is not yet proven. Thus, for example, when Peter Stretch inherited the shop of Abel Cottey there was listed in the inventory a case of parts of cast clock-works valued at two shillings per pound. Some writers, nevertheless, assert that Stretch was a brass founder who made clockworks although the sheet brass mentioned in several inventories was for clockfaces. Evidently colonial clockmakers imported parts which were, in fact, interchangeable; and then, after some minor work was done on them, they were assembled.

Contemporary newspapers, when properly read, are not ambiguous. They suggest that the term "clockmaker" meant repairman of clocks in the same way that today shoemaker means one who repairs shoes. In Christopher Sauer's paper for February 16, 1754, is this note:

Martin Schneider, thoroughly trained watchmaker, born in Nürnberg, and Johann End, clockmaker, trained here, have formed a partnership to sell old and new clocks and to repair clocks and watches in Germantown.

This notice clearly states that timepieces were sold and repaired, even though both men were well trained repairmen. By the same token an advertisement in Heinrich Müller's *Staatsbote* for April 7, 1772, says that Augustine Neisser continues to make all kinds of clocks and to repair clocks and watches. A few months later the same paper carried this notice:

John Ebermann, Jr., dealer in clocks and watches, Lancaster, has removed from King Street to a house opposite the Black Bear Inn.

This suggests that Ebermann made no clocks although his name has been found painted on several clockdials. This also seems to be true of another notice in the same paper, April 25, 1775:

Johannes Lind opens a store for the sale of clocks and watches at Arch and Second Streets, Philadelphia, formerly occupied by Edward Duffield, clockmaker.

Duffield's name frequently appears on clockfaces although it is hard to prove that he actually made them.

The problem is not easy. There obviously was a common source of parts, for most colonial clocks follow much the same pattern and if the several early clockmakers actually made their own works there would be much more individuality evident and greater adaptation. The best guess is that cast parts were imported, some work was done to finish them, and then they were assembled and put in a tall case and sold, often with the seller's name on the dial.

Some works bearing Pennsylvania names on their faces also have the names or marks of British manufacturing firms on their works. The Christian Bixler clock in the Historical Society of Montgomery County has Bixler's name in German-style lettering on the face, while

Fig. 97.   Fig. 98.   Fig. 99.   Fig. 100.

Fig. 97. Clock by Peter Stretch, Philadelphia, circa 1740.
Fig. 98. Clock by David Rittenhouse, circa 1765.
Fig. 99. Painted clockcase, 1785.
Fig. 100. Clockcase from Philadelphia.

Fig. 101. Clockcase from Reading,
David Rose, circa 1795.

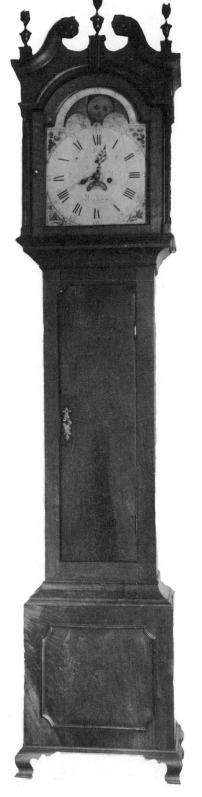

Fig. 103. The most famous clockcase made in early Pennsylvania. This piece was made in Easton around 1823 as a present for the Marquis de Lafayette, on the occasion of his second visit to America. It has a bas-relief of the Marquis carved on the door. The works are by Daniel Oyster.

Fig. 102. French works in a Philadelphia-made clockcase, circa 1790.

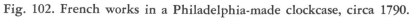

the moon at the top has Roman style lettering. It is not yet proven that the person whose name appears on the clockface did anything more than assemble parts made in Europe and sell the clock.

Even wooden works are dubious. Many of the wooden works surviving in rural areas come from cheap New England clocks which were peddled all over rural America near the beginning of the nineteenth century. However, it also is known that some clockmakers, like David Rittenhouse, made wooden works.

Clocks placed in steeples were probably of American manufacture. In 1742 when the middle building next to the *Gemeinhaus* in Bethlehem was built, its tower was furnished with a clock made by Augustin Neisser of Germantown. Its turret had three bells cast by Samuel Powell. Likewise it is claimed that the clock on the first *Bethaus* at Ephrata had been made by Dr. Christopher deWitt although this gentleman died much earlier and although it is known that Peter Müller's father sent a clock from Germany as a present.

Books dealing with early clockmakers list a hundred for the city. The 1790 Census, however, classes many of these as merchants.

Thus we have to go behind the name on the face if we are to find who actually made the works. We include this account of the early Pennsylvania clock under furniture because we believe that, with few exceptions, there were no true clockmakers in early Pennsylvania and that the parts were manufactured abroad and shipped knocked-down, assembled here, and then fitted into American-made cases.

We do know, however, that several "clockmakers"—whatever is meant by this term— were working in seventeenth-century Pennsylvania. The first man who is credited with making a clock is the already-mentioned Dr. Christopher deWitt who worked about 1710. At this period William Chandler, born in Ireland in 1685, is also said to have worked on clocks in Nottingham. Phillip Syng, Jr., the silversmith, put his name on several clockfaces in the 1730s, and in the next decade Christopher Sauer's name also is found. Versatile as Sauer was, he most likely merely assembled the works. In the years of the 1730s Joseph Elicott also made clocks in Horsham and the Richardsons, celebrated for their exquisite silver, also worked on clocks. In the 1740s Edward Duffield, Franklin's friend, worked in the city and in Lower Dublin. And the celebrated David Rittenhouse, with his brother Benjamin, is known to have made works.

One interesting feature of early clockmaking was the migration of craftsmen from the piedmont to the city. Huguenot clockmakers were working in Oley as early as 1720 and certainly this frontier region did not have the brass founding facilities necessary for making clocks. Many provincial masters moved towards the center of population. Christian Bixler went from Reading to Easton and his son to Philadelphia. Adam Brandt's son went from New Hanover to the city, Charles Campbell from Carlisle, the dePuys from Reading and Johann Endt from Germantown to Philadelphia and then to New York. George Faber went from Sumneytown to Reading and Jacob Heilig from East Norriton to Philadelphia. This movement of piedmont clockmakers suggests that they were not tied down by elaborate brass-founding machinery; indeed, the piedmont was not yet industrially developed.

However, if we assert that clockworks were merely assembled in early Pennsylvania from interchangeable parts manufactured in Europe, the same is not true of Pennsylvania clockcases. British cases of this period are drab and monotonous. However, our Pennsylvania clockcases betray an imaginative realization and adaptation which is characteristic of all our other crafts. Where the works in our clockcases are all alike, the cases vary.

We present some Pennsylvania clocks, representative of several styles. One (Fig. 98) is a David Rittenhouse clock made about 1760-1770 and shows the characteristic brass face of this craftsman, some of which were engraved. Another (Fig. 101) shows an English works in a case decorated in the Germanic style sometime around 1795. Another clockcase (Fig. 103) is indeed one of the historic pieces of American furniture. It was made in Easton sometime around 1823 for the second visit of the Marquis de Lafayette to America. It has a bas-relief of the Marquis carved on the door, another bas-relief just above, an American eagle at the top with other floral carvings. The works are signed with the name of Daniel Oyster, a Reading clockmaker. Oyster was active in Reading at this time, and the clockcase he made for his foster parents—his masterpiece when he became a master craftsman—still survives in the family and its decoration is similar to this Lafayette clock. Without question the Lafayette clock is the finest Pennsylvania product of the period.

FINE ARTS

European art altered immeasurably as the eighteenth century moved to its close. The century had really begun with Antoine Watteau (1684-1721), French master of the age, and it ended with Jacques-Louis David (1748-1825) who shared the Revolution. In Watteau we see artificial pictures of uncontaminated happiness where, under eternally blue skies, shepherds and shepherdesses sported in innocence, where murmuring springs and gentle zephyrs spoke the same sweet melodies of peace—the "best of all possible worlds!" All this was manufactured beauty for under these smiling skies all human desires were fulfilled—the same pastoral perfection which contemporary poets were writing about. In David, on the other hand, we have a man who was to share the revolutionary mood, who was to become Napoleon's court painter and the founder of French classicism—albeit somewhat dry and strenuous without either life or form in his drab works.

Classicism was, though, only another form of artificiality. The painters—like architects and poets—went back to Rome and to Athens for their inspiration. In 1748 a commission was sent out from Paris to Italy to study the marvels of antiquity. In 1751 the English architects Revett and Stuart reached Athens and sought here for true beauty. In 1755 J. J. Winklemann's *Thoughts on the Imitation of Greek Works* appeared which laid down the task of following the Greeks in the creation of pure spirit and form. In 1763 he published his *History of Ancient Art,* the meaning of which lay in its new approach to the conditions of artistic creation for he traced artistic work back to its roots in the life-forms of soil, climate, race, religion, society, and the like.

The whole eighteenth century was dichotomous: in religion one was either deist or evangelical; in art one was either elaborating idealist projecting a hoped-for world or simply honestly realistic. Under Calvinist influence, Dutch painting, especially landscapes, had moved away from portraying imaginary scenes to realistic interpretation of the countryside. So the century saw the tension mount between those who, like Gainsborough, painted the fashionably aristocratic world and those who, like Hogarth, painted life as they saw it with caustic irony. However, the same year, 1771 which saw Thomas Gainsborough paint *The Blue Boy,* masterpiece of English rococo portraiture, also saw a Pennsylvania Quaker-born painter paint the *Death of General Wolfe at Quebec* which pictured British soldiers as they really were. Gainsborough's piece was artificial and stilted; the work of Benjamin West, while

Fig. 104. Water color of a Sunday school class, circa 1840.

technically inferior, was marked by the honest simplicity of a Pennsylvania Quaker's search for the simple truth.

Here we discover the character of the artistic traditions that were developing in Pennsylvania for it is clear that the three earliest painters in this province—Gustavus Hesselius, Valentin Haidt, and the younger Benjamin West—were already painting in a mood quite different from that which prevailed in Europe. There was in short a Pennsylvania tradition of realism and honesty which had developed independent of European art, for these three painters—all originally members of sectarian groups—were painting with realism at a time when this was not fashionable in Europe.

European painters still were rouging elderly people to make them look younger and powdering younger people to make them look older. Both Hesselius and Haidt, already in the 1740s, were trying to show the spirit which lurked behind the countenance. In truth, Valentin Haidt, the Moravian, was painting his subjects dressed in the same clothes and his effort, as his more than thirty portraits show, was to catch their spirit. In distinction to European art of the time, early Pennsylvania portraiture was not an atlas of silks, full of shimmering velvets, warm furs and fiery jewels. No! When Hesselius painted the Indian chief Tishcohan, he showed *the man!*

Already in the age of Louis XV this dichotomy of European art was clear. Bourgeois art was indeed emerging, nourished by Flemish elements which were realistic and which showed subjects naturally. Early Pennsylvania art was given to realism which did not show in the other colonies, and it may perhaps be said that in the person of Benjamin West this Pennsylvania realism came to influence, in a small way, the artistic traditions of Europe.

Like the inhabitants of early Pennsylvania, religion also pervaded the fine arts which ran the gamut from crude primitives like the mystical portrait of Johann Kelpius by Dr. Christopher deWitt (Fig. 105) to the American work of Benjamin West who became President of the Royal Academy in London.

In this art-impoverished century tidewater Philadelphia with its modest pretentions to elegance was a back eddy in the main stream of culture. Even painters in Europe were poorly supported by their patrons and our provincial towns were far worse. Art during this century was largely conditioned by the demands of these patrons for what they seem to have wanted were good likenesses of themselves, their wives, their families and perhaps landscapes of their rolling acres which showed their estates with representational accuracy. And surely our early painters were glad to oblige; for in the end as the century came to a close the subjects began again to pose as noblemen and during the Federal period plain Pennsylvanians were caught on canvas in moods that were hardly egalitarian.

Gustavus Hesselius and the Early Masters

First among Pennsylvania artists who were professionals in attitude was the Swede, Gustavus Hesselius, painter of portraits of planters, religious compositions, classical myths, landscapes and portraits of American Indians. Early in Pennsylvania history Hesselius set an inspiring example for native artists, showing the road that leads from religious dissent to artistic realism.

Gustavus Hesselius was descendent of a family of Swedish dissenters, a kinsman of the mystic Emanuel Swedenborg. This religious point of view is clearly mirrored in his life and work. Born at Folkarma Dalarne, Sweden, in 1682, he arrived at New Castle, Delaware, with his brothers who had been commissioned by the Swedish king, Charles XII, to preach the Gospel in America. Soon after his arrival he married Sarah Wallrane.

In probably the first commission on record for a work of art for an American public building, the vestry of the parish of St. Barnabas, of Prince George County, Maryland, in June, 1720, commissioned Hesselius "to paint ye Altar piece and Communion Table, and write such sentences of Scripture as shall be thought proper thereon." September 5, 1721, the same vestry agreed with "Mr. Gustavus Hesselius to draw ye history of our Blessed Saviour and ye Twelve Apostles at ye last Supper, ye institution of ye Blessed Sacrament of His Body and Blood, proportional to ye space over the Altar piece and to "find all other necessaries for ye same." In 1725 he painted "the Altar and Railes of ye Communion Table."

Philadelphia was growing fast; so, in 1735, Gustavus Hesselius arrived in the city and soon thereafter purchased a lot on the north side of High Street below Fourth Street where

Fig. 105. Portrait of Johannes Kelpius:
Dr. Christopher deWitt.

Fig. 106. Self-portrait: Gustavus Hesselius.

Fig. 107. *Chief Lapowinza*: Gustavus Hesselius.

Fig. 108. *Rebecca Doz*: James Claypoole.

he resided until his death May 25, 1755. On September 26, 1740, he was naturalized at the Supreme Court of Pennsylvania, an event which implies that he had already resided in the province for seven years. *The Pennsylvania Gazette* for December 11, 1740, carried the following notice:

Painting done in the best manner by Gustavus Hesselius from Stockholm and John Winters from London. Viz., Coat of Arms drawn on Coach, Chaises, &c or any kinds of ornaments, Landskips, Signs, Show Boards, Ship and House Painting, Guilding of all sorts, Writing in Gold or Color, old Pictures cleaned and mended.

Gustavus Hesselius reflected the unsettled religious life of early Pennsylvania. He had come to America a member of the Swedish Lutheran Church, and in Maryland he is known to have been a member of the Church of England. His countryman, the Reverend Abraham Reinke, induced him to turn to the Moravian Church. Between 1743 and 1750 his name appears on the Register of the Moravian Church in Philadelphia, and he is frequently referred to in the correspondence between Bishop Cammerhof and Count Zinzendorf. During this period, when Moravian theology was cross-centered and when the piety of this group became mawkish and sentimental in its concentration on Christ's passion, Hesselius exhibited in one of his windows his own painting of the Crucifixion which attracted much attention from the inhabitants of Philadelphia. He also is said to have been a maker of organs for he had as his assistant Johann Klemm who became one of the first organbuilders in Pennsylvania, the teacher of David Tannenberger. This gives rise to the speculation that Hesselius may have made musical instruments—a fact, however, not as yet established.

Few of Gustavus Hesselius' paintings have survived. Two of his portraits are of unusual interest. These are his likenesses of Chiefs Lapowinzo and Tishcohan, the two leaders of the Lenai Lenape. These portraits were in the Penn family for many years until Granville Penn presented them to the Historical Society of Pennsylvania. They were made at Pennsbury, May 9, 1735, while John and Thomas Penn were the Proprietors and at the conference where two other Indian chieftains, Lesteconk and Nutimus, were present. Lapowinzo, the chieftain who lived near Hockendocqua, now Northampton, was the great orator of this conference—a noble man of the forests—and the artist shows him, indeed, as a noble savage bearing all the weight of his tragic race. Tishcohan lived along the Delaware near Riegelsville. There paintings by Hesselius show the red men neither in romantic poses nor as beasts but rather as human beings with strong individuality and character. Their noses are almost Roman. Lapowinzo (Fig. 107) has a large mouth, slanting almost oriental eyes, a wrinkled brow and rugged frame—a native American who shows the oppression and deep despair of his people. Tishcohan means, according to the Moravian missionary Heckwelder, "he who never blackens himself" and on this portrait by Hesselius no daubs of color disfigure the noble image. Tishcohan did not stay long in Pennsylvania after this conference, where the notorious "walking purchase" was arranged, and the Moravian Post met him in the Ohio country in 1758.

Fig. 109. *Portrait of Hugh McClolloch*: Matthew Pratt.

Fig. 110. *Mrs. William Penn*: John Hesselius.

In addition to the Swedish sectarian Gustavus Hesselius other artists also were working in the rapidly growing capital city of Pennsylvania. One of the earliest of these was James Claypoole (1720-1796), son of a house painter and glazier who, besides painting portraits, also did gold lettering on sign boards as well as painting canisters and sugar loaf. His somewhat stiff portrait of Rebecca Doz (Fig. 108) shows him to have been a competent but uninspired workman whose awkwardness in composition denies him high rank. Claypoole also was an engraver and during his later years he gained considerable stature as a public figure in the city, being elected Sheriff of Philadelphia as well as holding other offices.

Another early artist in the city who has been called the first distinctly American portrait painter was Matthew Pratt (1734-1813) who was listed as a "painter" in the 1790 census of the city. He was born in Philadelphia in 1734, and between the years 1749 and 1755 he was working with his uncle, James Claypoole. In 1758 Pratt began to paint portraits, and in 1764 he went to London where he spent two years with Benjamin West, followed by another two years of itinerant study. After returning to America in 1768 he did much portrait work, travelling over the Middle Atlantic area. In 1772 he was in New York City and the following year in Virginia. His portrait of Hugh McColloch (1719-1817) (Fig. 109) was done about this time. Pratt painted tavern signs also as well as a portrait of Benjamin Franklin and another of Benjamin West's wife, probably done while he resided in London.

John Wollaston, about whom not even the dates of birth and death are known, was also working in early Philadelphia. The studies of critic William Sawitsky have established that many of the paintings attributed to other early American artists, including Benjamin West, were actually the work of Wollaston who has been proven to be the painter of portraits of Judge William Peters and members of the Coxe, McColl, Oswald, Ritchie, Swift and Turner families, all prominent in the city. Wollaston was working in Philadelphia before 1754, and authorities now are able to define the technical features of his work.

Another shadowy figure in early Pennsylvania who did painting was the itinerant Welshman, William Williams, who also was musician and writer as well as artist. He is known by only a few pieces, which have been proven to be his work. He arrived in the city sometime around 1747 and soon established himself as a portraitist as well as the person who painted the scenery for the first theater in the city. This was in 1759. Williams lived in the city from 1763 on, and he was still painting in 1775 although it is known that he returned to the land of his birth in 1780. It was Williams who loaned books on painting and other artistic subjects to the young Benjamin West.

John Hesselius (1730-1788), son of Gustavus Hesselius, also has to be counted among early Pennsylvania painters although he was later to become a resident of Maryland. He grew up in Philadelphia where he did some painting before he began his travels at the age of twenty. One of his Pennsylvania portraits is his likeness of Mrs. William Penn (Fig. 110), a somewhat stilted picture of a kindly Quakeress with wrinkled countenance and an undersized right hand. As a wandering artist John Hesselius painted throughout most of the Middle Atlantic region, returning to Philadelphia for several periods of work during the 1750s. Some of his paintings are now beginning to be identified by the experts who have isolated his technique.

By the middle of the century, as classical themes were appearing in architecture and as European standards of taste were beginning to overwhelm the plain mood of the early colony, a young painter from Germantown did a charming self-portrait which some critics feel marks the start of a distinctly American school. John Meng's (1734-1754) picture of himself as a self-assured young man, proud of his musical abilities, may have been an expression of an original spirit of a native Pennsylvania school, but his portrait does have a mood of artificiality often found in the baroque portraits of Europe. The conventional background is rococo in mood. However, William Sawitsky has shown the influence of Gustavus and John Hesselius on the work of Meng who died at the age of twenty, thus putting an end to what may have become an indigenous school of early Pennsylvania portraiture.

Robert Feke (1705-1750), although a native of Long Island, must be listed among Pennsylvania painters too because he frequently worked in Philadelphia. He did portraits of Phineas Bond, Mr. and Mrs. Tench Francis, Thomas Hopkinson, William Peters, Edward Shippen, Jr., James Tilghman, and others. Feke's work is recognizable by its formal and sometimes still composition, which Belknap has shown was based on European engravings.

These then were the chief artists who were working in early Philadelphia. Not all artists are known to students of the period. Thus the October 7, 1761 issue of Christopher Sauer's newspaper has this notice: "Jacob Boehm, German artist, Philadelphia, in Queen's Alley, with Franz Seener, German tailor, and opposite the Rossmühle of Nicholas Bogard, is ready to undertake any art work." This is the same "Jacob Böm" who had arrived in the ship *Phoenix* in September, 1743. None of his work has been identified.

Two other persons working as artists in early Philadelphia are known, John Winter and John Green. Also it is known that Georg Michael Weiss, pastor of the Goshenhoppen Reformed Church, did portraits which he sent to Holland, of the Indians. This was as early as 1740.

During these early years painting meant portrait work. Most of the pigments were used to record the physical likenesses of the burghers of the city that then was coming to maturity along the banks of the Delaware and Schuylkill rivers.

Johann Valentin Haidt

A center of colonial painting, smaller than that of Philadelphia, arose among the early Bethlehem Moravians. In 1740 Johann Jakob Müller arrived in Pennsylvania. He was a professional portrait painter who had been trained at Nürnberg and who served as secretary to Count Nicholas von Zinzendorf, leader of the renewed Brethren. In 1743 Müller returned to Europe, having spent three years in America. No proven memento of his Pennsylvania painting has survived, but it is known that he furnished the first ornamentation for the chapel in the Community House in Bethlehem; and, as several early travellers reported, there were original paintings on the walls which were his work.

The one artist among the Moravians whose work has come down—and whose paintings were unique not only in Pennsylvania but in American colonial art—was Johann Valentin Haidt. His studio was in the Horsfield House in Bethlehem and he was without question the best-trained painter working in Colonial America who reflected in his work the blood-and-wound theology of his sect. Haidt was a thorough-going Pietist.

Valentin Haidt was born in 1700, the same year as his patron Zinzendorf, son of the court jeweler and goldsmith in Berlin. Before he was thirteen years of age, he had won the prize for painting at the Royal Academy in Berlin for three years, and as a result he was given a scholarship from the Prussian king to study painting. In 1714 the king died, and the youth had to forgo his stipend so he adopted his father's craft, goldsmithing. However, he laid a solid foundation in his drawing and studied at Dresden, Augsburg, Prague, Vienna, Rome, Sienna, Florence, and Paris—where he was put in touch with the practicing masters of the time. He was beyond question the best trained artist in Colonial America. Also, Haidt came to be under the influence of the Awakened, a pious devout man and it is not surprising that he became a convert to the Moravian Brethren. In 1740 he arrived at the Moravian center of Herrnhaag, and here he did several portraits for Zinzendorf. He arrived in Pennsylvania on the *Irene* April 22, 1754.

Haidt's work has survived in bulk, and at least seventy examples have come down, and now and then a new one is found. His work falls into two groups: Biblical scenes and portraits.

In the first category are included works of majesty and almost classical character, like the *Crucifixion*, and pieces which exhibit incidents with poignant devotion. His subjects reflect with rare sincerity the deep piety of his nature. Fundamentally baroque in mood, he portrayed scenes vibrantly alive depicting religious emotions with skilled touch. In a work like *Abraham Prepares to Sacrifice Isaac* (Fig. 111) the anguish on Abraham's face and the deep resignation of youthful Isaac have been fully realized, showing Pietist realism on a theme Kierkegaardian in mood. The Abraham theme was popular among the Moravians, for he was held to be prototype of resignation to the will of God. Haidt's religious paintings show more than visual literalness; they express religious themes and really are sermons in oil. *Eliezer Meets Rebeccah* (Fig. 112) is a work rich in oriental luxury and voluptuousness done with the restraint that Pietism suggested. Rebeccah, who before she became wife of the patriarch Isaac, was "fair to look upon," had gone with her pitcher to the well to draw water. According to the Biblical passage a man took "a golden earring of half a shekel weight, and two bracelets for her hands of ten *shekels* weight of gold; and said, whose daughter *art* thou?" (Genesis 24:22-23). Here Eliezer, seeking to win the chaste Rebeccah with his gifts, offers the lascivious counterfoil to the virtuous young lady.

Fig. 111. *Abraham Prepares to Sacrifice Isaac*: Johann Valentin Haidt.

Fig. 112. *Eliezer Meets Rebekah*: Johann Valentin Haidt.

Fig. 113. *The Pierced Side*: Johann Valentin Haidt.

Fig. 114. *"Father" David Nitschman*: Johann Valentin Haidt.

Even more meaningful, it seems, for the history of Moravian piety is Haidt's painting *The Pierced Side* (Fig. 113). At a time when Moravian poetry in America was characterized by what has been called the "blood and wound theology," when hymns were being composed by Bethlehem Moravians about the hole in the side of Jesus' body, Haidt painted this piece which, compared with the poetry, shows remarkable restraint, being free from gore, chaste and clean for so bloody a theme. Yet the artist has conceived not the anguishing Christ of the Passion but the loving Christ whose compassion and warmth are plain.

In 1755 Haidt painted a large canvas depicting the first group of converts to Moravianism, which must have been somewhat imaginative as he was not acquainted with them. Fourteen of his religious works hang in the Museum of the Moravian Church in Nazareth.

The second category of Haidt's work consists of more than thirty portraits of contemporary Moravians. Thirty-two hang in the Archives of the Provincial Synod of the Moravian Church in Bethlehem and a few in other places. All these portraits are much alike for his subjects posed much the same, and the composition is similar. Here was a portrait technique not born of practical needs but from congregational mood. All are dressed alike—the men in their sectarian clothes and the women in the Sisters' garb. Here is no individuality, but community of feeling. However, in spite of this congregational spirit the artist let the individual nature of the subject come through, as in the portrait of *Father David Nitschman* (Fig. 114), where the genial character of the old father is evident. His good and kindly face shows his spirit.

Valentin Haidt was one of America's finest painters during the eighteenth century, but he suffers from the neglect which most Pennsylvania German cultural achievements suffer—and he is almost unknown in the main stream of American studies.

In addition to Müller and Haidt, Nicholas Garrison, Jr. is also known to have painted both in Bethlehem and Reading. He was an English sailor who dabbled in oils. None of his work has been identified.

Benjamin West

On October 10, 1738, there was born in Springfield Township, Delaware County, on what is now part of the campus of Swarthmore College, a Quaker lad who grew up to become President of the Royal Academy in London. Benjamin West not only succeeded Sir Joshua Reynolds, author of the celebrated *Discourses on Art* and style-setter for the time, as President of the Academy, but he also was to become the father of American painting for many of our early limners received instruction in West's London studio. When he died in 1820, over eighty years of age, his fame was such that he was buried among the great of the British Empire in Saint Paul's Cathedral.

Benjamin West was one of the three early "plain" painters working in Pennsylvania, the others being Gustavus Hesselius and Valentin Haidt. West's aesthetic integrity was such that he was able to introduce a new realism into the artistic tastes of his age, a realism which surely issued from his Quaker simplicity and honesty, and his hatred of sham. Although later in life he succumbed to fashionable modes and reflected the various fashions of the age, there can be no question that in his earlier portrayals he was scrupulously honest in a good Pennsylvania Quaker way. Did he not have the courage, even in face of the king's wishes, to paint British soldiers as British soldiers in his famous painting, *The Death of General Wolfe?*

Although his later work in Europe came to reflect more fashionable tastes, West's American work, focus of our interest here, shows that he was an honest realist concerned with drawing what he was seeing rather than what his subjects thought. We believe that West's honesty, coming from Quakerism, came to be influential for the long line of Americans who studied with him in London; he came to be he guiding spirit of the American school in which a marked degree of realism stands in contrast to European artificiality. Truly, the Quaker-born Benjamin West helped to give realism and representational integrity to American art, keeping it from falling into the extravagances of European modes. Although West lived in Britain, winning a place there, he never lost his interest in his homeland.

We may then believe that the Philadelphia merchant who gave the young Quaker lad a paint box knew what he was about for he started a remarkable and influential career. In 1747 also West met William Williams, a shadowy figure in early Pennsylvania art, who seems to have introduced the youth to European theories of art. West also seems to have known the work of James Claypoole who was working in the city before 1750 and whose ideas seem to have been quite influential although none of his work has been identified. And finally the peripatetic New Yorker, John Wollaston, who was intermittently active in Philadelphia between 1749 and 1767, appears also to have been formative for some of West's earlier work, giving him formalized subject matter and the almond-eye technique. West's active Pennsylvania period, spent partly in the town of Lancaster and partly in the city, was between 1756 and 1763; in the latter year he was already in London after having spent some time in Italy.

After trying his skill with several landscapes—both copied and originally composed, wherein his future gifts already were apparent—West turned his attention to portraits. He did likenesses of Jane Morris and her brother Robert which show the awkward style of an

Fig. 115. *Self-portrait*: Benjamin West.

aspiring limner. His portraits of William Henry and his wife, dating from about 1755, show that the young portraitist had not yet overcome his stiffness. All of his earlier portraits are sharply formal, with unnatural poses, and with heavy almond-shaped eyes staring at the viewer. Sometime in 1756 West did a stunning miniature self-portrait on ivory (Fig. 115) with water-colors in which he portrayed himself as a somewhat prim, yet serious, young man. Set in a silver locket it shows an eighteen-year-old lad with brown hair and brown eyes, holding a three-cornered plain hat on his left arm. The portraits he did in the year 1757 show his emerging skill; the portrait of *Ann Inglis*, painted about this time, manages to convey a sly sense of humor; with the Mary Inglis and Jane Galloway portraits, however, the smiles are broader.

Probably the most important of Benjamin West's American work is his three-quarter-length portrait of Thomas Mifflin (Fig. 116), done in 1758-1759 when the subject was about fifteen years of age. This same Mifflin (1744-1800) was to become an important figure in early Pennsylvania, being a member of the First Continental Congress, Aide-de-Camp to George Washington, Major General in the Continental Army, and Governor of Pennsylvania during the years from 1790 to 1799 when Philadelphia was also the federal capital. West's portrait of young Mifflin is a compromise between the stilted elegance of Europe—here tempered, it seems, by a realism which European works do not show. The dog swimming in the lake and the covey of fowl, while not as representationally accurate as later naturalists, are still not

Fig. 116. *Portrait of Thomas Mifflin:* Benjamin West.

Fig. 117. Pencil drawing of David James Dove: Benjamin West.

Fig. 118. Pencil drawing of Francis Hopkinson in conversation with a lady: Benjamin West.

imaginary. And the rifle looks very much like a pre-Revolutionary Pennsylvania piece.

Also of considerable interest to students of early Pennsylvania art is Benjamin West's sketchbook now in the Gilpin Library of the Historical Society of Pennsylvania. Here too is realism and sometimes a hint of caricature in the mood of the British satirist, James Sayers. The sketch of David James Dove (Fig. 117), instructor in English at the College and Charitable School in Philadelphia, now the University of Pennsylvania, shows a mood similar to the sketch of Dr. Samuel Johnson and James Boswell done by Rowlandson. The sketch of Francis Hopkinson in conversation with a lady (Fig. 118) shows just a hint of caricature; the foppish dilettante is posed in a posture just not quite elegant and the lady has informally postured herself, suggesting perhaps that West may be drawing with his tongue in his cheek. These pencil sketches, however, have the promise of the artist to be a craftsman too kind to really caricature and too honest to be elegantly elaborate.

Fig. 119. Robert Fulton's self-portrait after an oil by Benjamin West.

In Benjamin West's American work the Quaker spirit of honest simplicity still is clearly evident, along with the promise of the greater skills yet to come.

Among the young men associated with Benjamin West was the celebrated inventor of the steamboat, Robert Fulton (1765-1815), who was born in Lancaster, Pennsylvania in 1765, and who studied with West while in Philadelphia. Probably during this period he painted miniatures, possibly the self-portrait done in oil after a picture by West (Fig. 119). The portrait also may date from the London sojourn of Fulton.

Another young Pennsylvania who studied with West in London was Thomas Spence Duché, son of the Reverend Jacob Duché, one time Chaplain to the Continental Congress. Little of Duché's American work has been identified.

Fig. 120. *Lafayette at Valley Forge*: Charles Willson Peale.

The Peale Family

One family dominated the artistic life of Pennsylvania during the last third of the eighteenth century and the first two decades of the nineteenth—the Peales. Taken as a group the Peales recorded the likenesses of several generations of ladies and gentlemen in Philadelphia and the Chesapeake region.

Altogether the Peale family produced over thirty-five portraits of George Washington who, according to a French volunteer officer, "dressed in the most simple manner without any marks of distinction of a commanding officer." Although a Virginia aristocrat Washington felt himself in the plain tradition and Charles Willson Peale became the painter of portraits of the patriots, men famous in American and Pennsylvania history, depicting plain Americans in unsophisticated poses at a time when European elegance marked the Tory. For there is no doubt that plainness was a Whig characteristic.

Charles Willson was born in Queen's County, Maryland, April 15, 1741, son of a schoolmaster who later moved to Chestertown. First apprenticed to a saddler, Charles Willson Peale married at the age of nineteen and set up shop on Church Street in Annapolis. On a trip to Norfolk he became interested in making pictures and he began a portrait of himself and of his family. Then advertising himself as a painter he began to receive commissions almost immediately, not refusing to do also the pedestrian coach and chaise painting which was in demand. Visiting Philadelphia he met James Claypoole, saw his pictures, and at Rivington's book store he picked up a copy of *The Handmaid of the Arts*. At that time only a few artists were working in the city—Hesselius and Wollaston—and business troubles hounded him, so he returned to his Maryland place. Because he was of the debtor class, when the political troubles started around 1764, he joined the Sons of Liberty, an ardent patriot group. His financial troubles continued to mount so in 1765 he left Annapolis in deepest secrecy for Virginia. Then he travelled to Boston where he visited Copley's house and began to paint portraits, including miniatures. Upon his return to Virginia he was commissioned to paint a portrait by James Arbucle.

Being now determined to become a painter, Peale set out for England, arriving in London February 13, 1761. Here he sought out the studio of Benjamin West and was the first of a line of Americans who learned from this Quaker the art of painting. Hardworking, though lonely, he found favor with the Archbishop of York; finally he was asked to paint Mr. Pitt,

Fig. 121. *Staircase Group*: Charles Willson Peale.

America's friend, which he did in truly conventional style as a Roman senator, showing that he too could do what was thought to be elegant.

In 1769 Charles Peale returned to Maryland determined to pursue his art. In Annapolis he found professional success, and he taught his brothers how to paint. His attentions, however, were directed towards Philadelphia—a rapidly developing city which he visited each year until 1774 to paint its distinguished burghers. Finally in 1776 the Peale family moved into their new Philadelphia home.

On his visits into the south he already had met Washington and had painted his portrait as a young colonel in 1772. Charles Peale, not yet fully established as a painter, became an ardent patriot. He was essentially unwarlike in temperament; yet this warm and gentle man bought a suit of regimentals and had a new rifle made for which he provided a telescopic sight. In this martial atmosphere he painted George and Martha Washington and John Hancock—cleaning Hancock's watch too! On August 9, 1776, after the break with Great Britain, Peale enlisted as a common soldier in the Associators of Philadelphia and on the October 3 he was commissioned a lieutenant. Thus did the gentle painter become a patriot, fighting with the Pennsylvania Militia in several subsequent campaigns.

During the winter of 1777-1778, while the American army was at Valley Forge, Charles Peale took the opportunity, which the military inaction afforded, to paint what appears to be a series of portraits of the leading patriots. Most of these canvases show similar composition and are nearly of equal size, about twenty by twenty-four inches, and from the historical point of view they could have been done only when the subjects were gathered in one place.

Fig. 122. *Still Life*: James Peale.

His biographer Sellars credits Peale with a group of miniature portraits made during this time including likeness of General Nathanael Greene and his wife, Colonel Clement Biddle, General Varnum, Colonel Thomas Proctor and Colonel William Grayson. Peale also painted, according to his biographer, miniatures of several physicians attending the army. However, in addition, portraits on canvas and linen, all similar in size and composition, seem to date from this period, suggesting that Peale spent the months at Valley Forge doing portraits of Washington, Lafayette (Fig. 120), Colonel Daniel Morgan, Chevalier du Portail, Colonel John Hazelwood and General Varnum. The larger portrait of General Steuben was done later. In addition to the Washington portrait known to have been done at Valley Forge, two other "Washingtons" also may date from this period. Were Peale's diary for this period extant these matters might be cleared up.

So if these military portraits may be grouped together, they form the largest single phase of Peale's work, and he then emerges as the painter of the patriots in America's hour of deepest gloom. It is unfortunate that he did not paint his own commanding officer, Colonel William Will, the Philadelphia pewterer who has been called the Paul Revere of Pennsylvania.

These early portraits by Peale, however, are sufficient to establish his artistic credo. Although he was acquainted with the elegant mode and actually had painted in it, when he came to depict Washington and other patriots it was in their plain Continentals. He did not make them into Roman legionaires. He was not interested in fashionableness but in solid construction and sound designs. His painting was never sophisticated or artificial; he believed that nature was the best teacher, model, and guide—that nature and beauty were bound together. His ideal was fidelity and as early as 1772 he was experimenting with mechanical devices like the painter's quadrant to attain it.

When the Revolution was over Charles Peale designed the triumphal arch for the victory celebration in the city, but it was prematurely burnt. Already he fancied himself painter to the patriots for in 1783 he wrote:

I have between 30 and 40 portraits of the Principal Characters [of the Revolution]. This collection has cost me much time & labour and I mean to keep adding as many of those who are distinguished by their actions or office as opportunity will serve.

New Washington portraits were begun, full-length studies. Rivals were bound to appear to capitalize on the revolutionary success; so when Robert Edge Pine announced that he meant to do a series of portraits of Revolutionary leaders, Peale took a dislike to him, although he was generally encouraging to other young painters like Robert Fulton. Pine, who died a few years later, was but a forerunner of many artists who came to Philadelphia during the post-Revolutionary period.

In 1784 Peale conceived the idea of establishing a museum of curios, including his precious collection of patriot likenesses. About this time he also experimented with pictures that moved, invented by deLoutherbourg, "Perspective Views with Changeable Effects; or, Nature Delineated and in Motion." These moving pictures were shown at his museum. At this time too he divided his professional interests; his brother James doing the miniatures, which Charles' eyesight would not let him do.

With the death of his wife Rachel in 1790 the first phase of the life of Charles Willson Peale came to an end. His museum was, in truth, born in an attitude of experiment. As his ideal always had been to show what his subjects looked like, he now turned to landscapes, painting them with realistic regard for accurate portrayal of animals in their natural habitat —for this too was the age of Audubon and Wilson, the naturalists who were stimulated by the Peale museum, then largest in America, to an expression of the new interest in ornithology then gripping the American people.

The 1790 census of Pennsylvania listed James Peale, Charles' younger brother, as a limner. He was a painter of miniatures and still life. He introduced the Dutch tradition of still life painting to America, and his work tends to be rich in color and elaboration. James Peale settled in Philadelphia and married Mary, the daughter of James Claypoole, fathering seven children. His still life painting (Fig. 122) is strikingly colorful, with deft arrangement of light.

Raphaelle Peale, eldest son of Charles, was a jolly man of much talent—musician, entertainer, but addicted to drink—and by many critics thought to be the best of the still life painters in the Peale family. His famous painting, *After the Bath,* was so realistic that his patient wife tried to pluck the cloth from it, not realizing that it was painted on the canvas. His portrait of Washington (Fig. 123) taken from Houdon's bust, shows his visual sensitivity and a firm and sure objective sense.

Another member of the Peale family, Charles Peale Polk, is also mentioned in the 1790 census as a limner. He was a portraitist and general painter who advertised himself as "house, ship, sign painter." He made copies of portraits of Washington, Franklin and Lafayette.

Painting in the Federal Period

After the American Revolution was over and the new country an on-going affair, Philadelphia became the capital of the new land. Then all sorts of artists, European and native-born, flocked to the city to paint the great and near-great. Although Charles Willson Peale was the dominant figure, others were working too. Not all of these artists are well known, but among them the following have to be listed: John James Barrolet, painter and engraver; William Russell Birch, painter and engraver; Joseph Ceracchi, sculptor; J. Frederick A. Eckstein, painter and engraver; John Eckstein, Jr., painter and engraver; Robert Field, painter and engraver; Samuel Folwell, miniature painter; Gilbert Fox, engraver; William Groombridge, landscape painter, Pierre Henri, miniature painter; A.O.H. deLoutherbourg, miniature painter; Cotton Millbourne, painter, George Isham Parkyns, artist and designer for engravers; Jeremiah Paul, portrait and landscape painter; James Peale; Raphaelle Peale; Rembrandt Peale; Robert Edge Pine, painter; Walter Robertson, miniature painter; William Rush, sculptor; Gilbert Stuart, portrait painter; St. Memin, painter; James Thackara, engraver; Thomas Thackara, engraver; Adolph Elric Wertmüller, painter; and Jacob Witman, portrait painter. Little of the work of most of these artists has been identified.

One of the most interesting figures in this list of artists in he city during the early Federal period was Charles Balthazar Julien Fuerit de St. Mémin who brought to the city a strangely rational instrument for making portraits in profile, the physiognatrace. This was a device for making silhouettes in profile. The subject pressed his cheek against a concave wooden plate while a large brass gnomen was lightly run about his profile; then, by a pantograph-like device, the profile was reduced in size on a double folded sheet of paper. Thus identical silhouettes could be made. St. Mémin, using this device, then made small oil paintings of profiles thus obtained. First from large portraits he made these smaller profiles and filled in the features. He also made small medallion-sized engravings on copper. From these he struck a dozen or so prints. St. Mémin, who had come to America in 1793 for political reasons, was active between 1798 and 1804. After Napoleon he returned to France to become curator of the Dijon Museum.

Although New York and Boston papers were complaining about the vulgar feeling towards the fine arts in Federal Philadelphia, Gilbert Stuart, like many other painters, came to the city to do portraits of the great. Here Stuart began the most famous portrait painted in eighteenth-century America, that of George Washington, which by now has been seen all over the world on American postage stamps.

Stuart first lived at Fifth and Chestnut Streets, at the center of things near the State House, but he was here interrupted so much that he could not work. So he removed to Germantown, to the Morris-Deshler house. Here the burghers of Germantown remembered him for his eccentricities, how he bought wine, gin and brandy by the cask, how he kicked a large

Fig. 123. Portrait of George Washington after the Houdon bust: Rembrandt Peale.

piece of beef across the street to butcher Diehl's complaining that the beef was not fit to be handled. Here too he painted a tavern sign for the King of Prussia Inn—a likeness of that monarch. Using the barn as his studio he also painted here the so-called "Boston portrait" of Martha Washington, and also a likeness of Mrs. Chew.

Here also he painted portraits, we believe, of Col. David Deshler and his wife (Fig. 124). David Deshler (1734-1796) had been born in Northampton County and became a prominent figure in the Indian wars. In 1764 he was a shopkeeper in Allentown and several years later he was operating a gristmill and sawmills. During the Revolution Col. Deshler was Commissary of Supplies, and with Col. John Arndt of Easton he advanced money from his private funds when the United States and Pennsylvania were low. He was a member of the Provincial Conference which met at Carpenter's Hall, January 18, 1776, and he was elected one of the judges of election for Allentown. In 1787 he became delegate to the convention to ratify the Constitution.

There seems to be little doubt that the portrait of Colonel Deshler, as well as one of Deshler's wife Susanna, were painted by Stuart during his stay in Germantown. As they show the Colonel late in his life they fall into the proper period.

Along with the general awakening of interest in realistic and naturalist painting, Pennsylvania attracted students of natural history. The Peale Museum was indicative of a new view towards nature, one which owed much to the interest of Pennsylvania dissenters in the

Fig. 124. *Colonel David Deshler*: Gilbert Stuart.

Fig. 125. John James Audubon's painting of a fishhawk.

natural world. Both in England and America the religious dissenters had showed a deep concern for nature. Fox, Penn and the London Quaker, Peter Collinson, were naturalists, the last having far-flung interests in North Carolina, Virginia, Maryland, New England, and Pennsylvania. Collinson was in correspondence with the botanist Linneaus, and he was a friend of Joseph Priestly, Richard Price and John Pringle, all honest Whigs. In Pennsylvania interest in science was alive among English and German settlers. James Logan, John Bartram, William Bartram, John Woolman and Benjamin Franklin were prominent; among the Germans, George deBenneville who constructed a pharmacopoeia, Wilhelm Jung, Abraham Wagner, David Rittenhouse and John David Schoepff. During the Federal period Alexander Wilson and Johann James Audubon were working in Pennsylvania. Two of the drawings of Audubon's have been identified as having been made while he was residing at Millgrove in Montgomery County—his drawing of the Fish Hawk and his drawing of the Wood Thrush (Figs. 125, 126). These are the only two drawings by Audubon that were drawn in Pennsylvania, as far as our present knowledge goes.

Another painter working in Philadelphia during this period was the Swede, Adolph Ulric Wertmüller, born in 1750. He had studied painting at home; then he went to Paris where he worked with Roslin and his cousin Vien. He became a member of the Royal Academy of Sculpture and Painting in both Paris and Stockholm. In 1794 he arrived in Philadelphia where he married the granddaughter of Gustavus Hesselius and settled at Marcus Hook where he died in 1811.

Fig. 126. John James Audubon's painting of a woodthrush.

Fig. 127. Portrait said to be of Benjamin Franklin: unknown artist.

Fig. 128. *Johann Arndt*: unknown artist.

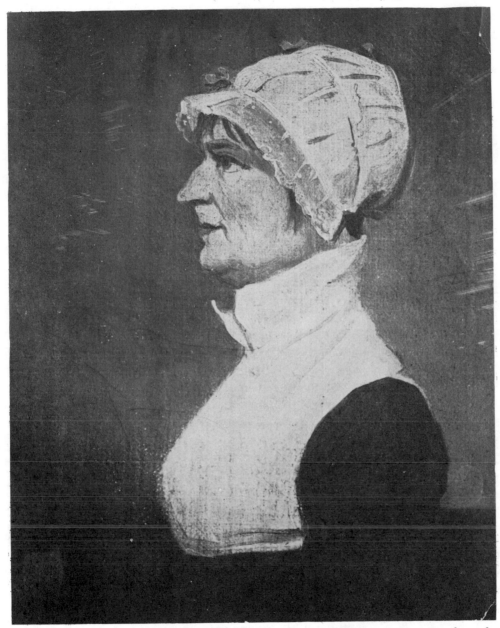

Fig. 129. *Aunt Polly Knox,* family tradition ascribes the portrait to a member of the Peale family.

In 1784 a middle-aged British painter, Robert Edge Pine, arrived in Philadelphia to record the likenesses of persons involved in the historic events just concluded. He is best known for his *The Congress Voting Independence, July 4, 1776,* which now is in the Historical Society of Pennsylvania. During his four years in America he painted the illustrious scenes of the late Revolution in realistic rather than idealized pictures. His picture of the signing of the Declaration of Independence is an effective composition which includes thirty-two persons with most of them depicted somewhat older than they were at the time of the event itself. Pine was protégé of Robert Morris who gave him a studio in which to work. He died in 1788.

The Fine Art of the Tavern Sign

As early as 1715 European magistrates ordered innkeepers to show signs so that travellers might know where to find refreshment and rest. This distinguished public from private houses. So all over western Europe—and in the American Colonies—public houses came to be distinguished by painted, carved, or gilded signs which were a mixture of fine and folk arts. As serious a painter as Benjamin West was not above the pedestrian bread-and-butter work of painting tavern signs.

Early Philadelphia really was not an artistic city and professional painters often could not find patrons. Thomas Pratt, son of portraitist Matthew Pratt, wrote in a *Memoranda* that in the year 1785 the fine arts were "very poorly encouraged in Philada" and that his father, having little to do in that line, was encouraged by his friends to turn to sign painting. What a remarkable experience, then, these eighteenth-century signs must have been. Walking down Market and Chestnut streets was almost like being in an art gallery!

One sign painted by Matthew Pratt was entitled *The Representation of The Constitution of 1788.* It hung at the southwest corner of Fourth and Chestnut Streets and presented fine portraits of the gentlemen who had composed the famous Constitutional Convention held just a short distance away, with good likenesses of Washington and other notables, along with this verse by the artist:

> These 38 great men here signed a peaceful Deed
> That better times to us, should very soon succeed.

The portraitist was not the only one unemployed in these early and difficult years.

Another tavern sign by Matthew Pratt, entitled *The Fox Chase,* hung on the north side of Arch Street, near Sixth Street. It pictured a gentleman on horseback in full pursuit of a fox with a pack of hounds and the verse:

> Our Hounds are good and horses too
> The Buck is quite run down,
> Call off the Hounds, and let them blow
> Whilst we regale with BROWN.

Yet another artistic sign hung at the old Lebanon Gardens on the southeast corner of South and Tenth Streets. It portrayed a ship on a calm sea on one side and Neptune riding triumphantly in his car on the other. Each side had a verse by the artist:

> Neptune in his triumphant Car
> Commands the ocean to be silent
> While universal calm succeeds.

And on the other side:

> Of the waters of 'Lebanon'—
> Coffee, Chocolate, Tea,
> And kind entertainments
> By John McGavney.

Fig. 130. Tavern sign by Jacob Eicholtz.

Up-country taverns, painted by less skillful artists than masters like Pratt, generally had simple representations of the name of the inn. Traveller Schoepff wrote of these country tavern signs as follows:

The taverns in the country are recognizable even at a distance by a sort of gallows arrangement which stands out over the road and exhibits the patrons of the house. So far we have observed many times the counterfeit presentment of Frederick the Second, King of Prussia, hung up in this

Fig. 131. A carving by an unknown carver, served as a sign for the Golden Swan Inn, Easton.

Fig. 132. Carved tavern sign circa 1800, possibly by William Rush.

way, that monarch having been a great favorite of the Americans ever since the war before the last. We still found a few Georges, let hung perhaps out of sympathy; but Queens of England we saw a good many. We have as yet seen no king of France, but a number of Washingtons and still more Benjamin Franklins—the latter makes a particularly alluring sight if everything is well-kept.

From these tavern signs many Pennsylvania villages got their names: Black Horse, Blue Bell, Blue Ball, Three Tuns, King of Prussia, etc. Jacob Staudt's tavern in Kutztown was The Washington.

Like the Philadelphia taverns, competition was keen and verses were painted on the signs to attract business. Sometimes the Germans were more direct in their approach, as Gabriel Schuler near the Trappe who put this couplet on his sign:

Ich verkaufe Bier und Wein	I sell beer and wine
So billig wie mei' Nachbar Klein	As cheaply as my neighbor Klein.

Unfortunately, hanging outside in all the weather, exposed to wind and rain, frost and snow, few of these painted tavern signs have survived. Several faded ones are in the museums and they are not even worth photographing with the exception of the portrait of William Pitt, Earl of Chatham, which was painted by Jacob Eicholtz in Lancaster in 1808 (Fig. 130).

Painting, however, was not the only technique in which the tavern sign was expressed. Many early Pennsylvania inns were named for tangible things like birds, beasts, bells, and the like. Many were represented by carved replicas of their names. Several magnificent carved pieces have survived, a few of them dating from before the Revolutionary War, and they suggest that carving was one of the finest expressions of the fine arts in early Pennsylvania. The golden swan (Fig. 131) which stood on top of a post in front of the Golden Swan Inn in Easton (then Northampton) is, plastically speaking, a magnificent piece of work. Who carved it is a question. We do know that members of the Demuth family of Lancaster were carving pieces as early as 1770 when they did a figurine, twenty-four inches high, of a pre-Revolutionary gentleman holding a hand of tobacco. They also carved Indians. Emmanuel Demuth (1770-1820), known as the snuff taker of the Revolutionary days, may have done work like this Easton swan, but if he did carve it, it is later in date.

We do know that William Rush, who has been called the first sculptor in America, did carved eagles which obviously were tavern signs. His shop was at 172 North Front Street in the city where he did work which allows him to be called America's first sculptor. Here he made portrait busts, anatomical models, ship figures, and tavern signs. The magnificent golden eagle tavern sign has his touch (Fig. 132). Rush also carved the eagle in the St. Johns Lutheran Church in Philadelphia, and three of his tavern signs have been identified.

Suffice it to say that the tavern sign was an artistic medium of Pennsylvania's best painters and carvers and were more known about their work, and if more identifiable pieces had survived, it would form a fine chapter in the history of our fine art. From the pieces which survive, we can see that the Colonial scene—from the city with its interesting signs to the country inns— was of more than passing interest to the traveller.

Reverse Painting on Glass

A Pennsylvania art form which never rose to great heights here, but which remained quite crude and even primitive in its mood, was the ancient technique of reverse painting of portraits on glass.

Fig. 133. Reverse portrait on glass.

Fig. 134. Reverse portrait on glass.

Fig. 135. *General Jackson, Hero of New Orleans.*

This technique can be traced back to the fourth century B.C., to the Hellenic period; and during the time when it flourished from 1500 onwards, in Germany, Holland, Italy and Spain, it was used chiefly for religious pictures. Basically it was a Catholic art form and was widely utilized for devotional pictures; in Protestant lands it was used in the Bible corner of the house where a portrait of Luther or some other Protestant hero replaced the Roman Catholic saint. In Germany these votive pictures were widespread.

The technique was simple. The artist placed a sheet of glass between his eye and the subject and then drew in water colors or in crayon the subject as he saw him. This gave him a direct image which then was painted on the back side of the glass with more permanent materials. Or, if the artist was copying an engraving or similar reproduction he would simply lay the glass directly on the reproduction and draw the image.

During the eighteenth century this technique was employed by many formal artists who sometimes even reversed the reversals and gained positive images. After 1725 this technique came to be used by folk artists, and this is the way it was used in Pennsylvania. No proven portraits by formal artists made in this way have come down.

In Pennsylvania this art remained quite primitive; it had nothing of the brilliance shown by the European masters of this method. The crude but still recognizable portrait of William Penn (Fig. 133), which was a substitute for the Protestant portraits of Luther and other reformers, does not go much beyond the primitive in mood while the romanticized portrait of an unknown young lady (Fig. 134) suggests a lithograph by Currier and Ives. Yet in both of these reverse portraits on glass done in Pennsylvania, an American spirit is clearly evident.

The Fine Art of the Silversmith

Silver showed the formal elegance of tidewater merchant and professional classes for it was almost wholly confined to this area. In the beginning, though, it was even used for primitive forms and the native Pennsylvania gourd or calabash was dried and then made into cups and dishes which were silver-tipped.

Philadelphia silver, which has been greatly admired and widely exhibited, was made by a group of talented, even brilliant, silversmiths for well-known American figures like George Washington, Thomas McKean, John Penn, Jr., Abraham Kinsey, Bishop William White, Charles Thompson, and Aaron Burr. While at least one hundred and forty silversmiths plied their art in the city between 1680 and 1800, there were hardly a dozen known to be working in the piedmont. Of these three were in Lancaster during the 1760s: Phillip Becker, Charles Hall, John Price. In Bethlehem were Johann Georg Weiss, Abraham Boemper and Adam Andreas. In Reading John Keim may have been doing work with silver for it is known that he trained Christian Bixler, Sr. After 1810 William Mannerbach was working there. The 1790 Census lists at least sixteen silversmiths working in the city.

The same pattern prevailed over most of British America. Few silversmiths were working beyond tidewater port areas and the Hudson valley probably because the sources of metal were abroad. But this was also probably due to the fact that the demand was from tidewater areas. Even silver used for ecclesiastical purposes was generally limited to tidewater churches for the interior parishes had pewter communionware made by the Philadelphia craftsmen. Philadelphia silversmiths made communionware for the First Baptist Church, the Memorial Church of Saint Paul, the First Presbyterian Church of Northern Liberties, Saint Peters in Lewes, Delaware, Saint Johns in Salem, N.J., and for Saint Annes in Middletown, Delaware. No denominational patterns are visible, but tidewater groups used silver chalices and plate while pewter was used by piedmont churches.

Moreover, the German *Hausfrau* was satisfied with her pewter, which she could afford. Craftsmen like Jeremiah Boone, nephew of Daniel Boone who had been born in Oley,

Fig. 136. George Washington's Silver camp mug: manufactured by Humphreys.

Fig. 137. Silver group by Philip Syng, Jr.

established themselves in the city close to both European sources of metal and to their market.

Silver did indeed imply a way of life different from that of the piedmont farmer—sugar tongs, waste bowls, and pots—and a custom foreign to the ways of the farmers. And when a group of Boston patriots pitched overboard a shipload of the "cursed stuff," the

> fated plant of India's shore,
> Whose vaunted steam shall rise no more,
> In Freedom's sacred land,

tea became a political issue. In Charleston, tea was consigned to damp vaults to foul; and the captain of a ship with tea aboard was not allowed to proceed up the Delaware to bring his load into port. Patriots rejected everything that tea implied while tories seem to have welcomed it. The farmer said farewell to

> the teaboard, with its gaudy equipage
> Of cups and saucers, cream bucket, sugar-tongs;
> The pretty tea-chest, also lately stored
> With Hyson, Congo and Best Double-Fine . . .

Fig. 138. Silver patch boxes by Joseph Richardson.

Indeed, many hours were spent at this tea-table—not a part of the furniture of piedmont farmers

> Hearing the girls tattle, and old maids talk scandal,
> And the spruce coxcombs laugh—maybe—at nothing.

Patriots, from piedmont to frontier, bulk of new Americans in Pennsylvania and western Virginia, rejected tea bowls loved by the merchants and professionals of the city.

In matter of fact, German Pennsylvania came to be known as the place of the "Coffee-mantia" as the German scholar Fabricius called it, for coffee was a Germanic drink, especially in the southern areas. Tea was the drink of Friesland. In Pennsylvania beer and schnapps,

Fig. 139. Philadelphia silver pieces made by Abraham Carlisle.

and of course the homemade applejack, were popular. Also much brewing and distilling went on in rural Pennsylvania, replacing traditional German wines, for where the Rhinelanders had been among the best vintners of Europe their American descendents became good distillers; in Pennsylvania the grape did not grow well but grain did. And the first rebellion against the new government was the Whiskey rebellion, fomented by Pennsylvanians who hated the new tax.

Moreover, snuff was not used by the piedmont farmer in the same degree as among fashionable dandies of the city. Hence the snuff boxes were not needed. Nor were ladies of the piedmont prone to wear patches on their faces; hence patch boxes were unnecessary.

These cultural differences gave piedmont settlers disinclination for the silver which was used with tea, snuff, and face patches.

All this however cannot detract from the brilliant craftsmanship of the Philadelphia silversmiths who created some of the finest art of early America. Richardson, Humphrey, Neuss, Syng, and others achieved an elegance equal to anything that the old world could show. The celebrated inkstand made by Phillip Syng, Jr., used when the Declaration of Independence was signed, is a precious piece of Americana. George Washington's camp mug, made by Humphreys (Fig. 136), is likewise rooted in our history.

By the turn of the century silver began to catch on in the larger provincial towns and Bethlehem, Reading and Lancaster had good craftsmen working.

Related to silversmithing was the art of the goldsmith. Little of this early Pennsylvania gold seems to have survived. We do know that gold was being worked in the city even before the American Revolution from the following advertisement in the *Staatsbote;* February 15th, 1774:

Jacob Ludwig Videbant, former royal Prussian coin assayer, is now prepared to test metals, at the Golden Swan Inn, of Widow Kreyberin, Third Street, Philadelphia.

Also in the same newspaper there is an announcement that Gottfried Schwing was in business as goldsmith and jeweler; this under date of March 3, 1779.

The 1790 census lists four goldsmiths working in the city: Abraham duBois, William Haverstick, Joseph Anthony, and J. Friedrich Reiche; little of their work has survived.

Early Nineteenth Century Painting

After the federal capital had moved from Philadelphia the province settled down again and the excitement which had accompanied the great events of the founding of the new nation gave way to soberer moods. The traditional religious themes of early Pennsylvania art returned as the masters who had flocked to Philadelphia to paint the American leaders went elsewhere.

It will be remembered that both Gustavus Hesselius and Valentin Haidt had painted pictures on the Crucifixion. This theme was much loved by the sectarians who were followers of the *theologia crucis,* that is those religious groups whose faith was centered in the Passion. This viewpoint was widespread in the interior and it led Friedrich Krebs, the itinerant who was active in Berks County between 1790 and 1815, to present the figures of the Roman captain, Mary, John, and Caiaphas in eighteenth-century costume (Fig. 140). The theme of the pierced side from with blood flowed is plain.

In contrast to the Krebs *Crucifixion* is the painting in water colors by Samuel Reinke. a Moravian minister. He was son of Abraham Reinke, Jr., and grandson of Abraham, Sr., the person who introduced Gustavus Hesselius to the Moravian sect. Samuel Reinke had studied at Nazareth Hall, taught school in Bethlehem in 1813 and later in Lititz and Lancaster. This work, it seems, was painted in Lancaster. Here blood flows in quieter drops than in the Krebs painting, and the whole tone of this work communicates a mood of disturbed agitation, the earth-shaking nature of the events being pictured (Fig. 141).

About this time another Moravian schoolteacher named George Fetter, who also taught in the Bethlehem schools but who likewise removed to Lancaster, is known to have been painting portraits in water color. None of his work has been seen, and no opinions on it are possible.

The most celebrated "primitivist" in early nineteenth-century Pennsylvania was the Quaker, Edward Hicks (1780-1849), travelling minister of the Society of Friends and coach painter whose picture, *Peaceable Kingdom,* is widely known in many versions. The one illustrated is the version in the Historical Society of Bucks County (Fig. 142).

Hicks, however, was more than a mere coach painter; he was a religious mystic whose interest seems to have been more in what he was trying to communicate than in the way in which he did it. His painting is in truth mystical vision—but mysticism in a soundly American sense, mysticism in which the upsurging Gothic has been replaced by a worldly unon of contraries. Hicks was a Pennsylvanian who was not like Dante climbing heavenly ladders to transcendent ecstasy; rather he was seeking to bring this Kingdom of Peace to the Pennsylvania soil. This is a thoroughly earth-bound paradise which he pictures; it is not the enclosed heavenly garden which the medieval master of the upper Rhine painted. For here

Fig. 140. *The Crucifixion*: Friedrich Krebs.

we can see the Delaware Water Gap in the distance and William Penn is treating in a brotherly way with friendly Indians while Quaker and other officials are quietly purchasing the land.

The painting is an exposition of several verses from Isaiah. The upper third grouping is a representation of this passage from the prophet:

The wolf shall dwell with the Lamb, and the leopard shall lie down with the kid; and the calf and the young lion and the fatling together; and a little child shall lead them.

The central portion of the main grouping of figures illustrates these words:

And the cow and lion shall feed; the young ones shall lie down together; and the lions shall eat straw like an ox.

Fig. 141. *The Crucifixion*: Samuel Reinke.

And the lower tier of figures, below Penn and the Indians, expresses these words:

> And the suckling shall play on the hole of the asp, and the weaned child shall put his hand in the cocatrice den.

Here this Biblical version of an earth-bound paradise is rooted in the Pennsylvania countryside and a this-world vision of American mysticism is plain.

As his *Journal* indicates, Hicks was indeed a religious mystic, sharing in the dialectical nature of Protestant mystical experience, the experience of light and dark, and good and evil in one moment—thus gaining the longing for a kingdom where peace prevails and where the cosmic conflict between Yes and No and the contradictions of life has been permanently stilled. Hicks's great painting presents this longing for an earth-bound Pennsylvania paradise and so contrasts sharply with the Gothic mood of medieval mysticism which sought its ful-

Fig. 142. *The Peaceable Kingdom:* Edward Hicks.

Fig. 143. *Penn's Treaty with the Indians*: Edward Hicks.

Fig. 144. *Penn's Treaty*: unknown artist.

fillment in transcendent glory. Traditional mysticism was in truth looking for the beatific vision; Hicks was seeking the peaceable kingdom in Pennsylvania.

Pennsylvania was then a mystical dream too. Some of the incidents of its founding have become part of American folklore. Parson Weems, author of the early American best-selling life of Washington, also published his *The Life of William Penn, The Settler of Pennsylvania,* which was widely circulated in the rural areas of the state. In this book he spins out at some length the story of the Proprietor's treaty with the Indians. Although New York also was "bought" by Peter Minuit—and named Manhattan by the Delawares, meaning "the place where we got drunk"—the story about Penn's dealing with the Indians is famous. Voltaire helped to spread its fame when he characterized this treaty as the only one never signed and never broken.

More influential than the myths of Weems or the wit of Voltaire was the celebrated picture which Benjamin West painted on this theme and which, engraved on the Boydell print, came to be widely copied. Edward Hicks already had introduced this theme in the *Peaceable Kingdom,* symbol for him of the new age of the brotherhood of man and the philadelphian world; but Hicks also treated this theme on a separate canvas (Fig. 143) which shows its roots in the nineteenth-century romantic world which is joined with a technique almost cubist in style. The story of William Penn's dealings with the aborigines was part of early Pennsylvania legend, and several other treatments, apparently based on the engraving of West's painting, were made. One of these is the anonymous work (Fig. 144) which was once owned by the silversmith William Ball and which may perhaps be earlier than the work by Hicks.

Religion continued to be a dominating motif in provincial art. John Landis, a sectarian from Lancaster, drew his picture of the resurrected Jesus appearing before his followers in which the Lord shows his scarred hands to a kneeling and longer doubting Thomas (Fig. 145). Here we have folk art in almost a pure form—stylized figures, unsophisticated composition and deep piety.

Patriotism also was soundly grounded in the popular mind. The stirring events of the Revolution had lingered long in the provincial consciousness and old soldiers, both Continentals and Militia, kept the great days living in imagination. Grandchildren were regaled with heroic tales. As late as 1842 the deeds of Revolutionary patriots under Washington were memorialized by children as in the anonymous drawing of General "Waschington," here surrounded by patriotic and folk designs, protected by the same "fat angels" which also appeared on contemporary birth certificates. This was entirely typical of the new mood which exalted the freedom, equality, unity, and brotherhood of the new American experiment (Fig. 146).

Surely the greatest of the folk artists of interior Pennsylvania during these early years of the nineteenth century was Lewis Miller, the carpenter of York, whose notebooks and

Fig. 145. *Jesus Shows Himself to Thomas*: John Landis.

Fig. 146. Child's drawing of a military and patriotic theme with the inscription:
"Freedom, Unity and Brother-Love," 1820.

drawings form an intensely interesting commentary of the life of his time. In the year 1841 Miller visited Europe and drew sketches of the cities he visited, fascinating vignettes of places like Worms and Heidelberg. However, his drawings of his York contemporaries and his sketches of his fellow citizens are the most interesting of his work. His drawings were accompanied with commentaries which more than illuminate the time. Here are illustrated: his sketch of himself (Fig. 147); his drawing of the yearly market in York in 1801, when the patriots of the town burned the black cockade on the election of Jefferson as president (Fig. 148); his fascinating study of the interior of the old Lutheran Church in York showing the altar in the center of the room, organ on the balcony, and the panel portraits of the evangelists and Biblical figures on the balcony (Fig. 149); his drawing of Anthony Ritz, the unfortunate man who sawed off the limb he was sitting upon (Fig. 150); and finally, as an example of the several dozen portraits in similar style, Miller's sketch of Jost Harbaugh, father of the celebrated Pennsylvania Dutch poet, Henry Haubaugh (Fig. 151). In Lewis Miller's

Fig. 147. *Self-portrait*: Lewis Miller.

notebooks we can find an illuminating and indeed fascinating commentary on the life of a provincial Pennsylvania town in the early years of the nineteenth century.

Meanwhile in Lancaster, which for a time had been the capital of the American nation, a native Pennsylvanian was painting formal portraits with an uncommon skill, works which were not in the folk tradition. Jacob Eicholtz was in truth a piedmont artist, who like the artists of interior Connecticut and interior New York, had turned from craft work to the fine arts. Eicholtz was a humble man, unmoved by grandiose dreams of elegant art; he was a tinsmith and coppersmith who during his earlier years had painted on shingles. Naturally skilled, he was and remained a man of the people for whom art was never a means to fashionable glory as it was to become with Benjamin West.

Unlike many others, Eicholtz did not study with West. Rather he was influenced by the figure regnant among American artists, Gilbert Stuart. Eicholtz also had met Thomas Sully

In 1801. march 4. the administration of Thomes Jefferson commenced
in York the bury the Black Cockade. riband worn on the hat. democratical.
by George Spangler. Fred Rockey. Conrad welshans. Henry weiser. Salmon Myer.
michael Edward. at furry's tavern. John Sturd. John Stroman. John weyer.

Mr Barnhard. A vender give
to little Lewis Miller, the first
Barlo-Knife as A present.
1799.

Yearly Market, or publick fare.

Held in the Borough of York, June 9.th 1801,
the had privilege of a Stated yearly market,

In 1816. the prohibited the holding of fairs within the
Borough of York. and declared Such holding a common
nuisance in Some dispute at Lewis Wampfler, tavern —
michael Hahn. Stop. Robert Dunn, and at the Same time
nickolas Scheffer cut Barnhard with a Knife, at Eberhart, tavern.

Fig. 148. Yearly market in York, 1801.

who was to dominate Philadelphia painting for many years and who, on a visit to Lancaster, saw the work of Eicholtz and praised him for the use of his time, stolen from making copper pans.

Eicholtz has left a brief autobiographical sketch in which he recalls his struggles to become a successful painter. After removing to Philadelphia, where around the turn of the century there was a mania for portraits, Eicholtz began to paint those who came—as well as relatives, friends and neighbors— with a fine sense of character. His likenesses of children retain a sweet innocence which is almost—not quite— sentimental. Eicholtz was a good craftsman, in sure control of his materials, and the more than fifty pieces which survive give us adequate material to judge his work.

Two of his pictures here are illustrated: his *Portrait of a Mennonite Lady*, and *Dorothea*, which dates from 1841 (Figs. 152, 153).

Fig. 149. The Old Lutheran Church in York, 1800.

Fig. 150. Anthony Ritz sawing off the limb underneath him.

Fig. 151. A Lewis Miller portrait of the father of Henry Harbaugh.

Fig. 152. *Portrait of a Mennonite Lady*: Jacob Eicholtz.

Fig. 153. *Dorothea*: Jacob Eicholtz.

Fig. 154. A portrait of Conrad Weiser III, grandson of the Indian interpreter, who was an officer in the Continental Army. Here he wears the emblem of the Order of the Cincinatti. As Weiser was a resident of York, the portrait may have been painted by Samuel Enredy Stettinus (1768-1815).

Among the problematical figures working in early nineteenth-century Pennsylvania was Edward Enredy Stettinius who was Silesian born and who had arrived in America in 1791, first settling in Baltimore but later in Hanover and York. Some of the paintings ascribed to him—and few are indeed authenticated—show him as a mechanical workman, skilled in making laces, whose composition hardly varied, for he nearly always painted in profile. The portrait of Conrad Weiser, III (Fig. 154) is ascribed to him because of the technique around the laces and hair and because Weiser was, at the time this portrait was painted, a resident of York. Moreover, the technique of profile painting matches other work of the same artist.

With the work of Thomas Sulley, which is illustrated by his portrait of Sarah Franklin Bache (Fig. 155), we come to the end of early Pennsylvania fine arts. Here, with this genteel and kind man, who like so many of the painters of early Pennsylvania, studied with Benjamin West, we come to the leading portrait painter of the nineteenth century, dominating the Philadelphia scene until 1872. He marks the end of the first period.

Fig. 155. *Sara Franklin Bache*: Thomas Sully.

Music and Musical Instruments

Among the fine arts widely practiced in early Pennsylvania was music. In spite of Quaker plainness and opposition to music in worship, Pennsylvania, especially the German piedmont, became what may have been the musical center of Colonial America. Surely it was the center of the manufacture of musical instruments. Unlike New England Puritans for whom church music was somewhat "high," most Pennsylvania sects, even the plainest, did much singing and even the conservative Amish continued in their homes their traditional worship distinguished by musical modes ancient already when they came to Pennsylvania. Their hymnal, *Die Ausbundt,* is the oldest unchanged Protestant work in continued use, and its religious ballads are accounts of Anabaptist martyrdom during the sixteenth century, from which time they date. The melodies are equally old, some even older. Many of the more formal German churches sang the Lobwasser metrical psalms to tunes which are related to the German chorales. So the need for instruments was plain and men like Gustavus Hesselius were building instruments quite early in the history of Pennsylvania.

The most musical place in Pennsylvania, however, was Moravian Bethlehem. Music gave the community character and tone, and perhaps even social structure too for the congregational village was organized into "choirs." It is not known just when organized music was first performed there but in 1743, in the second year of the town's history, Moravians used musical instruments in worship.

Benjamin Franklin, in a letter to his wife in 1756, reported that he had heard very fine music in the Bethlehem church, that "flutes, oboes, French horns and trumpets accompanied the organ." Thus we know that both instrumental and organ music were in evidence, combined after the acquisition of the organ in 1751.

Bethlehem music, as would be expected, was church-centered. Instruction was free and participation was almost universal for no one was excused; everyone belonged to a choir, if only for vocalizing. On festal occasions trombone choirs announced the festival from the church steeple. Various services were opened from the steeple by a quartet of four trombones: soprano, alto, tenor, and bass. Oratorios and anthems were being written, words as well as music, dedicated to various leaders of the Moravian Church, European as well as American.

In 1780 Bethlehem had an orchestra—the names of the performers are now lost—consisting of two first violins, two second violins, one viola, two cellos, two French horns, two flutes, two trumpets and two oboes. In 1785 Joseph Haydn's quartettes, then quite new, were performed and soon thereafter his *Creation* was rendered.

One of the earliest organ builders in Pennsylvania was Johann Gottlob Klemm graduate of Leipzig University, who had had an interesting association with Count Zinzendorf in Herrnhut, Germany. After a short period of building organs both in Philadelphia and New York, Klemm returned to Bethlehem in 1757 and was associated with David Tannenberger in building an organ for the Nazareth Church. In 1759 they made a large organ for the Bethlehem Moravians, and in 1760 they established an organ factory in Nazareth. In 1762 Klemm died and Tannenberger continued to build organs, becoming the best known member of his craft in Pennsylvania. Later he moved to Lititz, another Moravian village in Lancaster County, there plying his craft, making organs for most of the larger Pennsylvania churches, including several in Philadelphia.

Meanwhile organ builders began to work also in the city. In 1762 Phillip Frying built an organ for Saint Paul's Church. He had learned his trade with Tannenberger. In 1763 George Schlosser offered pianos for sale. John Behrent announced in Müller's *Staatsbote* that he, a

Fig. 156. Organ by John Jakob Diffenbach, 1776.

joiner and instrument maker, of Third Street, Campingtown (Northern Liberties), opposite Coats' Burial Ground, was offering to sell a piano he had made. In 1776 in Bethel in Berks County, within a few miles of the Blue Mountains and along one of the busiest Indian trails, Johann Jakob Diffenbach built an interesting piece (Fig. 156). Baroque in mood and Germanic in inspiration, this piedmont-built Pennsylvania organ betrays a spirit far removed from the frontier just a few miles beyond. What did the Indians who passed by Diffenbach's workshop think of the culture which, rather than conquering nature, spent its energies making musical instruments?

After the Revolution the Lancaster town of New Holland became the center of the manufacture of pianos, organs, spinets, hand organs, and many advertisements in contemporary newspapers show how widespread this art was. The instrument which David Tannenberger made in 1790 for the Zion Lutheran Church in Philadelphia was unsurpassed for its time, showing that piedmont craftsmen, filling the needs of Pietist sects, also served tidewater patrons.

Fortunately we can document the sources of the Germanic skill of making musical in-

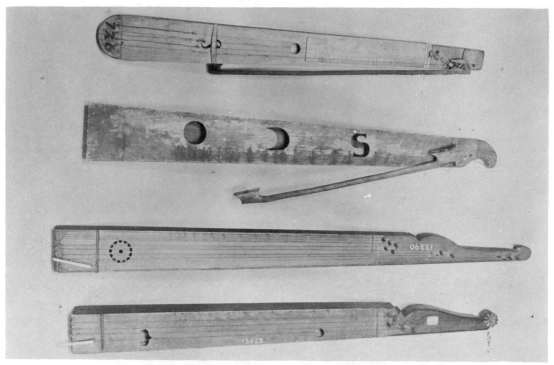

Fig. 157. Pennsylvania musical instruments.

struments. In the Schwenkfelder Library is the manuscript measurement book for making organs. This book was brought to America from Dresden, where they had learned their craft, by the Krause family of the Perkiomen. Then went out of business around 1790. Organ building then was not seriously affected by the demands of the American environment, but took skills already well-established and used them to produce instruments equal to what was being made in Europe.

The point where innovation came was not in the instruments but in the music. The instruments, like those traditionally German zithers, were made along old patterns, but the songs sung and composed reflected the new environment. Many times the old chorals were retained.

We do know, however, that new words were being written to the fine old German tunes by the Bethlehem Moravians to celebrate birthdays, ordinations, departures, liturgical events, and other special events. The words of the anthem Georg Neisser wrote on January 16, 1745, survive, suggesting that he also wrote music. The same also is probably true of the anthem he wrote later the same year for Peter Böhler's departure for Europe.

THE CRAFTS

The vigorous growth of craft activity in early Pennsylvania was due to the interaction of two forces, one negative, the other positive.

The first was the disappearance in the new world of the conservative and tradition-bound guild system. In Europe the guilds had been regulated with uncommon strictness. Ancient patterns of work were jealously preserved. In Pennsylvania this old system was not followed. European trained workers here did not need a *Wandersbuch* to get a job. Mittelberger suggests in his *Journey to Pennsylvania* that this removal of guild regulations had a liberalizing result on American creativity. Here indeed was the true American Revolution as far as the crafts were concerned and the American worker's imagination was freed to cope with the problems that the new environment presented.

European guild traditions were old, some of them even going back to Roman times, and they preserved some values which even a Christian-dominated culture could not eradicate. The *collegia fabrium* of the Rhine and Danube valleys were well-established in medieval times, and the Church used them in erecting the cathedrals. Research into the character of these guilds is hampered by the secrecy of their rites, and thus little is actually known about them. Around the end of the seventeenth century, just as Pennsylvania was being settled, the movement to open up the guilds was under way. Whether there was any relationship between this movement and the migration to Pennsylvania has not yet been studied.

Guild life had been marked by a strict set of rules regulating the life and work of man through apprentice, journeyman, and master stages. These stages already had appeared in the thirteenth century, and the various princes protected workers. Four kinds of regulations were enforced. First the entering apprentice had to be of honorable birth and he had to produce a birth certificate as illegitimacy was a barrier to craft status. In 1733 Prussia forbade a guild from keeping a person out of a trade because of an irregular birth. Second, a journeyman was put under the strict control of a master who in turn protected him but who also demanded obedience. This was almost chattel slavery. Third, the guild, by many initiations and rites of instruction, preserved the ways of working. These rites consisted of almost endless sermons in rhyme which transmitted the old ways. These could not be changed easily, thus making the crafts traditional. And finally, the initiatory rites also contained acts—some

Fig. 158. Pie crust marker, 1753.

serious, others humorous—with symbolic and psychological meanings. On the whole the guild system was tradition-bound. Journeymen had to work at specific places and were assigned by masters to duties which were hard and onerous. When they finally settled down in a community they worked within a strongly conservative craft-fellowship.

Coming to Pennsylvania meant freedom from all this. Here European-trained workers needed no master's approval to get a job. Here old ways were not mandatory. Here too they could forget the long-winded speeches at guild meetings. In coming to America, however, old skills were not forgotten for here what counted was workmanship. By thus freeing skilled workers and allowing their imaginations to work, Pennsylvania let them face the demands of the new environment with creativity which replaced the conformity of Europe in the labor-hungry economy of early Pennsylvania. This allowed competent workmen, trained in the best systems of Europe, to work within a new environment.

This leads to the second force which invigorated the Pennsylvania crafts—the indenture system. Here a worker was bound only for his debts. This made it easy for out-of-work European craftsmen to come to Pennsylvania and make places for themselves. They were not here bound for life to established patterns. From the employer's point of view this was advantageous; a few extra dollars, a trip to dockside in Philadelphia, and the planter had a skilled workman.

The many advertisements in early newspapers regarding indentured servants point to a labor system able to produce both imaginative craft work and vigorous agriculture—the dual economy of piedmont Pennsylvania. This land attracted skilled and intelligent workers from the ruined and sacked villages of Europe. So city and country became a mecca for these workers; the city indentured served the great and near-great, while the country indentured worked for established planters.

While most indentured workers were of humble origin, here and there a nobleman appeared, reduced to beggary, hiring himself out for passage money. Also the educated. This advertisement appeared in Christopher Saur's newspaper for June 1, 1750. It tells its own story:

Johann Heinrich Sickmann, unmarried, born in Hanover, Lutheran, is confined to the Philadelphia prison because he owes £20 passage costs, etc. He offers himself to anyone; is capable of teaching; he taught school the past winter with Peter Reiff and Jacob Treibelbitz of Oley.

Although temporarily pauperized, Sickman was not without hope; he could foresee new freedom.

Thus George Merkel of Richmond Township, Berks, advertised in Heinrich Miller's *Staatsbote*, August 31, 1773, that his servant, Leonhard Miller, had left him for another master. Miller was twenty years old, Swiss born, and spoke German, French, and Latin. Also, Peter Hausenclever, New York iron-master, had a servant, Alexander Burkhardt, who spoke German and French.

Sometimes the planter-master got a worker who was a problem, as in the following notice from Sauer's paper for September, 1750:

Ernst Sigmund Seydel, of Oley, gives notice that last year he became security for the passage of a Swiss named Schnäubeli, and eventually had to pay the costs. Two small children of Schnäubeli were indentured. Schnäubeli had another son who has coaxed away the younger brother from Seydel's service, pretending he was going to raise the money to free him. He has collected three times the sum required, and has bought a fiddle and a cow with the money.

Whatever the faults and injustices of the indenture system—and they were not moral like those of the southern slave system—the Pennsylvania pattern, temporary as it was, liberated European-trained workers from the guild system and made for quick assimilation into the developing farm-craft economy of the piedmont area.

All one has to do to grasp the meaning of this new freedom is to study the tools which these workers invented to perform their tasks. Henry Chapman Mercer and the Landis brothers saw the full significance of the tools that were made here.

Moreover we must study our Pennsylvania crafts chronologically. We are now beginning to understand that many forms appeared in Pennsylvania before they were known in Europe. The firing mechanism of the Kentucky rifle was made here before it was known in Europe. So we must be cautious when we compare European pieces with American, and we have to go beyond saying that this was a memory craft—that is that our Pennsylvania workers were merely doing what they had known at home.

So, heirs of the skills which Europe could teach, freed from a conservative guild system, these competent workers migrated to a new world where they faced a new environment which made new demands on their imagination. And when this new freedom was supported by one of the most productive agricultural systems the world had yet known, the elements were present for an expansive development of the Pennsylvania crafts.

One further result of this new freedom was the transference of skills. The worker was not limited to his trade. A pewterer was more than a worker in metal, for he also carved his own patterns and made plaster casts therefrom. Ironmolders also were carvers, as were silversmiths. Sharp individualization in tasks was not yet firm and this allowed for easy movement from trade to trade.

New freedom, shortage of labor in early Pennsylvania, and a demanding new environment joined to make one of the most creative periods in the history of American labor when Pennsylvania, city as well as country, became the center of men who were using their new freedom with astonishing imaginative vigor, producing things which reflected Old World skills adapted to the news of the new.

The Cast Iron Bible

Earliest of the crafts to show itself in Pennsylvania as a fully-developed cultural form was the cast iron five-plate stove. It is clear, even to a beginner, that these pieces of molded iron, some decorated with realistic scenes and conventionalized motifs, employed a style and imagery somewhat different from that used in illuminated writing and painted furniture. Here in this first phase of the Pennsylvania crafts, which was already over by the time of the American Revolution, we find a craft form which takes us back in mood to the century of the Protestant Reformation.

By the time of the Revolution at least half a hundred iron plantations flourished in eastern Pennsylvania, like the one now being restored at Hopewell Village, making interesting iron pieces, although by the time of the founding of the American republic the period of the German-type stove already was over. Making iron stove plates cannot be done at home and so a developed industrial organization came into being with some capitalization and labor organization. So for the development of these iron plantations, a system was worked out which is of interest because it marks the start of American industry, a combination of agriculture, craft, and mercantile interests. At these furnaces all kinds of things were made for household use along with miscellaneous iron products as many blacksmith shops arose, clustered about these furnaces. In these iron plantations were manor houses, forests, offices, stores, gristmills, sawmills, blacksmith shops, bake ovens, barns, grainfields, gardens, meadows and orchards.

English Quakers and Scotch-Irish started the iron industry about 1716, and they were the first owners of these plantations. However, Germans were associated with many of them. In 1726 a Mennonite named Kurtz erected along the Octorora in Lancaster the first German furnace. Many furnaces arose in Berks County—Oley in 1745 and Tulpehocken in 1749. The German iron industry is linked with the colorful figure of Heinrich Wilhelm Stiegel, of whose origin we know nothing, but who resembled Peter Hasenclever, the New York iron manufacturer. After Stiegel's marriage to Elizabeth Huber he inherited a furnace in Lancaster which he then called Elizabeth furnace. Expanding his activities in 1760 he acquired Charming Forge, and in 1762 he established a partnership with Carl and Alexander Stedman, acquiring 730 acres near Mannheim. Here he made both iron stove plates and decorated glass.

Along with glassmaking, making stoveplates was one of the crafts which were brought to America unaltered. It remained a traditional craft, experiencing little basic change until about 1760 when portable stoves were introduced and the old German wall stoves were abandoned.

September 1, 1749, Christopher Sauer's newspaper announced that the Reading furnace was making stoves, an example of which was being shown at the Germantown printing office —further evidence that crafts were developing in the piedmont. This notice further said that this stove could heat a large room and that cooking, frying, and baking could be done without spreading offensive odors. Benjamin Franklin, himself credited with inventing a stove, as illustrated, described the German stove thus.

[It] is like a box, one side wanting. 'Tis composed of Five Iron Plates scru'd together and fixed so that you may put the fuel into it from another room or from the Outside. 'Tis a kind of Oven revers'd, its Mouth being without and Body within the Room that is to be warmed by it. This invention certainly warms a Room very speedily and very thoroughly with a little fuel.

The Franklin stove was made to set the fireplace with an end opening towards the room to be heated, while the open end of the German stove, as shown, faced the fireplace from the adjoining room. Into it were placed burning logs, and the smoke escaped through a small flue.

Although Franklin called this German stove an "invention" it dates from the sixteenth century. Similar stoves, also showing Biblical scenes, had been cast in the Rhineland from that time. The Brunswick Museum in Germany had plates with the following scenes and dates: Lazarus and the rich man, 1599; Adam and Eve, 1567, 1569; Levi and the tax gatherer, 1577; Joshua and the kings, 1577, 1598; the good Samaritan, 1598; Samson and the Lion, 1592; Bathsheba, 1593; and so forth. The Hessian Museum of Folk Art in the Ernst von Hülsenhaus in Marburg has plates of considerable elaboration, and we should not conclude that our Pennsylvania pieces gained in richness for they simply cannot match these European pieces in elaboration of detail. In the Palatinate and Alsace the art of casting stoveplates was centered: in the former at Schönau, Bergzabern, St. Ingolt, Landau and Trippstadt; in the latter region at Zinsweiler. So the casting of iron stoveplates arose in those Reformed lands just at the time when religious issues were dominant. In 1563, Fredrick the Pious brought a full-blown Calvinism to his Palatinate lands, and these areas were soundly Reformed. So the Bible was put on iron.

Bible scenes likewise were cast on the stoveplates of early Pennsylvania, especially between the years 1740 and 1765, in a variety that is truly astonishing. Comparing Pennsylvania with European plates discloses that the same themes were also cast here, but with some decrease of elaboration, and our styles were not as rich as the European. Here are the American themes: Samson carrying away the city gates, Samson being shorn, the Pharisee and the Publican, Abraham offering Isaac, the woman at the well, seeking Joseph, the miracle of Cana, Adam and Eve, "judge not that ye be not judged," Cain and Abel, the four horsemen of the apocalypse, and Christ and the woman at the well. Quotations from the German Bible, especially the Psalms, also appear on the plates.

Other religious themes also appear. Thus one plate illustrates a theme which takes us back to the sixteenth century when one of the more popular literary and artistic ideas was the *Totentanz* or *dance macabre,* the frolic with death (Fig. 159). This theme appeared in the drawings of Holbein where life and death dance in explication of Luther's hymn; in the midst of life death surrounds us. This theme arose, during the late medieval period, from the folklore idea that at midnight the spirits leave their graves and lead a dance. The most celebrated of these, the *Tod von Basel,* is on the wall of the cemetery of the Basel Cathedral. This theme was especially popular among wood carvers and so was easily transferred to the stove-plate. The plate here illustrated bears the verse:

Nun achtet myt mit die Doht   Now death contends with me,
Und bringt mich in grosse Not   And brings me into great need.

Not all scenes were religious. Sometimes we find battle scenes between mounted *jaeger,* a man and woman dancing to a fiddle, grenadiers and all sorts of animals. After 1760 classical themes began to appear showing that although this form arose in the sixteenth century it was also being accommodated to the classical age.

Fig. 159. German stove with *Todtentanz* or Dance of Death, 1749.

Fig. 160. Stove plate with Christ and the Woman at the Well.

Fig. 161. Stove plate from Shenandoah Valley with hunting scene.

Fig. 162. Stove plate with the arms of the city of Philadelphia and a German language inscription.

Fig. 163. Cast iron stoveplate from the Stiegel Furnace in Mannheim.

One of the most delightful of American plates, here illustrated, was made somewhere in the Shenandoah valley, and it depicts a hunting scene. Here are indeed Crevecoeur's crude men of the woods with hunting dogs, chasing deer, and a bird giving an intrusive serpent a going over (Fig. 161). Purely American themes also were molded, like the arms of the city of Philadelphia (Fig. 162).

However, the art of the stoveplate was really that of the woodcarver who made the pattern. Before iron was poured into sand the matrix had to be shaped by means of a carved mold. So the traditional carving art, so widespread in the Old World, and which did not show too forcibly in American furniture, came forward in the casting of stoveplates.

Generally speaking, while there is fundamental similarity, the iconography of the Pennsylvania stoveplate differs from that of the other crafts. It was Calvinist and soundly Biblical in a literal sense, rooted in those areas of Germany where the Reformed Churches were strong. Thus these stoveplates differ from other Pennsylvania designs, especially those of illuminated writing, where we meet the world of the baroque, the mystical imagery of the seventeenth century. That Pennsylvania stoveplates thus betray another world than that of the *Vorschrift* and dower chest is clearly shown by the highly conventionalized flowers diamonds, hearts, and other devices on Baron Stiegel's plate here illustrated.

The Baron's Glass

Glass was produced early in Pennsylvania history. In 1693 a glass house was in operation in Philadelphia for we know that Joshua Tettery, glassmaker from New Castle-on-Tyne, was employed in that capacity by the Quakers. We also know that around the year 1707 a member of the Pennypacker family at Schwenksville had established a glass-house which continued active for about five years, producing bottles and other wares. Also, sometime around 1739, Caspar Wistar founded his glass-house in Salem County, New Jersey, producing the celebrated Wistarberg glass.

All of these early efforts, however, were overshadowed by the products of a glasshouse established by one of the most colorful figures to appear in early Pennsylvania. Heinrich Wilhelm Stiegel, who called himself "Baron" and sometimes even signed his name "von Stiegel," was not a nobleman; he had been born on May 13, 1729, of middle class parents in the Rhineland city of Cologne. He arrived in Philadelphia from Rotterdam on August 21, 1750, having most likely already been in England for he seems to have been conversant with British methods of making glass. On November 7, 1752, he married Elizabeth Huber, daughter of a Lancaster furnace master, and so he acquired an interest in the Huber furnace situated on the eastern slope of the northern spur that divides Lebanon and Lancaster valleys at the place called Middle Cut or Furnace Run. By 1756 Stiegel was operating Elizabeth Furnace, named after his wife; and in 1760, the year he was naturalized, he bought Charming Forge in the Tulpehocken region. During these years he made no glass.

In 1763, however, the Elizabeth Glasshouse, first of three which he was to operate, began to make wares. On September 18, three glass blowers, Christian Nasel, Martin Grenier and Benjamin Nisky, began to produce bottles and window glass. Soon after he had opened this glasshouse Stiegel journeyed to Britain where he studied British methods of blowing glass, probably even going to Bristol, center of the British industry. The work which was produced at this first Stiegel glasshouse was still somewhat plain and crude and lacked the sophistication of his later work. When a piece of this glass turns up most students seem to attribute it to another maker. In truth, early Stiegel glass is hard to identify.

In January of 1765 Stiegel began *Ledger A, No. 1,* the record of his second establishment, the Mannheim Glasshouse, whose ovens were soon finished and which began operation

Fig. 164. Enameled Stiegel glass.

Fig. 165. Enameled Stiegel mug.

on November 11. The first glass blowers at Mannheim were Martin Grenier, Christian Nasel, Christian Gratinger, Conrad Walts, and Jacob Halder. This glass made at Mannheim during this first period was imitative of the work of European glass cutters with whom Stiegel was in competition for the American market. The pieces made were window glass and bottles "gallon, half-gallon, quart and pint" which were sold by merchants in Reading, Lancaster, and York. The first season of work at Mannheim was over on April 14, 1766 and the fires were started up again on November 15, 1766, when Stiegel began operations on an expanded basis. He hired more workmen and made many new forms. Now he produced "quart, pint, half-gallon' tumblers" and "Electer glasses." In 1767 the British Parliament put a tax on American-made glass through the notorious Townshend Act, and Stiegel's business was depressed. He found it hard to work in competition with untaxed European ware.

The irrepressible "Baron" Stiegel, however, was not the man to let a small matter like a tax on glass keep him down. He became a patriot. His answer to the Townshend Act was to open his third glasshouse in 1769. He enlarged his work force to one hundred hands, a cosmopolitan group of workmen that included English, German, Irish, and Italian blowers. Thus did Stiegel seek intercolonial recognition, and in this new glasshouse, it must be said, he produced wares as fine as that being made in Bristol. He even came to imitate Venetian glass forms, employing William and John Rugo for this purpose. However, he advertised in colonial papers that he was offering:

> American Flint Glass, made at Manheim
> equal in quality with any imported from Europe.

Fig. 166. Etched Stiegel glass.

He stressed the first word! It was American, made in Pennsylvania! And then it was equal, too—equal in hardness, decoration and in the variety of its forms. An advertisement in the *New York Gazette and Weekly Advertiser* for February 8, 1773, lists the kinds of glass he was making:

quart, pint and half-pint decanters; pint, half-pint, gill and half-gill flint and common tumblers; carrots, enamel'd, mason, and common wine glasses, jelly, cillabub glasses with and without handles, mustard and cream pots, flint and common; salts, salt linings and crewets, widemouth bottles for sweetmeats, rounds and phyals for doctors, wine and water glasses, ink and pocket bottles.

A well-rounded assortment! In truth, Heinrich Wilhelm Stiegel was twitching the British lion's tail when he expanded his work and the forms he made. This was a patriotic gesture for those perilous pre-revolutionary times which, because he refused to pay the tax on his glass, could only end, as it did, in his bankruptcy.

Stiegel was always alert and energetic. He gave an exhibition of his glass, with a description of how he made it, before the American Philosophical Society. Benjamin Franklin brought back for him from Germany some "pulse glasses," showing Stiegel how to make them—pieces in which the heat of the human hand was enough to make water boil under the low pressure of the vacuum. David Rittenhouse is said to have preferred Stiegel's glass tubing to the British in making barometers.

Stiegel's glass was one of the first truly colonial products. He had established agents in Philadelphia, Lancaster, York, Lebanon, Heidelberg (Tulpehocken), Brickerville, Hagerstown, New York, Baltimore, and Boston. Some men who were to become celebrated in the patriot cause were among his agents: Paul Zantzinger of Lancaster who was to become procurement officer for clothing, and Michael Hillegas who was to become first Treasurer of the Continental Congress. There can be little doubt that Stiegel Glass was one phase of America's rebellion against the hated Townshend Acts; and to buy a piece, of course without paying the tax, was about the same as helping to pitch a crate of tea into the harbor.

Faced by overexpansion, and by British pressures, it was inevitable that Stiegel would land in debtor's jail. He even tried to raise money to bail out his fortunes by the "American Flint Glass Manufactory Lottery." Note again the word "American!" Not even this helped. He was bankrupt, and imprisoned. His enterprises collapsed, and the stores where his glass was being sold without benefit of the tax were closed.

As a product, Stiegel glass is, then, not just American in mood, but it was really good glass. The processes and decorations were as fine as anything done in Europe. And it was not wholly Germanic in spirit for the workmen were a cosmopolitan lot: John Carey was a cutter and flowerer as was also Edward Farrel—Irishmen. Sebastian Witmer and Martin Yetters were enamelers—Germans. Other enamelers were Henry Nissle, Sebastian Witmer, Joseph Welch and others. No one yet has successfully identified the work of these artisans.

Stiegel glass was widely circulated in eastern Pennsylvania. Today, however, caution must be taken when collecting for unscrupulous dealers have imported much European ware and palmed it off as Stiegel. Qualititatively it is hard to distinguish between them. So most persons today say "Stiegel type." There are two ways to determine if a piece is Stiegel. If the piece has remained in the same family before 1910, when the first Bohemian glass was brought in, and secondly by careful comparison with the known fragments which were dug up on the dump of the Mannheim Glasshouse. Fortunately, several museums have not only proven pieces of Stiegel but also fragments recovered from Mannheim. In this way comparison is easy and a student, if he wishes to work from known pieces to the unknown, can easily develop a good sense for the genuine.

The Frontiersman's Friend

Surely the finest craft-product made in piedmont Pennsylvania, one which was to become symbol of frontier America, was the Kentucky rifle, so named because of where it was used rather than where it was made. As a cultural form it was as new and as fresh—and as American— as the forests and praries where it was used, a clever marriage of several European forms, a hybrid like the frontiersman who used it.

It was in truth virtually a new instrument. It joined the rifled German snub-nosed gun from the Black Forest region with the British smoothbore musket. It was the main possession of the man of the frontier, a prized tool which defended him against the savages, which put meat on his cabin table, which helped to keep European armies out of the New World, and which was even a source of his sport. In the frontiersman's hands it expressed the virile individuality of his character for even without bayonet it was, along with knife and tomahawk, part of a deadly threesome of weapons.

However, like many other cultural forms of early Pennsylvania, the Kentucky did not experience its golden age until after the American Revolution. There was, in fact, over half a century during which the gun was being developed. We do know that by the time of the Revolution already a characteristic Pennsylvania rifle had emerged for a British soldier, writing after the Battle of Long Island, said that the Pennsylvania Germans were "shirt-tailed men with their cursed twisted guns—the most fatal widow-orphan-makers in the world." This refers not to the Kentucky but to its prototype, for long before the golden age of the Kentucky there was a cruder Pennsylvania rifle in existence which was already a recognized cultural form. Extremely plain, with little or no carving, of native woods chosen for utilitarian rather than ornamental value, this thick-stocked Pennsylvania rifle was not a work of art like the later Kentucky. However, it was the Kentucky's ancestor, the common prototype of all schools which made Kentuckys.

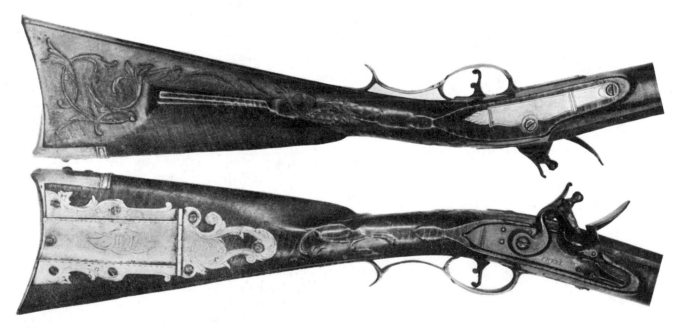

Fig. 167. Carved stock of a Kentucky rifle.

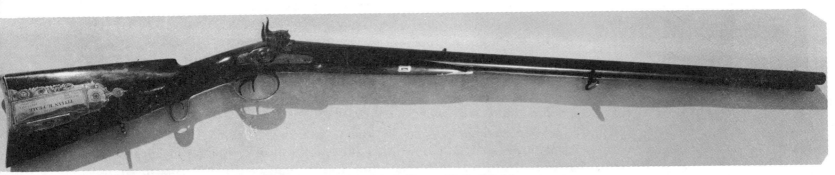

Fig. 168. Double-barreled Kentucky rifle made by J. Kunz, Philadelphia.

The development of this earlier Pennsylvania rifle took place between 1740 and 1765. The first German rifles had been brought into Pennsylvania by the earliest piedmont settlers in the first two decades of the century. The British smoothbore long musket did not show on the frontier until the Scotch-Irish brought it along in the 1730s. So about 1740 the early Pennsylvania rifle began to appear, joining these two in a plain weapon out of which the Kentucky was to come. By the time of the Revolution this was already an established instrument which joined the chubby German gun, with octagonal barrel, and the long smoothbore English piece, producing the Pennsylvnaia rifle with brass patchbox, invented here, to store the patches which had been invented in Lancaster sometime about 1725.

So the Kentucky was a product of several traditions as it was also the product of several skills. First the gunsmith had to be ironmaster adept at forging, rifling and finishing metals. Then he had to be a woodworker too, capable of shaping stocks and carving designs, some of which are as fine as the work of the Chippendale furniture carvers of the city. And finally he had to be a worker in brass, making butt plates and trigger guards. Some of the materials he bought wholesale. The barrel blanks came from boring mills where they were made in bulk. The gunsmith made a breech plug, rifled the bore, finished the outside, added sights and lugs to receive the pins which held the barrel in the stock, added ornamentation, and put the flint lock in. Most of the flint locks were imported from Germany and Great Britain. However, the gunsmith did one more thing. He was the artist who gave the Kentucky rifle its balance and "feel," the individuality which suited the gun to the personality of him who was to use it. Here is where the gunsmith became the real artist, for each weapon was matched to its man, filling the demands of the purchaser, making it a highly personal and individual achievement.

Gunsmithing was not a recognized European trade. Pennsylvania gunsmiths, from one point of view, were merely assemblers who took parts made elsewhere and fashioned an individualized instrument. However, one authority suggests that Pennsylvania gunsmiths were descendents of European families established in the gunmaking trades and that there was much intermarriage among them. Common family names have been found, suggesting that perhaps European traditions did form the basis of this American craft.

Moreover, one authority has discovered at least nine schools of gunsmiths, each with characteristic features, which seem to have appeared independent of one another after the American Revolution. Here they are with the number of gunsmiths known to have been working in each school: Lancaster (19), Bethlehem (12), Womelsdorf-Reading (9), Lebanon (5), Dauphin (4), York (26), Littlestown (8), Emmittsburg (7), Chambersburg (8). Several individual makers cannot be classified. Moreover, it has been asserted that these schools arose with little connection between them, developing regional characteristics. Although they were never made on the frontier itself, the making of these rifles tended to move westward as the frontier receded. They were made in western Pennsylvania and in the Virginia Shenandoah.

The final instrument which emerged was a work of high art. Nearing its peak after the Indian wars and reaching its zenith in the post-Revolutionary period, this remarkable instrument, made in the Pennsylvania piedmont, was the triumph of our arts.

As a work of art, however, the Kentucky is related not to traditional folk arts—although here and there tulips, birds, and geometric patterns show—but more to the rococo style of furniture. Perhaps some hidden movement of cultural forms took the elegant carving of Chippendale furniture and transplanted it to the Kentucky, making this symbol of the American frontier a truly elegant instrument in the hands of the frontiersman, helping him not merely to win a place for himself in a raw wilderness but also to repel the best European troops in the battle at New Orleans.

The Potters' Craft

Earthenware pottery, the poor man's porcelain, was a universal craft which was practiced among nearly all peoples. Roman forms had come to dominate early German pottery but gradually their influence waned. Vessels of the Frankish period had been decorated with stamped ornaments and those of the Carolingian period were orange-brown in color with designs stamped on them. Rhineland pottery was formally richer than that of other regions. Palatine slip ware, however, dates from the nineteenth century although such ware was being made in southern and eastern Germany much earlier.

In Pennsylvania the craft of pottery went through an expansion and development which moved through three stages.

First there was the primitive stage in which unglazed pieces were made. Of this period only a few pieces survive. The oldest seems to be the unglazed cake mold (Fig. 169) made by Georg Adam Weidner of Oley who died sometime before 1745. Traditional designs here were applied in incised form: hearts and simple floral motifs. Weidner also made many roof tiles in the European manner, and some Oley structures, like the springhouse on the John Hoch farm, still have roofs of these tiles. Tiles made by Weidner even have wandered to Ephrata where architects have put them on roofs in spite of the fact that Weidner was not in favor with the Ephrata people because of his religious views. The few other unglazed pieces that survive for this first period of Pennsylvania pottery are quite primitive in feeling.

The second period of Pennsylvania pottery began about 1760 and lasted well into the 1830s. This period consisted of glazed pottery. Most of this ware was not decorated but rather was utilitarian in character. The unusual pieces—gifts or mementos—were decorated in one or two ways: either by tracing a design in slip or by cutting through the glaze to reveal the clay beneath. It is, perhaps, interesting to note that slip-decorated pottery does not seem to have appeared in the Rhineland until after the beginning of the nineteenth century so it may be fruitless to speculate about the origin of our Pennsylvania pottery in the Palatinate.

Of the slip ware pieces here illustrated, the first (Fig. 170) shows a poorly executed bird plucking its breast—the traditional posture of the pelican in old Christian lore which bleeds itself to nourish its young and which was used in the fourteenth-century building of the St. Elizabeth's *kirche* in Marburg. Drawn with boldness and surrounded by stylized flowers, this pelican was a Pennsylvania version of an old theme. The second of these slip-traced pieces is the barber's basin (Fig. 171) with its highly stylized flower in the center and the verse running around the edge, reading in translation:

> Come, sir, I'll shave you,
> And you shall no longer want me!

Fig. 169. Tile cake mold by George Adam Weidner of Oley, circa 1740.

This grim note is fully in accord with the folksy mood of humor associated with Pennsylvania pottery. In this method of decoration the designs or inscriptions were applied by means of a cup of glaze to an already glazed piece, covered with transparent glaze. These pieces were generally made before the Revolution.

The second technique for decorating pottery during this second period is called sgraffito which described a technique of incising the design by cutting through the glaze which has been applied to the entire surface of the piece, thus allowing the design to show in natural clay. The earliest surviving piece is also one of the finest; it was made in 1762 by Jacob Staudt of Perkasie and is signed with his monogram (Fig. 172). Jacob was born October 13, 1710, in Gimbsweiler, the Palatinate, and he arrived in Philadelphia in 1737 and died in 1779. His wife was a physician's daughter. This plate is remarkable because this Palatine-born potter placed an English inscription on it:

> Be not Ashamed I advice Thee Most
> If one learneth Thee what Thou not knowest,
> The Ingenious is Accounted Brave
> but the Clumsy non Desires to have.

Fig. 170. Slip ware plate with pelican motif.

A bit awkward was Jacob's verse but it reflects the language and mood of William Penn Charter School, which he attended.

These pieces reflect the humble world of the folk. Here we are in the peasant's world, one far removed from the elegance of fashionable society. The inscriptions on these pieces range from Biblical quotations to almost bawdy humor. Here are a few:

Wer etwas will verschweigen haben
Der darf es seiner Frau nicht sagen

He who wants something kept secret
Dare not tell it to his wife.

Ich fert die breid stross hin und her
Und doch wirt der beitel ler.

I rode the broad way far and wide
And still my pocketbook is empty.

Ich koch was ich kan,
Est mein sau net so est mein Mann.

I cook what I can,
If my sow eats not my husband will.

Es ist mir bang   I fear
Mein wieschtes Tochter   My ugly daughter
Grigkt kein mann.   Will get no husband.

Wer des lieben ungesund   If loving were unhealthy
So thätens Doctor meiden;   Doctors would forbid it;
Und wan die weibern weh thät,   And if it harmed wives
So thätens sie nicht leiden.   They would not endure it.

The classical inscription on a pie plate was made on September 14, 1778, by Georg Hübner of the Perkiomen:

Wann das männgen und des hengen nicht wehr,
So ständen die wiegen und die hienkel heusser lehr
Were there no men and no roosters
Then cradles and hen-coops would be empty.

And perhaps the saddest of all, one in which the trials and tribulations of Henry Henpeck break through, is the pie plate made for Elizabeth Reiser on January 10, 1827, probably as an engagement gift, which says:

Lustig wer noch ledig ist   Happy he who is still single,
Traurig wer versprochen ist.   Sad he who is betrothed.

Fig. 171. Slip ware barber's basin with inscription.

Fig. 172. Jacob Staudt's pie plate, 1762.

Other inscriptions convey similar folksy sentiments: "This dish is made of earth; when it breaks the potter laughs." "All maidens on earth gladly would become wives." "Rather would I stay single than give my pants to the woman." "A pipe of tobacco is as good as a dollar spent on the girls." "I have ridden over hill and dale and still have found no wife." And finally this parody on the Lord's Prayer:

Leiber Vatter in Himmelreich   Dear Father in Heaven,
Was du mir gibst das ess ich gleich.   Whatever you give me I shall eat.

Sometimes designs appear without description and these bring on, we believe, an even profounder meaning—one that is more deeply ingrained in the folk mind or in religious consciousness. Consider the plate depicting three fish. In early Christian art the fish was a symbol of Christ because, living in water, it was early associated with baptism. Sometimes three fish were shown having only one head, a symbol of the Trinity called *Trinacria,* as in the keystone of the Benedictine Abbey at Luxeuil. In folklore the fish became the symbol of fertility and life and an index of ability to bear children. In some places, notably Italy, the fish also bears erotic meaning, and one of the oldest love charms, that of Brother Rudolphus, suggests that to make love sure one has to take three fish, one in the mouth, one beneath the breasts, and a third at the lower parts, leaving them there until they die. Then they must be ground up and fed to the man on whom the woman wants this charm to work and he will be duly smitten. Whatever the meaning, three fishes were incised on this Pennsylvania pie plate (Fig. 173).

One of the more interesting designs that appeared on the pie plates is the figure of the rider on the white horse. In German this rider of the white horse is the *Schimmelreiter.* In

Fig. 173. Sgraffito pie plate with three fish.

Fig. 174, 175. Two plates by Johannes Neesz of Tylersport, Montgomery, showing the rider of the white horse (*Schimmelreiter*). One of them has an inscription identifying the motif.

Saint John's Revelation 19:11-16, we read of the rider upon the white horse who "was called Faithful and True" and who bore a sharp sword and ruled with a rod of iron and who was the king of kings and lord of lords. Early in the history of European folklore we find this image of a ghostly rider on a ghostly horse leading "armies which were in heaven" and which followed also on white horses. Here (Fig. 174) is one of the horsemen of the apocalypse on this plate made by Johannes Neesz, clearly identified by the inscription:

Ich bin geritten über berg und thal   I have ridden over hill and dale
hab untreu funten über all   And have found unfaithfulness everywhere.

Another plate (Fig. 175), also by potter Neesz, shows the horseman with pistol and sword. Here we are reminded of the Greek legend of Apollo, god of bow and arrow, who chased Daphne who was sometimes transformed into a tree. Washington Irving has immortalized this figure in *The Legend of Sleepy Hollow;* Ichabod Crane was chased by the headless horseman. This image of the rider on the white horse, originally an apocalyptic figure, easily became a myth for George Washington also rode a white horse and here we can see how this image, like the eagle of Revelation too, became Americanized.

The environment of early Pennsylvania pottery, then, reflects the varied worlds of folklore, Scripture, peasant life and the American scene. But the old world was not forgotten for Hansel and Gretel (Fig. 176) also appeared:

Fig. 176. Hansel and Gretel plate.

Fig. 177. George Washington plate.

Fig. 178. Military celebrating a "Battalion Day."

Fig. 179. Sugar bowl by George Hübner.

Fig. 180. The famous "Joined Birds" plate by George Hübner.

Hansel und Gretel,   Hansel and Gretel,
Zwee luschtige Leit,   Two lusty people;
Der Hansel is naarisch,   Hansel is crazy,
Die Gretel net gescheid.   And Gretel not all there.

After Baron Steuben had written the drill manuals for both the Continental Army and the Militia of Pennsylvania his regulations were drilled into the minds of the village yokels who paraded each Battalion Day in the village square. This was a favorite holiday. Not only the rustic soldiers but the whole family was on hand to watch father play soldier with the

Fig. 181. Sgraffito pie plate.

Fig. 182. Sgraffito pie plate with pelican motif.

Fig. 183. Plate with floral designs.

other farmers who were his neighbors. And when one of these soldiers was engaged a Pennsylvania potter reminded him of his military duties, depicting him executing one of the orders in Steuben's drill manual (Fig. 178). The spelling in it was folksy too.

Other pieces of Pennsylvania sgraffito and slip ware—the second phase of our Pennsylvania pottery—depicted the traditional birds, stylized flowers, wind-blown tulips, urns, lilies and Georg Hübner's magnificent rendering of the phrase from Solomon's Song: "My Beloved is Mine, He feeds among the Lilies!" (Fig. 185).

For those who would argue that Pennsylvania pottery derives from Sweden we have but one rebuttal: read the language that appears on these plates. Is it Swedish?

The third phase of Pennsylvania pottery was almost an about-face. Not only did this appear in another geographical area, and half a century later, but it expressed an altogether different mood and technique. This was the highglazed ware made in central Pennsylvania

Fig. 184. Plate with floral designs and humorous inscription.

around Waynesboro, Pennsylvania, and as far south as Winchester, Virginia, by members of the Bell family. Here is the earliest brightly-glazed pottery made in America, exactly imitative of contemporary pottery in the Palatinate, in which figures were molded in naturallistic form—dogs, lions, human figures, angels, and the like. Here we are no longer in the world of symbolism or folklore but have crossed the divide from symbolic and traditional to the representational and realistic. Still it was pottery of high quality, able to rank with the best folk pottery then being made in Europe.

Fig. 185. "My Beloved is mine, He feeds among the Lilies."

Carving

Of all forms in which wood, by its structure, may be shaped the commonest was by carving, generally with a knife. Indeed, one of the chief crafts on the farm was carving pieces for house, kitchen, laundry, inn, barn, and field. This domestic carving was not the work of specialists—carpenters, cabinetmakers, patternmakers—but of individuals. It was therefore a sound folk art and was not commercially promoted. The boy carved his own toys—weapons, pipes, and sticks—and the man carved household objects as well as the pieces which he, the craftsman, was making. Wood was a material easily worked by fire, axe, saw, and knife.

European carving was highly developed, for in almost every forested region of Germany it had grown to become a house industry. North German carvers were partial to hard woods while southern carvers used their softer woods. In Roman Catholic areas religious figures, especially those depicting Christ's Passion, were made. The carving of Christmas scenes originated in Silesia from whence it spread to other areas.

Pennsylvania carving never became as developed as the German, and it never evolved into a home industry, although this was a heavily wooded land and materials were at hand. While there was some early carving, little of it has survived and most of it, like the pie marker (Fig. 158), was utilitarian in character. The most ambitious carving in Pennsylvania was quite late, the best of it being the group of patriotic and religious figures done by Noah Weiss which stood for many years in the Siegfried's Inn in Northampton. Weiss also painted barns.

Wood was not the only medium in which carving was expressed. Bone also was sometimes used. A magnificent carved pie marker dating from around 1760 is known, but it has no decoration and is strictly a utilitarian piece. A most interesting category of carving is the powder horn, the accompaniment of the long rifle, on which military and naturalistic designs were etched (Fig. 186). Many of these horns must have been made, and there is some evidence that traditional folk designs were used on this medium.

Of course the American eagle, both as a religious symbol and as a patriotic device, was an excellent subject for the carver. The Pennsylvania eagles is as good as any in America. A large bird with outspread wings is magnificent in the sweep and plastic conception, a fine example from the knife of a Philadelphia carver late in the eighteenth century. Smaller eagles also were carved to be placed as ornaments on the top of organs, as the one carved by a member of the Krause family of the Perkiomen sometime before 1790 (Fig. 187). Far more celebrated than these early pieces are the eagles carved by Wilhelm Schimmel (1865-1890) who, while not really belonging to the early period still is much sought after. His pieces are more primitive and less elegant. (Fig. 188) Late in the nineteenth century this Pennsylvania carver was making eagles in abundance, an interesting example of how primitive work follows more traditionally executed pieces.

Carved forms for baking, another one of our inherited cultural forms, were widespread in Pennsylvania. These were used to impress designs in pastry although in the process sharpness of designs was lost. Unlike European examples, our Pennsylvania springerle molds were not limited in design but showed wide variations. Thus the springerle mold made in 1843

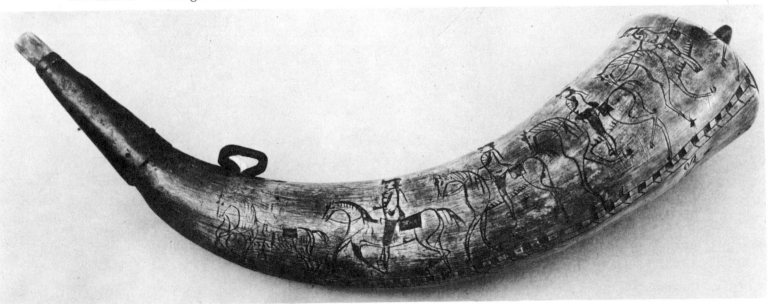

Fig. 186. Decorated powder horn, made before 1770.

Fig. 187. This carved eagle once graced the top of an organ built by the Krause family, near Palm, who ceased making organs around 1790.

Fig. 188. Eagles carved by William Schimmel.

Fig. 189. Carved wooden springerle mold, early nineteenth century.

(Fig. 189) pictures a dozen birds in quite realistic fashion, and we can tell what these birds represent. Here is realism in carving only a few years after Audubon was drawing birds. There is no symbolic ambiguity here; we know which species is depicted.

Pennsylvania carved toys also were among our earliest carved pieces. Here ingenuity is noteworthy. The set of toys (Fig. 190), probably carved by a young boy, reveals a mood almost modern in character with its bold and suggestive lines and strong detail. The carved toy was

Fig. 190. Carved toys, late eighteenth century.

Fig. 191. Nineteenth-century carved toys.

Fig. 192. Butter molds, nineteenth century.

the instrument of childish imagination, the prop for young fantasies, and thus it was destined to show the deep love for animals, generally the common ones around the home. Thus the birds and squirrel (Fig. 191) are characteristic of a tradition which passed when commercial manufacture of toys came.

Another common form of carving was the butter mold (Fig. 192). This was a strictly utilitarian piece. Each family had its own design which was pressed on the butter it sold at market. Much like a coat of arms, this design served to identify the butter from each farm. So purchasers as well as sellers could tell what butter they were handling. Butter molds with hearts, tulips, *Sechsstern,* acorns, and other designs were common in the Palatinate during the eighteenth century. Butter molds in every shape and size have come down, dating from the middle of the eighteenth century to the last decades of the nineteenth.

The spoon rack is not yet proven to be a specifically Pennsylvania piece. Few, if any, have been authenticated, and most of those made in early America come from New Jersey and the Hudson Valley. It simply was not a part of the Pennsylvania way of life to display silver or pewter spoons; and the carved wooden spoon, which was common in Germany, was not made in early Pennsylvania, or, if it was, none has survived. German carved spoons, which were presents for baptism, wedding and other festivals, were rarely if ever made here. Experts

Fig. 193. Carved spoon rack, early nineteenth century.

have doubts about the spoon racks as in Fig. 193, although the one illustrated here has Pennsylvania designs.

Mangle boards likewise are problematic. These were strong sturdy pieces of wood, often carved, used to pound the laundry. In Germany those which show richest decoration come from Schleswig-Holstein, Lower Saxony, and Pomerania. Some Bavarian pieces are also

Fig. 194. Sawed and carved box, late nineteenth century.

Fig. 195. Child's rocking horse, mid-nineteenth century.

carved. Those claimed to have been made in Pennsylvania show tulips, double eagles, crowns, palms, mermaids, and horses. Little information about mangel boards is accurate, and those which were found here are suspect; some unscrupulous dealers imported them, probably the same unprincipled merchants who palmed off Bohemian as Stiegel glass.

With the coming of power tools the jig saw supplanted the carver's knife for shaping flat wood into bas-relief figures. This was a development during the latter half of the nineteenth century. Here carving is at a minimum, as in the cigar box illustrated (Fig. 194).

Painted Objects

Decorated small objects, known in German as *Kleinmöbel,* also were made in interior Pennsylvania as they had been made in Germany. Here too traditional designs common to Germanic folk arts reappeared, producing an interesting decorative tradition which repeated, with little change, in Pennsylvania the folk art traditions of the Old World. However, it must be said that our Pennsylvania pieces were simpler and fewer types are known; some European types did not appear in Pennsylvania for as yet no painted cradles have been found and no decorated flax boards are known.

Chief among the designs used on this smaller furniture was the traditional tulip or lily which had come into Europe from the Orient just before 1560. By the third decade of the seventeenth century most central European folk art had come to be dominated by this floral device which because of the simplicity of its form and the richness of color variations came into wide use. Joined with this floral device was the turtledove, known in Germany as the *Herrgottsvogel.*

Decorated hatboxes (Fig. 196) raise serious questions for the student of Pennsylvania folk art. We cannot be sure that they were made in Pennsylvania. Many authorities assert that they are strictly European while others admit that a few may possibly have been made here. The one illustrated here bears a European flavor and its inscription, which seems to have been taken from an old world bit of proverbial lore, has nothing of the Pennsylvania dialect about it. It reads:

Ich liebe was fein ist,	I love what is fine,
Wens gleich nicht mein ist,	Though it be not mine;
Auch mein nicht werden kann,	And though it cannot become mine,
Hab ich doch mein Freud daran	Still I shall take pleasure from it.

And the clothes worn by the figures here depicted are European in style, suggesting that this box may have been imported, being made in Europe early in the nineteenth century.

Bible boxes were used to store the massive family bibles and other much-used books. They resemble small chests and many of them were made in rich walnut and never decorated. Those which were painted were miniature dower chests and seem to be small replicas of the larger chests (Fig. 197). Tulips appear here along with the conventionalized six-lobed design (*Sechsstern*) which the ignorant call a hex sign. The early nineteenth-century Bible box (Fig. 198) shows a highly conventionalized use of the tulip or lily motif.

Pennsylvania salt boxes were made in traditional European form and decorated style, even including the carved or shaped back by which the box was hung on the kitchen wall. European salt boxes made in northern Germany and in the Alpen lands were generally carved while those from central Germany were painted. Our Pennsylvania salt boxes were never as elaborate as those which survive in the German museums and none were carved. Also no inscriptions have been found on them, and none of our pieces have added embellishments

Fig. 196. Painted hatbox with inscription.

like clock faces and other devices. Sometimes small drawers for pepper or other spices were added, as in Fig. 200 where a cut-out back reminds one of more elaborately carved German pieces. This box, dating from the second decade of the nineteenth century, has brass drawer pulls. Most Pennsylvania salt boxes were quite simple both in form and decoration, and as a class this aspect of Pennsylvania folk art never reached the development of European pieces. The Berks county box (Fig. 201) is quite simple, almost crude, in its execution.

The candle box was different from the Bible box and salt box in form because instead of having a hinged lid the candle box had a sliding lid. But the same designs were employed —tulips, *Sechsstern,* and other floral designs.

The dough box was a receptacle, usually made of soft wood like poplar or pine, in which dough was placed to rise. The Pennsylvania *Hausfrau* made her own bread and her speciality, *gegangene kuche* (raised cakes), which necessitated that dough stand overnight in a warm place so the yeasty mass could rise. Sometimes, but not always, these boxes were decorated— especially when they were portable and without legs—although some of the latter kind are known to have been painted. The piece from Dauphin County (Fig. 203) shows two panels and the influence of the dower chest is here apparent.

Fig. 197. Decorated Bible box.

Fig. 198. Decorated candle box.

Fig. 199. Decorated Bible box.

Fig. 200. Spice box with drawers.

Fig. 201. Decorated spice box.

Fig. 202. Decorated candle box.

Fig. 203. Dough box.

Fig. 204. Painted wooden tray.

Fig. 205. Decorated footstool.

Fig. 206. Pin cup turned and decorated by G. Lehn.

Fig. 207. Lehn ware.

Other decorated pieces of small furniture also were made in interior Pennsylvania such as painted trays of wood (Fig. 204) and small footstools (Fig. 205).

Late in the nineteenth century, around the year 1870, the Lehn brothers of Lititz in Lancaster County, produced a type of decorated small stuff now known as Lehn ware. They shaped these pieces on a power lathe and then decorated them with old designs. They made pin cups, spice boxes, buckets, all decorated in soft colors almost like pastels (Fig. 206, 207).

On the whole there was far less decoration of small pieces in interior Pennsylvania than in Germany, although again we must say that our stuff was either contemporary with, or earlier than, similar European pieces, and the great mass of Pennsylvania stuff remained undecorated.

Iron

From the eleventh century on metal working was one of the more highly developed crafts in Europe, especially in the agricultural villages surrounding the large noble estates. At this period the blacksmith made arms as well as a large assortment of household and craft objects.

However, even during the medieval period, an interesting division of work was apparent, namely that iron, because it was essential to agriculture, was made chiefly by rural blacksmiths while other metals like pewter, copper, brass, bronze, silver, and gold were fabricated chiefly by urban or town craftsmen. This division of work was to remain in Pennsylvania where both cast and wrought iron were mainly products of the piedmont.

Fig. 208. Wrought iron hinge from the entrance door of the Dunkard Meeting-house, Blooming Grove Colony, Lycoming.

Fig. 209. Wrought iron hinges.

Because of its durability, much early Pennsylvania iron has survived. Yet in spite of this, we know little about the work of the Pennsylvania blacksmiths; the definitive work on this craft has not yet been written. However, we may speculate that in this new land where our forebears were struggling to bring civilization, the blacksmith was an even more important craftsman than in medieval Europe. His heavy muscles were able to create light and delicate forms, some of which in truth equaled the work of the silversmiths. Like the medieval blacksmith the Pennsylvania workers in iron made weapons too for many of the so-called gunsmiths who created the Pennsylvania rifle were in reality blacksmiths. One of the unsung creations of the Pennsylvania blacksmith was the balanced American broadaxe, that instrument which was so essential in building cabins on the frontier.

During the eighteenth century a technical revolution changed the iron industry. Abraham Darby, an Englishman, invented coke in 1735. Thirty years later Cranages invented the reverberating furnace which made the use of untreated coal possible in smelting. However, large iron and steel mills did not appear in Britain until about 1780, although already in 1762 Samuel Potts and Company had built a steel furnace at Pottsgrove which continued to work through the American Revolution. Thomas Potts made steel which he openly advertised as cheaper than British steel, and Whitehead Humphreys of Philadelphia was making steel before the American Revolution. The fact that so many of the ironmasters turned patriot and were leaders, civilian and military, in the Revolution shows how sensitive they were to British competition.

Those iron objects of interest to students of art were either cast at the furnaces or wrought by blacksmiths.

Casting was done at many furnaces scattered over the early Pennsylvania countryside, and forging was done at a thousand and one smitherys on farms, a phase of the agricultural-craft economy of early Pennsylvania.

Cast iron was mainly the work of the carver who made the patterns of wood which were used in making the molds in sand. It was thus a woodcarver's craft. The cast iron stove plates

Fig. 210. Wrought iron hardware.

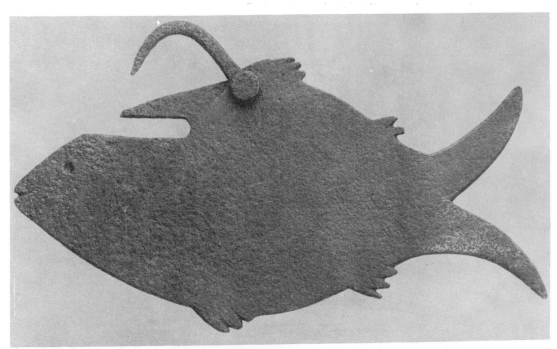

Fig. 211. Wrought iron hasp.

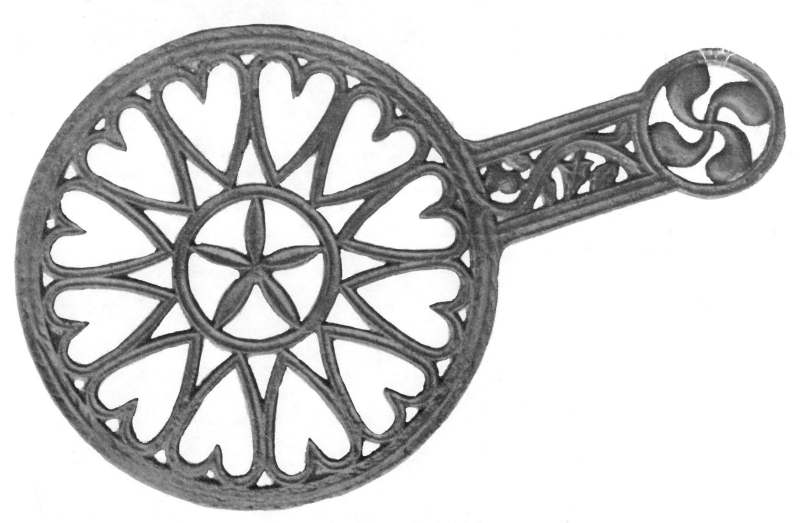

Fig. 212. Iron trivet in the Pennsylvania Farm Museum, Landis Valley.

Fig. 213. Cast iron triv

Fig. 214. Cast iron waffle mold.

Fig. 215. Cast and wrought iron waffle molds.

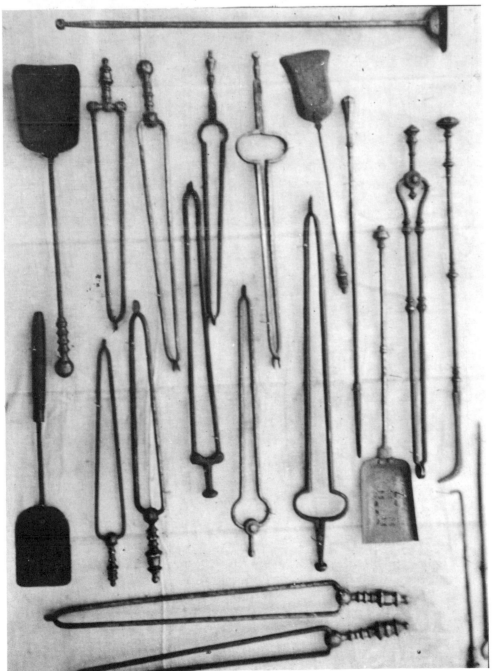

Fig. 216. Pennsylvania fireplace tools in the Farm Museum.

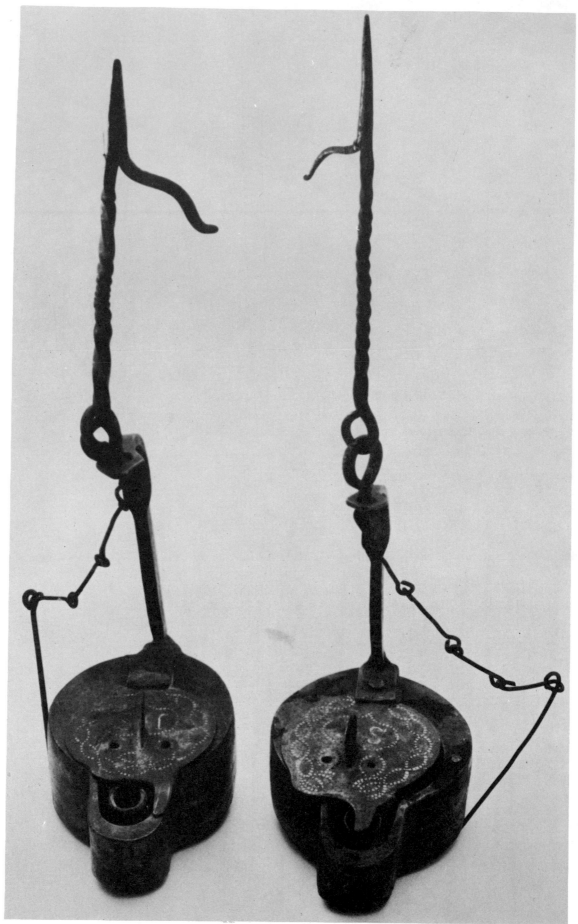

Fig. 217. Punch decorated iron fat lamps.

made in early Pennsylvania were not as elaborate as those then being made in Germany; the Pennsylvania casting industry was still not as well-developed as European. However, before the Revolution castings were already being exported from the province. An advertisement which Heinrich Stiegel ran in the *Pennsylvania Gazette* for May 4, 1769, said that he was making iron castings of all sizes such as kettles, or boilers for pot and ash workers, soap boilers, pans, pots from a barrel to three hundred gallons, kackels and sugar house stoves with cast funnels of any height for refining sugar, weights of all sizes, grate boxes, and other castings "for sugar works in the West Indies." His account books show that these West Indian orders were being filled.

Here are many implications. Already before the Revolution cast iron pieces were exported from piedmont Pennsylvania. Not only was the Pennsylvania iron industry producing enough to supply domestic needs, but it was well enough developed to supply West Indian sugar refineries at a time when Great Britain was imploring our ironmasters to supply her wants. Moreover, Stiegel's list of cast iron pieces shows the utilitarian nature of what he was making. The smaller pieces, which are of interest to art students, were made at smaller furnaces. On the whole early Pennsylvania cast iron was not as artistic as European work.

This cannot be said however of the work of rural Pennsylvania blacksmiths. Here cast bar iron was forged into surprisingly lovely shapes. The blacksmith was truly the most important craftsman in the community, but in Pennsylvania this was not yet the village blacksmith; the smithy was on farms, part of the rural economy. He was a true folk artist who took traditional designs and wrought them in hard iron. Pennsylvania blacksmiths made hinges for doors, chests, and the tool boxes of Conestoga wagons. They made ornamental weather vanes, runners for sleds, rims for wheels, hardware for houses, and nails. They even forged small votive figures like little iron cows which were placed in barns as talisman figures. In fact, as stated, it was the blacksmith who used all his skills to produce the Kentucky rifle; the Rupps of Lehigh were primarily blacksmiths who made guns as a sideline.

Although the cultural and historical significance of Pennsylvania forging cannot be known until basic research has been done on the whole work of early blacksmiths, we can still, surely, admire what they made. From them we can deduce their artistry. Thus the wrought-iron hinge from the entrance door of the Dunkard Meeting House in Blooming Grove (Fig. 208) shows the same skill as the pair of hinges in the Mercer Museum (Fig. 209). The interesting fish-shaped hasp and door catch (Fig. 211) has an almost classic shape. The two cast pieces illustrated here include a trivet (Fig. 212) with the barn design which dates from about 1820 and the waffle iron (Fig. 214) with equally traditional geometrical ornaments. And the pair of fat lamps (Fig. 217) with punched decoration show the skill of these early Pennsylvania blacksmiths.

Textiles

The same technological revolution which changed the iron and other industries also worked to transform the manufacture of textiles so that by the end of the eighteenth century a traditionally homebound craft had become, even in Europe, an industrialized venture.

A series of inventions created new cultural forms and altered these home-based crafts. Hargreaves invented the spinning jenny and thus freed women from the endless task of spinning single threads on a foot-operated wheel for now hundreds of threads could be spun at one time in a factory. Then too the "Crompton mule" allowed even finer yarns to be spun, thus making finer cloth possible, the fashionable muslins and calicos which supplanted the coarser homespun stuffs. In 1784 Cartwright combined the weaving loom with James Watt's steam engine, which had been invented in 1768, and by 1785 cotton, also now being produced faster because of the cotton gin, was being made at Papplewick near Nottingham. A Frenchman named Jacquard, from Lyons, gave homecrafts a boost, however, when he invented a loom on which linen and wool, the home-grown fabrics, could be woven into one piece.

For most of Pennsylvania early history, however, the production of textiles was a home industry and industrialization of this craft had to wait for the discovery of anthracite coal.

Next to production of foodstuffs, early Pennsylvania farmers grew much flax and wool. Already with the founding of Germantown the Pennsylvania textile industry was flourishing as a home craft and as the eighteenth century progressed the organization of these home-based looms into textile businesses developed. Already in 1750 weaving was a large scale craft in many centers of interior Pennsylvania; men like Peter Hausenclever became known as the "kings" of the craft. Paul Zanzinger of Lancaster emerged as a cloth broker capable of aiding materially in supplying Washington's army with uniforms.

Decoration appeared at three points in the pre-industrial production of textiles.

Fig. 218. Altar cloth, Woodstock, Virginia, 1767.

Fig. 219. Tablecloth with birth record, 1787.

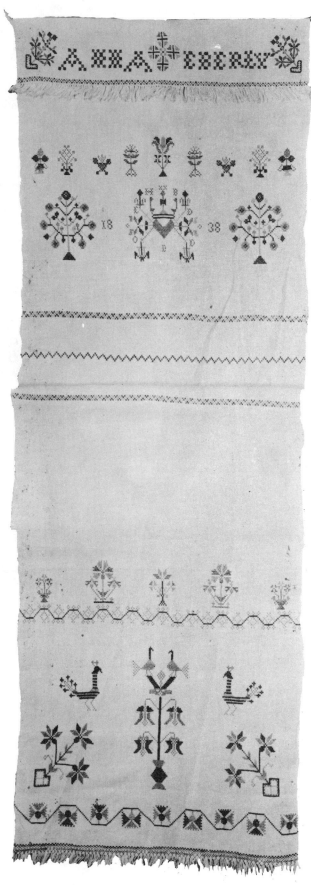

Fig. 221. Decorated towel.

Fig. 220. Towel decorated with cross-stitch and drawn work, dated 1820. The letters surrounding the central design in the third panel from the top are: *O E H B D D E,* an acrostic signifying: *O Edles Herz Bedenk Dein End.*

The first place where decoration appeared was in the old homecraft of making damask linen cloth. There is some vague historical evidence that damask was made in early Pennsylvania although no pieces of such fabric have come down. A few early letters refer to crude pieces of bleached and unbleached linen and the production of twilled table linens with some designs on them must have been done in early Pennsylvania.

The second place where decoration appeared was on the chairs, looms and weaving combs used by the craftsmen. The traditional weaver's chair—usually a high-legged piece, either stool or with arms—was often elaborately decorated with traditional designs. In addition there were also decorated weaver's combs (*Webkämme*), small instruments used to comb the wool before it was spun. Even in Europe these pieces had become traditional items for decoration; in northern Germany they were carved and in southern Germany they were painted. Carved European designs include crosses, six lobed stars, hearts, trees, horses heads, ships, and human figures. No carved pieces are known to have been made in Pennsylvania. German painted weaving combs contain designs as well as quotations from seventeenth-century poetry. Several Pennsylvania pieces are known which have decoration on them, especially Elizabeth Stauffer's which was made in 1794 and which is of special interest because it is one of the key pieces which joins words and designs. The verse at the lower panel of this piece says:

In den geliebten Rosen Thal	In the beloved valley of roses,
Viel Rosen Zeigen ohne Zahl,	Numberless roses grow;
Da wird auch sein das Lilien Feld,	There also is the lily field,
Dort in der Neuen Himmel-Welt,	There in the new heavenly world
Da alles wird in schönsten Flohr,	There everything is in heavenly bloom,
Nach seiner Art wachsen her vor,	Growing after its own kind;
Da werden zarten Feigen sein,	There too are ripe figs
Die Trauben bringen süssen Wein	And the grapes that bring the sweet new wine.

Now figs do not grow in Pennsylvania and the world that the artist was picturing was not earth-bound; here the baroque heaven has come down to earth.

The third point where decoration appeared in the making of early Pennsylvania textiles was in the printing of designs on linen. Again only a few pieces of printed linen have survived. By 1790 there were many fulling mills in eastern Pennsylvania, and the newspapers were full of advertisements about such mills in Lancaster, Berks, and Northampton counties. Associated with fulling was the art of printing designs on linen by means of wooden blocks. This craft, linked with dyeing, once was widespread and although little of the printed linens have come down some of these early printing blocks survive. In 1774 Joseph Barth advertised in Heinrich Müller's *Staatsbote* that he now could print linen in colors as fast as any found in Europe. This is a remarkable statement, and it suggests that even before the American Revolution our native Pennsylvania dyes were as fast as any imported from Europe. This implies the existence of a craft—dyeing—hitherto unrecognized. In the *Germantaun Zeitung* for April 3, 1787, Martin Appel announced that he had perfected a process for printing linen at his place in Upper Saucon, and he solicited work. He also was continuing his fulling and dyeing operations. This statement too is remarkable, showing the independent development of an American dye industry just after the American Revolution.

Some designs on these printed linen pieces were quite elaborate. At the sale of Governor Pennypacker's collection in 1920 there was a linen bedcover with the theme of American independence, showing block-printed portraits of George Washington and Benjamin

Fig. 223. "Show" towels.

Fig. 224. Drawn work on Catherine Hoch's towel, 1844. The *C.W.* is for Catherine Weidner, her mother.

Franklin along with other patriotic designs. Although most of this block-printed cloth has become dust, and we are much too ignorant about what must have been a highly-developed craft, the few surviving pieces, like the cloth in the Miller room of the Philadelphia Museum, show that printing linen must have been one of the finest phases of our early art.

Printing linen should not be confused with stenciling linen, chiefly feed bags, which was widely done during the earlier part of the nineteenth century. Many so-called printing blocks were merely stencils for marking the bags in which grain was taken to the gristmill and not blocks used to print designs on fabrics.

The common method by which textiles were decorated during these early years was through cross-stitch. This was work done in the *Spinnstube*. One of the most interesting of these pieces, and an early one too, is the altar cloth given by Friedrich and Eva Margaretha

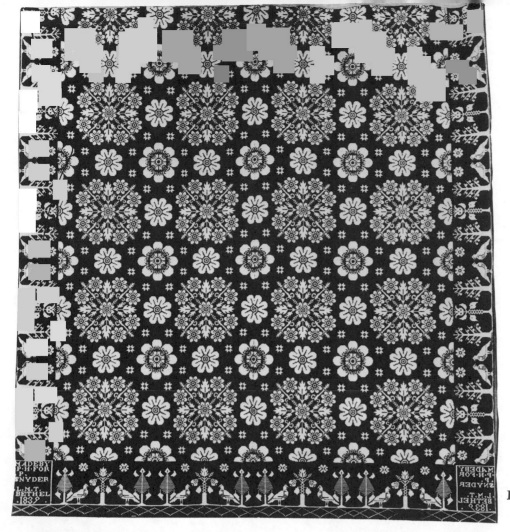

Fig. 225. Blue and white coverlet.

Fig. 226. Red and white coverlet.

Fig. 227. Coverlet made in 1854 by T. Marsteller, Lower Saucon Township, Northampton County.

Fig. 228. Tablecloth woven of bleached and unbleached linen.

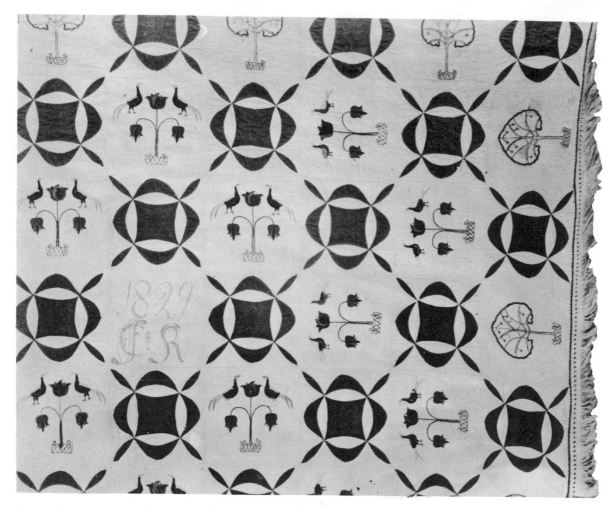

Fig. 229. Patchwork quilt, 1829.

Fig. 230. Field of lilies on a patchwork quilt.

Fig. 231. Patchwork quilt.

Fig. 232. Patchwork quilt with the American eagle.

Henger to the Woodstock, Virginia, Lutheran Church (Fig. 218). It is dated 1767. This cloth shows traditional crown and heart-bodied angels along with freshly-conceived floral designs. Another example of early cross-stitched linen is the tablecloth which, in addition to usual floral designs, also shows that Maria Katerina was born into this world on the thirteenth of August in the year 1787 (Fig. 219). Similar table cloth birth records have been found in northern Germany.

"Show Towels," called in German *Paradehandtücher,* were symbols of cleanliness and prosperity to the Pennsylvania *Hausfrau.* The custom of covering the guest towels that hung on racks behind the door in the company room with these ornately decorated towels came from Germany. These towels were quickly removed when company came, but they did keep the "use-towels" from collecting dust, and so they were soiled when company came; furthermore they reflected on the good housekeeping of the hostess. Surviving Pennsylvania towels are quite similar to and contemporary with European ones, especially those from Alsace, Tyrol, and Transylvania. Sometimes a special technique called drawn work was used by which designs were made by pulling threads from the fabric, as on Magdalena Alebrecht's towel (Fig. 220). Others were covered almost completely with designs like Mary Reist's (Fig. 221); and still others and often the earliest ones were simpler, like Barbara Landis' (Fig. 223). This last towel was made in Pennsylvania before any known surviving German counterpart.

Invention of the four-harness loom by Jacquard, by which contrasting materials like bleached and unbleached linen or linen and wool could be woven into large one-piece fabrics, gave additional life to home textile making. Itinerants acquired these looms and

Fig. 233. The Star of Bethlehem.

Fig. 234. Lily quilt, mid-nineteenth century.

Fig. 235. Patchwork quilt with portrait of a family, mid-nineteenth century.

Fig. 236. Patchwork pillowcase.

Fig. 237. Susan A. Yoder's sampler.

Fig. 238. Catherine Hoch's sampler, 1843.

Fig. 239. Catherine Hoch's sampler, 1821. This is a true sampler in that Catherine here "recorded" the designs she used or was interested in preserving.

Fig. 240. Helena Kutz's sampler showing the church and school in Kutztown.

Fig. 241. Margaret Hoch Peter's sampler, 1853. Here the transition from folk designs to formalized needlework has been made.

moved from farm to farm. Thus John Hausman of Lobachsville, Oley, wove a tablecloth for Catherina Hoch (Fig. 224) which used bleached and unbleached linens. Thomas Marsteller used wool and linen in the one-piece coverlet he made in Lower Saucon Township, Northampton County. (Fig. 227). Both pieces employed traditional designs. These Jacquard looms were carried from farm to farm by itinerant weavers who worked for periods as long as a month, making fabrics from the accumulated linen and wool thread which had been spun during the long hours. This itinerating of weavers lasted until as late as the Civil War.

The patchwork quilt brings us to another world. Here we are no longer in the craft world but have entered the world of manufacturing. Here remnants are used up. Patches

Fig. 242. *Gros point* cushion in traditional style.

were hoarded. The rag bag was raided and from what had been saved patches were cut, designs laid out, a spread made and then quilted at a party or at church. So the patchwork quilt is characteristic of nineteenth-century America and is in truth a product of the industrial revolution. However, what is surprising is that traditional designs continued to be used such as the lilies and birds of paradise and the paradisaical field of lilies (Figs. 229, 230). Sometimes even pillow cases were put together from the scraps which the rag bag held (Fig. 236). On the whole, patchwork, because of the manufactured materials employed, was later than older crafts.

In Pennsylvania only the German women made true samplers, that is they took a piece of linen and used it to record designs that appealed to them and alphabet letter which they intended to use. Generally speaking, the samplers of Anglo-Saxons were far more elaborate and less utilitarian. However, from this originally practical use the German sampler soon developed into a more elaborate thing. This development can be seen if one studies the samplers of mother, daughter, and granddaughter. If one starts with the samplers made around 1830, one will see that they are simpler, traditional, and nonrepetitive. Gradually, however, the sampler became an instrument for elaboration and for creative presentation, even pictorial designs, as in Helena Kutz's sampler (Fig. 240) which shows the St. John's Lutheran Church and school in Kutztown. The little eleven-year-old girl skipping rope under the maple tree may be Helena herself.

By the middle of the nineteenth century the Pennsylvania sampler had become, not a utilitarian piece, but one of high decoration. Thus Margaret Hoch Peter's sampler, dated 1858 (Fig. 241) was made in the Oley Select School taught by Sarah Boone, niece of Daniel Boone, who taught the children of the German farmers how to set tables, embroider, and other accomplishments. The initials on this sampler are Margaret's parents—Daniel Yoder Peter and Susanna Hoch Peter. Here we have come to the end of the Pennsylvania textile decoration.

Metal Work

In contrast to iron, both cast and wrought, which was in the main the product of country foundries and blacksmiths, work in other metals was chiefly the product of the towns and villages. As in Europe, so too in Pennsylvania; little pewter, copper, bronze, and brass were made in the country.

Pewter is an old medium, especially easy to work, malleable and capable of many forms and uses. Moreover, it was almost indestructible, and it found many household uses, even being adapted for sacramental use in churches of the Pennsylvania piedmont. Pewterers were clearly free from fashionable influences although here and there city workmen copied forms popularized by the silver-smiths. They were rather traditionalists and generally made pieces in patterns which had been in favor for years.

Pennsylvania pewter, like American pewter generally, is rare. This is due to several reasons. First a lot of our early pewter did double duty being first used as household ware, and then it was melted down and shot at the British redcoats. Secondly, it is also quite hard to identify. To counteract the British tax on American-made pewter many of our American craftsmen stamped the word "London" on it. And finally, the task of linking examples with known pewterers is a slow and tedious process.

Scholars are just now beginning to link pewter pieces with their makers and new finds are being made all the time. There are at least seven known Philadelphia pewterers for whom there are no identifiable pieces: Thomas Pashall who worked in the last decade of the seventeenth century and the first two decades of the eighteenth; Thomas Badcocks who worked in the first decade of the eighteenth century; William Cox whose work was done between 1715 and 1721; James Everett who worked in the second decade of the eighteenth century; Simon Wyer who worked about the middle of the eighteenth century; and Mungo Campbell and Johann Philip Alberti who worked in the middle of the eighteenth century. For these craftsmen no examples are identified.

Fig. 243. "Love" pewter tea pot.

Fig. 244. Unrestored pewter creamer by William Will.

At least ten pewterers are identified only by one piece, hardly enough to establish the characteristic forms: John Christian Horan, Philip Will, J. M. Uffen, L. Shoff, Robert Porter, Elisha Kirk, Christian Hera, John Hera, H. Dunlop, and Lewis Kruiger.

Among early Pennsylvania pewterers for whom several forms have been identified are: Simon Edgell, who worked between 1713 and 1743, for whom five forms are known; Thomas Byles, working between 1738 and 1741, for whom five forms are known; Cornelius Bradford, working from 1753 to the time of the American Revolution, for whom three forms are known. Among later Pennsylvania pewterers for whom a number of forms have been identified are: John Andrew Brunstrom, whose characteristic love bird appears on about forty pieces along with his initials; Benjamin and Joseph Harbeson, for whom seven forms survive; John Fischer, with seven forms too; John Christopher Heyne, who was working in Lancaster from 1754 to about 1780, for whom twelve forms survive; William Will who worked in Philadelphia from 1764 to 1798 for whom about forty forms are known; Parks Boyd, with twenty forms, and Thomas Danforth with about twenty-five forms.

Thus it is seen that little is known about the earliest period and not very much about the pewters of the second half of the eighteenth century.

The three-legged teapot (Fig. 243) is one of a type indigenous to the Philadelphia area. The two types are the ball and-claw foot type which was favored by William Will, and the pad-footed type as in this illustration. The one illustrated here bears the "Love" touch and was probably made by one or more of the presently unknown Philadelphia pewterers in the last third of the eighteenth century. This seems to be the only known specimen made from a mold that also was used by Cornelius Bradford.

The pewter sconce (Fig. 245) is a hammered and cut-out piece not made in the mold which employs traditional heart and tulip motifs. This art of punching designs on pewter seems to have been used quite early, as with the molded pitcher (Fig. 246). Here the grapes which bring the sweet new wine are molded. Sometimes these designs became quite intricate, almost as delicate as engraving on silver (Fig. 247). There may be a possibility that designs were added by craftsmen who did not fashion the piece.

Some authorities assert that there was little or no painting of tin among early Pennsylvania craftsmen; others, equally authoritative, say that there was. What we do know about decorated tin was that it was popular both in nineteenth-century Britain and nineteenth-century America. It seems reasonable to assume that Pennsylvania craftsmen painted tin, especially since our characteristic shade of red, called by some the Pennsylvania red, was used; still it is hard to separate our pieces from those made elsewhere. One of the finest collections of painted tin, which included a few pieces which most likely were made in Pennsylvania, is in the American Museum in Great Britain (Fig. 248). These pieces have a Pennsylvania flavor.

Not all Pennsylvania tin was painted. Tin was a widely used metal, being shaped into sconces, candlemolds, candleboxes, footwarmers, candlesticks, caddies, lanterns, bread trays, sand shakers, and many kinds of boxes. We are sure that much tin was being made in Pennsylvania, especially in the growing towns, for the 1790 census lists the following "tinmen" in Philadelphia: John Morrison, Alexander Balslend, Paul Metz, Martin Raiser, Conrad Hetter, Joseph Baker, Henry Hoover, and John Horton.

While painted tin is problematic, there can be no question that punch-decorated tin was soundly Pennsylvanian (Fig. 251). Here we sense a different mood than that of painted tinware. Often the owner's name was scratched on the bottom, and these pieces were decorated with traditional designs and were often given as wedding presents.

Cookie cutters originally were related to offerings given for the souls of the departed, and so they took on many interesting shapes. Religious forms seem to have been restricted to Roman Catholic areas of Europe although a few have been found in Protestant regions; however in the latter they usually took on more prosaic purposes. In Pennsylvania there no longer was any hint of this original religious purpose, except that they were used chiefly for Christmas cookies, and simple naturalistic shapes, human and animal, as well as flowers and hearts were employed (Fig. 252). Here symbolism has disappeared.

Painted trays come from the nineteenth century, although some persons profess to see a "Chippendale" style and then identify this shape with the Chippendale period of furniture. Most of these trays, however, were late, and in almost every phase they betray a style which

Fig. 245. Pewter sconce.

Fig. 246. Decorated pewter pitcher.

Fig. 247. Designs punched on metal work.

Fig. 248. Pennsylvania painted tin in the American Museum in Britain.

Fig. 249. Pennsylvania painted tin coffee pot.

Fig. 250. Decorated tin coffee pot and cream pitcher.

Fig. 251. Punched decorated coffee pot.

Fig. 252. Cookie cutters.

Fig. 253. Pennsylvania painted tray.

Fig. 254. Pennsylvania weather vane—Gabriel blowing his trumpet.

Fig. 255. Sugar tongs of silver made by Jeremiah Boone, nephew of Daniel Boone.

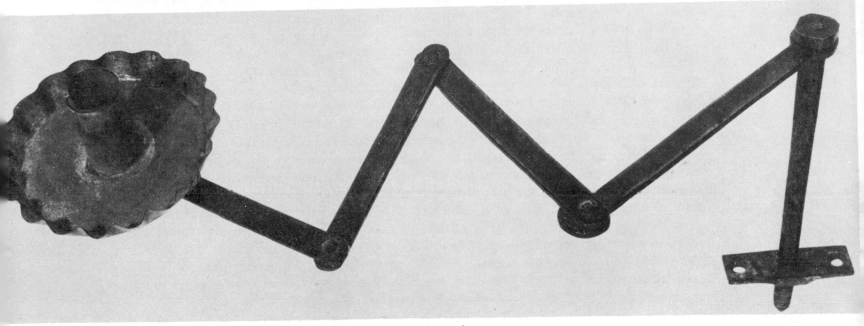

Fig. 256. Folding candle bracket, tree, and stand, mid-eighteenth century.

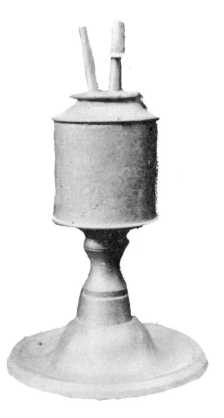

Fig. 257. Pennsylvania fire igniter.

was popular after the third decade of the nineteenth century. The one illustrated here (Fig. 253) is definitely mid-nineteenth century and has a characteristic Victorian look. These trays are, however, pieces of early American folk art.

As a metal, brass was not widely made in America before the beginning of the nineteenth century. Inventories of early furniture makers show that much was imported. The American brasscasters made some early articles—chiefly door knockers, a few candlesticks, door knobs, and some furniture hardware. From the beginning our American brass founding industry was imitative of European styles. However, several of the account books of early brass workers, notable the Ball family, still survive. One phase of the brass industry allowed opportunity for craftsmen and that was warming pan lids where scrolls, designs, and flowers were worked on the brass.

Little also is known about the copper industry and only a few pieces of early Pennsylvania copper have come down. Among these authenticated pieces is the delightful weather vane which once was on the Reformed Church at Maytown in Lancaster (Fig. 259).

By the last decade of the eighteenth century metal crafts came to be well-established and the foundations of American industry were thus laid. All sorts of craftsmen were beginning to work with power, that is to substitute engines for muscles. This was not universally true, however. Thus Jeremiah Boone, nephew of Daniel Boone, moved from Oley, where he was born, to Philadelphia and became a minor silversmith. While his work did not have the brilliance of the Richardsons and other great metropolitan silversmiths, still he was a competent craftsman who was not trying to imitate European styles. A pair of sugar tongs which he made (Fig. 255) show a somewhat American mood. Here we are no longer in the world of classical forms and we can see, perhaps yet dimly, the start of an American style. Also the folding candle bracket made of tin and steel (Fig. 256) shows the beginning of mechanical gadgetry and this collapsible bracket, dating from mid-eighteenth century, shows a new spirit struggling to come forth. And finally the lovely piece of pewter in Fig. 257 shows how one craftsman was using his molds to create beauty in a strictly utilitarian piece. Why should a craftsman make so lovely a base for so ordinary an object unless he was eager to create something both utilitarian and lovely—the essence of all craft art.

Miscellaneous Pieces

The imagination shown in early Pennsylvania crafts was unique in America. A spiritual force was present here which liberated man's spirit, allowing him to go beyond the patterns which he had inherited from the old world. This force was the liberty which William Penn gave us, his legacy to his province.

As long as early Pennsylvania craftsmen were imitating the styles of the old world they were not yet free in imagination and so were incapable of creating those new forms demanded by new environmental conditions. Not only freedom from guild restrictions, not only freedom from European tastes, but also frontier requirements, competitive work and conscious reaction against old-fashioned elegance combined to create the bloom of Pennsylvania craft activity.

The astonishing thing about Pennsylvania crafts, particularly those of the piedmont, was their comparatively tardy development. The first bloom of craft activity was between the founding of the province and 1730 when, chiefly in Philadelphia crafts flourished. In the piedmont, however, which was fully settled by 1750, the full flowering of craft activity had to wait until after the American Revolution. Those piedmont crafts plied by earlier generations—stove plates, glass and printing—were imitative of European work. The main period

Fig. 258. Pottery figurine.

Fig. 259. Decorated hand basket, mid-nineteenth century.

Fig. 260. A group of Pennsylvania German broom makers, 1905.

Fig. 261. Lintel in Allentown, mid-nineteenth century.

of piedmont craft activity fell between 1783, the end of the Revolution, and 1830, the heighth of the industrial revolution. This suggests that British Colonial trade policies worked to restrict rather than to liberate creative imagination. Only when total freedom was won did Pennsylvania craft activity come to full flower. Thus Pennsylvania crafts were the result of American cultural forces and not just "memory arts," that is transplanted European crafts done in America.

What this means is that the genetic approach to the problems of Pennsylvania crafts is insufficient to explain them. We cannot assume, for example, that because most Pennsylvania Germans came from the Palatinate their crafts were imitations of Palatinate work. Nor dare we be caught in the trap of tracing designs, assuming that because certain designs appeared in the Palatinate they were copied by Pennsylvanians. Surely the crafts were dependent upon European work but too much innovation and too many fresh things were made here to make these assertions of dependence more than foolish conjecture. Moreover, much Pennsylvania craft work was more closely allied to the crafts of other American regions than to European forms.

Then too the problem of chronology must be faced. We dare not suggest, as one writer has done, that Pennsylvania pottery made between 1785 and 1815 derives from Swedish pottery made between 1840 and 1860. Nor can we say that Pennsylvania weaving was dependent on Germanic forms when the Jacquard loom was not invented in France until about 1800. No! The truth seems to be, when we pay strict attention to dates, that much similar European craft art was either contemporary with or later than Pennsylvania work. Argue as we will, the facts still are brutally firm: much Pennsylvania work was done at the same time as European work.

Consider for example the small pottery horse and rider (Fig. 258). This was made in Pennsylvania around 1815. Similar figurines, done in highly glazed ceramics, were popular in Silesia, Thuringia, Swabia, Baden and Bavaria. Yet Konrad Hahm in his *Deutsche Volkskunst* pictures similar ceramic toys made in Hesse during the twentieth century! He found no older ones in the German museums.

Moreover, as the years progressed greater refinement came to our craft work. Eighteenth-century basketry, such as the work of Ephrata was uncomplicated while mid-nineteenth-century work was more sophisticated and hard to distinguish from general American work (Fig. 259). So too with painted tin and stenciled furniture: one is hard put to it to distinguish Pennsylvania from New England work. This can be done only on a technical basis.

From the beginning of Pennsylvania craft activity there was much sophistication in tools. Here our craftsmen really excelled. They did not just make the old tools they had known in the old world; they began all over again and used their imaginations to create new forms. Consider the broommaking craft (Fig. 260). As late as 1900 homemade tools still were used to ply this old craft. The broom in the hands of the seated worker is not yet flattened out. This shape is still common in Europe today. The workman on the right is operating a device which flattens brooms into the popular American shape. Here in this photograph the two stages of craft are clear; and the American advance in tools is apparent.

However, vestigal and craft arts survived. There was little architectural decoration of lintels and gables in the eighteenth century, but in the third and fourth decades of the nineteenth century, well after migration had ceased, carved lintels were put on homes in some Pennsylvania towns (Fig. 261).

What survived was a group culture out of which these crafts, arts and forms arose. Culture created the forms. Thus the custom of making a Christmas *Putz* (*Krippe*) originated in Renaissance Italy and appeared in Germany around the end of the seventeenth century. Figures were made of wood, wax, and papier-mâché which depicted the stall at Bethlehem, the

Fig. 262. Christmas *Putz* in traditional arrangement.

Fig. 263. The oldest example of Pennsylvania folk art, a date stone with rudimentary designs and the date 1734.

Fig. 264. Date stone near Pricetown, Berks County.

Fig. 265. A mason's shield erected by Heinrich Hertz in 1802. The inscription reads: "God can build and destroy; He can give and take as it pleases Him."

Fig. 266. "This is Eva Anna, Wife of Conrad Weiser." Beneath this smiling
angel lies the remains of the wife of the famous Indian interpreter.

Holy Family, oxen, sheep, donkeys, shepherds, and the Magi. Sometimes the flight to Egypt
also was shown. What survived was the tradition, not the craft; no carved figures made in
Pennsylvania are known but the tradition of erecting a *Putz* even with commercially produced figurines has come down (Fig. 262).

There can be no question that the Pennsylvania crafts underwent considerable expansion. This can be seen in three date stones. The earliest known piece of Pennsylvania piedmont decoration is a date stone dated 1734 with simple incised sunflowers, a heart, and a
single initial (Fig. 263). Another date stone from near Pricetown, Berks County, is more
elaborate (Fig. 264), having colored flowers and initials. Even more elaborate, including an
inscription, is the mason's shield erected in 1802 by a builder, Heinrich Hertz (Fig. 265).
Here folk art is emerging.

Fig. 267. Tombstone in the Ephrata cemetery.

Fig. 268. A gravestone in the Ephrata cemetery.

An even more dramatic proof of the development of craft activity in Pennsylvania is found in tombstones. Here we can see the death of one mood and the birth of another.

Gravestones form an interesting aspect of Pennsylvania craft art. Were more known about the tombstone cutter's guild we might perhaps know what traditions were maintained. The delightful monograph, *Pennsylvania German Tombstones* by Preston A. Barba, with drawings by Eleanor Barba, published by the Pennsylvania German Folklore Society, gives a comprehensive picture of early Pennsylvania tombstones. (These were confined mainly to the piedmont because Quakers did not erect large stones).

The personal tombstone was a late development, coming around the end of the fifteenth century. During the medieval period only nobility were personally memorialized—other persons were serfs and so not significant. Memorials usually were plaques in cathedrals or churches; graveyards also were not yet common. By the sixteenth century, due to the increased appreciation of individual personality, graveyards came into common use. At first,

Fig. 269. Stone in the Chestnut Hill Church cemetery, Lehigh.

during the sixteenth and early seventeenth centuries, skeletons and skulls were the usual designs but gradually baroque imagery brought another family of symbols, the angelic hosts who bore the soul to heaven.

Our earliest Pennsylvania stones also bear these grim symbols of human mortality. Thus in Dr. Barba's work, Maria Becker's stone in the Lutheran graveyard at Stouchsburg, Anna Hiestand's stone at Goshenhoppen, Leonhard Rieth's at Stouchsburg, and Walter Numan's at Stouchsburg—all dating before 1760—have skulls and bones. This related them to the time of the Reformation when the *Totentanz* was popular. About 1765 other symbols began to show, as on the stone of Conrad Weiser's wife (Fig. 266) and as on Herman Fischer's stone in Goshenhoppen where lilies, sun, moon, heart, and angels show. Here is a change of symbolic mood; the old dance of death has given way to the promise of new life, and the imagery of the grave has been replaced by the imagery of paradise.

Thus Anna Seiffert's stone in the Ephrata graveyard (Fig. 267) shows three lilies which, according to tradition, grew from Christ's grave. Another Ephrata tombstone is that of the innkeeper and member of the Householders. Heinrich Müller (Fig. 268). Surely the most elaborate gravestone was the magnificently incised marker for Catharina Stahlnecker (Fig. 269) in the Chestnut Hill cemetary, Lehigh County, where angels and lilies, the symbols of the new world that is to come, adorn an otherwise plain stone.

So from our tombstones we can see the change in symbolic mood which accompanied the development of the Pennsylvania crafts. The old world of the sixteenth century gave way to the new world of the eighteenth. The dance of death was replaced by the promise of life. Like the angels on the ceilings of baroque churches in Bavaria, heaven here descends to earth. So our old graveyards are themselves evidence of this new world, and the people are buried with their feet towards the rising sun so that when He comes in the clouds of glory they may rise up to greet Him face to face.

All this is clear from a humorous inscription which, they say, appears on a Pennsylvania tombstone. Even here the shrewish wife remained in the fold of grace and also waits for the general resurrection at the end of time; It reads:

Doh leit mei Fraa, Gott sei dank,
Hot lang gelebt und viel gezankt.
Nau, geh doh weck, mei liewe leit,
Schunscht steht sie uff und zankt mit
  euch.

Here lies me wife! God be praised!
She lived long and argued much.
Now good people, please go away,
Or else she will rise up and argue with
  you.

THE ILLUMINATING ART

Surely the most distinctive and colorful form of early Pennsylvania art was that of manuscript illumination. This *genre* of folk art here attained a degree of realization both in technique and imagery which was not present in European peasant art. While the basic forms were derivative, coming from known European prototypes, the illuminated manuscripts produced in early Pennsylvania show a vigor and intensity that was not present in European folk-produced manuscripts. Moreover, as one eminent German folklorist has said, Pennsylvania illuminated manuscripts, because of their close link with the religious poetry of the baroque, form the key which can unlock the symbolism of European peasant art.

The common name given to illuminated manuscripts is *fraktur*. This comes from a word which described a broken or fractured style of lettering. This style of writing, which was taught in the sectarian schools of early Pennsylvania, was an outgrowth of an older style known as *textura* which had been developed in the Rhineland, Alsace, the Palatinate, and Baden, where it was associated with religious writings.

Three periods of illuminated writing flourished in early Pennsylvania. The first was between 1745 and 1760 when the great manuscripts were made at Ephrata. The second period, a transitional one, lasted from 1760 to the beginning of the American Revolution. During this period illumination was still not ornate, being more directly connected with the matter which was being illuminated. The third period began with the end of the American Revolution and lasted until near the middle of the nineteenth century.

Except for the great Ephrata manuscripts, few pieces survive for the succeeding period, and this transitional time was when cultural patterns mixed; some pieces have English language and German, and in a few instances even Latin. As soon as the American Revolution was over the art of manuscript illumination experienced a revival, developing to heights unknown among the peasant arts of Europe. At the time of its flourishing this was not the art of an immigrant generation, nor even of the generation which made the Revolution, but it was a post-Revolutionary development.

The historical and social reasons for the development of manuscript illumination in post-Revolutionary America and for the elaboration of forms far beyond what had been known in Europe are not known. Apparently, revival of the art was linked to the social con-

Fig. 270. Page from a prayer book.

ditions prevailing in the Pennsylvania piedmont for this art form appears to have been limited to this area, although some later manifestations showed in western areas.

This art form seems to have developed in a cultural situation where there was some—but not too much—cultural stability. It seems to have come in the interim period between the founding of the sectarian schools and the establishment of printing offices. It was to some degree dependent on the schools and upon older methods of teaching penmanship. Whatever the social causes the art of manuscript illumination emerged in Pennsylvania as the most characteristic expression of the plain mood.

The word *fraktur,* derivative of *fractura,* describes an old style of penmanship in which capitals and many of the small letters were so formed that breaks, or fractures, appeared between the strokes of the letters. The whole class of writings, including pieces on which no lettering appears, has come to be known by this general name given to the style of lettering.

From the technical point of view *fraktur* is of two types: a) water color, made with paints and inks formed from berries and other vegetable matter growing on the farms; and b) tempera, made from similar home-grown pigments with a substantial base added of cherry, cedar, plum or peach gum applied moist. In most instances quills were used; if brushes were employed they were handled in the oriental way, with brush held upright, swinging freely away from the body.

Fraktur, or the broken-letter script, grew from medieval styles of lettering although the immediate parent style, as stated, was *textura,* a post-Reformation style chiefly associated with religious works like Psalters, Books of Hours and missals. Several examples of these manuscripts have been found in Pennsylvania, notably the Catholic Prayer Book in the Pennsylvania State Museum (Fig. 270), a page of which is illustrated. *Fractura* stressed the breaks between the letters and sometimes the ornamentation, which originally had been incidental, grew to become dominant, overpowering the piece. In some cases all writing disappeared and only designs showed. In Pennsylvania, as in Europe, *fraktur* continued to be associated with religious pieces although, with the exception of the Ephrata manuscripts and some Schwenkfelder manuscripts, few large ones were made here. Most Pennsylvania pieces were single sheets.

In Europe several of the sects which later came to Pennsylvania had not been allowed the privilege of print. This intolerance led them to do more handwritten pieces in an effort to preserve the religious materials felt to be vital. Among Schwenkfelders each house-father made his own manuscript hymnal and often his own prayer book. Not only did this make him a *fraktur* artist but it also served to make him expert on the traditions of religious poetry on which the meaning of this art rests. The many manuscripts surviving in the Schwenkfelder Library, large volumes in lovely hands, show how deeply these traditions were ingrained in the life of this group. So it seems true that the art of manuscript illumination came to be most highly developed among those Pennsylvania sects which had had no freedom to publish in Europe. So William Penn's tolerance was a factor in the development of manuscript illumination.

Furthermore, manuscript illumination was a social act. Useful pieces or significant events were thus memorialized. Ordinary run-of-the-mill papers and common events were not so embellished. On the whole illumination was reserved for important pieces, except legal documents which were made by official English scribes. Land surveys by civil engineers were neatly done but not illuminated.

Also, each piece of *fraktur* tells its story. A point is being made, and it is a mistake to separate the point from the designs. Words and designs both express one sentiment, and they must be studied together.

Finally, illumination was not universal. About 10,000 pieces have come down and at least twice as many have been destroyed. If we estimate that 30,000 pieces were made between 1760 and 1840 then we also have to say that at least 250,000 Germans lived in this time and in this area, making about one piece of fraktur for every sixth person. So it was a rarity.

The Art of Ephrata

First among Pennsylvania illuminated writings were the great manuscripts produced at the Ephrata Cloisters between 1746 and 1760. Here the illuminating art reached an early peak and here too a school was established where this art of *fraktur* was taught in a formal way.

Ephrata calligraphy was joined with music. A singing school had been instituted early in Ephrata's history where songs which dealt with the restoration of Adam before his division and hymns of androgynous humanity were composed and sung. During the thirty years of its existence Conrad Beissel, the Ephrata leader, composed more than a thousand melodies— tunes in two, four, and six parts. He evolved a unique theory of music for, a century before the Yankee tanner, William Billings, had published his *The New England Psalm Singer*, Beissel had written what appears to have been the first American treatise on harmony.

The celebrated preface to the 1747 edition of the *Turteltaube* hymnal, which contains this theory, says that these Ephrata hymns were "roses which have grown from among the piercing thorns of the Cross." Here the imagery is set forth which dominates the poetry as well as the art. As he says further, these hymns are

fields of flowers, grown forth of many different colors, and of varied fragrance. . . In some the spirit of prophecy sound above all mountains of the cross, bidding defiance to His enemies. . . In others the spirit had the inner court and exalted His voice in the holiest of all. Again, others have the pleasant odor of roses; others, on the contrary, spring from the myrrh mountains. . .

Here indeed is the imagery of Ephrata.

Fig. 271. Title pages of the Ephrata *Turteltaube* manuscript.

The three great manuscripts which were made at Ephrata were the work of one person, Sister Anastasia or, according to her family name, Margaretha Thomme. It was an Englishman named Ludwig Blum who had first taught the singing school, assisted by Conrad Beissel, but this school was disbanded because Margaretha Thomme fell in love with Beissel and "even tried to cut off his locks." For this she had to leave the Cloisters. Margaretha was a descendent of a well-known family from Basel in Switzerland, and Peter Miller described her as accomplished and well-formed.

In May, 1743, the Ephrata singing school was reopened and Margaretha returned to the Sisterhood. Not only did she assist Conrad Beissel in this school, but she also prepared the great choral books which were used in teaching. It was Margaretha Thomme who illuminated the three great manuscripts which came from Ephrata, two of which were dedicated to Beissel. When he died, Margaretha left the Cloisters and became the third wife of Johannes Wistar of Germantown.

The first of Margaretha's great manuscripts is the large *Turteltaube* manuscript now in the Library of Congress—a truly magnificent piece of American colonial calligraphy. Its title page, here reproduced (Fig. 271), reads in translation:

The Bitter-Sweet, Or, the Song of the Solitary Turtledove, the Christian Church here on Earth which Now in this Vale of Sorrow bewails her widowed state and, on dry branches and twigs, sings in hope of yet another betrothal. Ephrata in the Year 1746.

This hymnal was presented by the Sisters to Beissel as a testimony of filial esteem and surely, for Margaretha, this was a work of love too. The manuscript contains about four hundred tunes, each page with a headpiece, a dedication page which was especially wrought and many decorative end designs.

A companion manuscript, made by one of the Ephrata Brothers, and also specially wrought as a presentation piece to Beissel, is also known to have been made; it is now lost.

The second great manuscript made by Margaretha Thomme was entitled in translation: *The Christian ABC is Suffering, Patience, Hope . . . Whoever has learned this has attained his goal. Ephrata 1751.* This manuscript is a *Vorschriftsbuch,* a copybook, made to show the style of lettering and it contains specimens in several sizes, all in the *fractura* or broken style of lettering. The strokes of the letters are lily leaves, falling in the form of the German letters. Some have borders, others not. It is a work of rich symbolism, surely the most important *fraktur* manuscript made in early Pennsylvania. It is now in the custody of the Pennsylvania Historical and Museum Commission.

The four letters illustrated from this manuscript are *F, G, O,* and *V* (Figs. 274-277). Each contains vignettes which reveal the mood of the Ephrata Societies. The letter *F* shows two angels from the Revelation of Saint John, proclaiming by trumpet and Biblical text the character of this new age. And the lilies which symbolize this new time are omnipresent. The letter *G* shows an Ephrata nun, standing before the Mother of the Order of Roses of Sharon, who is instructing her from an open book. The letter *O* depicts Conrad Beissel being crowned as a "wonder Christian" as the dove of the Holy Spirit descends. And the letter *V* shows the symbol of the Heavenly Wisdom, known as the Virgin Sophia, that interesting conception which played so large a role in the thought of the mystic Jacob Boehme and which was also depicted on the manuscripts of the Shaker Societies where it is named. The winged head, then, represents the theological notion of the Wisdom of God.

The third of the great manuscripts made by Margaretha Thomme is entitled: *The Miracle-Play of Paradise, Which has come to the fore . . . in this Western World as a Prevision of the New Earth, 1751.* This manuscript is also in the Library of Congress. It contains one

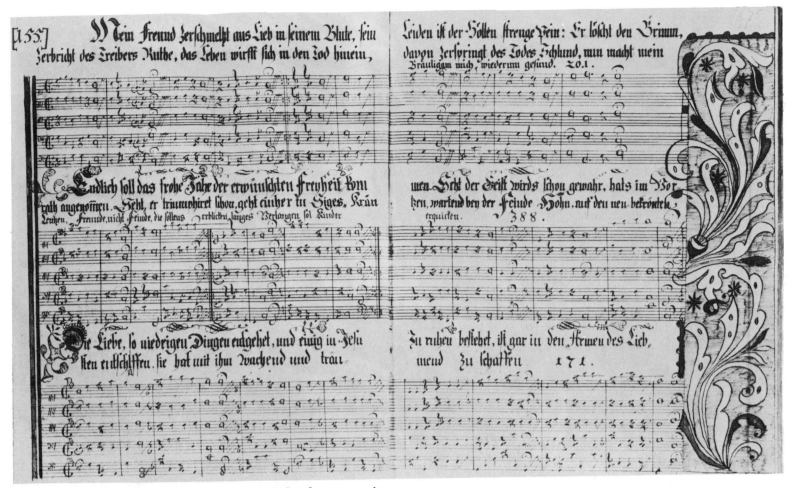

Fig. 272. Two pages from the *Turteltaube* manuscript.

hundred and forty sheets and is also richly illuminated. It was found in Bavaria.

Together these three manuscripts made by Margaretha Thomme form the first phase of Pennsylvania illumination. Other minor Ephrata illuminated writings also survive, like the illuminated *Rule Book of the Order of the Roses of Sharon* in the Historical Society of Pennsylvania, the various choral books, partly printed and partly illuminated, now in several archives and Museums, and the wall charts done in *fraktur* still hanging in the buildings at Ephrata.

Here with Ephrata illumination, at the beginning of a century of *fraktur* writing in early Pennsylvania, the spirit of the mystical baroque was already linked with the art of illumination. Two other art forms also were here joined—music and poetry—and it is foolish, if not impossible, to separate them for they express one spirit, one ascetic mood.

Conrad Beissel was trying to build the new age. He founded the singing school to manifest the wonderful harmony of eternity in a country only lately inhabited by savages. He said that God found no joy in bawling goats or screeching beasts, nor the crude scribblings of amateur writers, and the task of the singer was first to master the angelic life so he could in truth sing like the angels sing. Accompanying this discipline of voice and pen was bodily care for if the voice was to become angelic then gross foods have to be avoided. This meant that all animal products related to sex—milk, cheese, butter, eggs, honey—had to be shunned and those coarser foods like wheat and potatoes in which concupiscence was not so obvious were to be preferred.

Fig. 273. Title page of the Ephrata ABC book.

Fig. 274. Letter *F*.

Fig. 275. Letter *G*.

Fig. 276. Letter *O*.

Like the music and the poetry which it expressed, the calligraphic art of Ephrata prefigured this angelic life; yet, somehow, in the great manuscripts which Margaretha Thomme made, the imagery of bride-mysticism was clear and her passion for Conrad Beissel becomes obvious in every stroke of her clever pen.

Fig. 277. Letter *V*.

Fig. 278. Title page, Ephrata *Wunderspiel* manuscript.

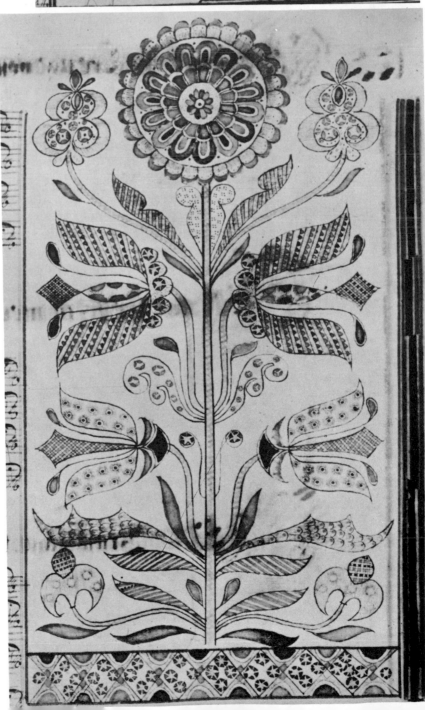

Fig. 279. Four designs from Ephrata manuscripts.

The Golden ABC For Everyone

All writing is based on the alphabet, so obviously the style of lettering which stresses the brokenness of the letters also is related to alphabet design.

However, as has already been suggested, we must not regard only decoration, ignoring the words although in some instances decoration overpowers them. The ABCs became a vehicle of folk piety and the words came to express sentiments fully as original and meaningful as those of the New England primer. Thus the Schwenkfelder physician, Dr. Abraham Wagner, who also was a religious poet, put together one of these ABCs from the minor works of Thomas a Kempis, *Das Kleine ABC in der Schule Christi*, which was printed both as a broadside and as part of the 1762 hymnal of his sect printed in Germantown. Here the mystical basis of the ABC tradition appears. Other ABC texts are known, and some of them were illuminated while others were printed. In these texts much of the ethos of the Pennsylvania piedmont, here expressed in somewhat proverbial form, becomes apparent.

If the emerging world view of the merchant-craftsmen of the city was projected in Benjamin Franklin's *Poor Richard's Almanac*, then the point of view of the farmer-craftsmen of the piedmont came to expression in the *Golden ABCs* (Fig. 280). Franklin's "morals" or Maxims, as they were called, became so popular that European manufacturers put them on porcelain, reflecting the prudent, penny-pinching values of an emerging mercantile class— the world of a penny saved is a penny earned.

The *Golden ABCs* of up-country Germans, on the contrary, projected a different mood, one which came from the folk piety of the post-Reformation period. Where Franklin's philosophy was rational and perhaps even deist that of the ABC was rooted in the baroque with its intensely mystical mood.

What does the *Golden ABC* urge us to do? We are to trust only in God, never in man. We shall guard honor and never be ashamed. We must not talk too much but listen more. We must be humble, avoiding vanity and pride, for these bring no man any good but have brought many to poverty. We are to be devout, generous to the poor, thoughtful, industrious (as Franklin also advised); we are not to be dismayed by setbacks but must persevere! We should moderate wrath at all times and give no cause for strife. As Xerxes (chosen because his name starts with X) relied on his armies and was beaten, so, if we must wage war we are to trust God or else keep the peace. We must not trust earthly things—temptations pass. The wise man trusts the Eternal God on Whom we shall call and He will help. When one would argue with us we shall be quiet and let him have his way, being wary, for deceitfulness is widespread.

Other proverbial lore was put in this easily remembered pattern which became part of the mental furniture of piedmont Germans. These maxims expressed a mood somewhat different from that of the emerging middle classes in the city and nowhere is the contrast between two cultural groups clearer.

The starry-eyed Virgin Sophia growing from a heart (Fig. 281) gives two of these verses from the *Golden ABC*. The verse in her wings is found on the printed broadside in the second line of verses before the ABC while the verse in the heart is found in the upper left hand corner of the broadside, second verse down. This proverbial poetry was widely known, and it often appeared as the basis of illuminated writings and in folk literature generally, showing how popular these lines were.

Susanna Hübner's ABC (Fig. 282, 283), made in 1810, next illustrated, presents poetry taken from the literature of her religious sect as it is a piece that was probably written by the

Im Namen der allerheiligsten Dreyfaltigkeit.

Das güldne A B C für Jedermann,
Der gern mit Ehren wollt bestahn.

Hüt dich, fluch nicht in meinem Haus,
Oder geh bald zur Thür hinaus,
Es mögt sonst Gott vom Himmelreich
Strafen mich und dich zugleich.

Ich kam einst in ein fremdes Land,
Da stund geschrieben an der Wand,
Bleib fromm und sey verschwiegen,
Was dein nicht ist, laß liegen.

Wer in sein eigen Herze sieht,
Der redt von keinem Böses nicht,
Denn an ihm selbst hat Jedermann,
Gebrech'n genug, wers merken kann.

Rede wenig und mach es wahr,
Borge wenig und mach es klar,
Laß einen jeden wer er ist,
So bleibst du auch wer du bist.

In diesem deutschen Alphabeth,
Viel guter Lehr geschrieben steht,

Es ist gestellt mit ganzem Fleiß,
Kürzlich und lieblich Reimenweis,

Drum solls ein jeder lesen gern,
Und was darinn ist, daraus lern.

A.
Allein auf Gott hoff und vertrau,
Auf Menschen Hülfe gar nicht bau,
Gott ist allein der Glauben hält,
Sonst ist kein Glaub' mehr in der Welt.

B.
Bewahr dein' Ehr, hüt dich für Schand,
Ehr ist führwahr dein höchstes Pfand,
Wirst du die Schanz einmal versehn,
So ists um deine Ehr geschehn.

C.
Claff nicht zu viel, sondern hör mehr,
Daß wird dir bringen Preiß und Ehr,
Mit Schweigen sich verredt niemand,
Viel Reden bringet Sünd und Schand.

D.
Dem Großen weich, echt dich gering,
Daß er dich nicht in Unglück bring,
Den Kleinsten auch kein Unrecht thu,
So lebst du stets in guter Ruh.

E.
Erheb dich nicht mit stolzen Muth,
Wenn du bekommen hast groß Gut,
Es wird dir nicht deswegen geben,
Daß du dich dadurch sollst erheben.

F.
Frömmigkeit laß gefallen dir,
Vielmehr dann Gold, das glaube mir,
Wenn Geld und Gut sich von dir scheid,
So weicht doch nicht die Frömmigkeit.

G.
Gedenk der Armen zu aller Frist,
Wann du von Gott gesegnet bist,
Sonst dir das widerfahren kann,
Was Christus sagt vom reichen Mann.

H.
Hat dir auch jemand Guts gethan,
So solle du stets gedenken dran,
Es soll dir seyn von Herzen leid,
An dir zu spür'n Undankbarkeit.

I.
In deiner Jugend sollst du dich
Zur Arbeit halten fleißiglich;
Hernach gar schwer die Arbeit ist,
Wann du zum Alter kommen bist.

K.
Kein'n Glauben geb nicht jedermann,
Welcher vor dir wohl reden kann,
Nicht alles geht aus Herzensgrund,
Was schön und lieblich redt der Mund.

L.
Laß kein' Unfall verdriessen dich,
Wenn das Glück gehet hinter sich,
Anfang und End oft ungleich sind,
Wie solchs sich mit der That befind.

M.
Mäßig' dein Zorn zu aller Zeit,
Um klein' Ursach erheb kein' Streit.
Der Zorn das Gemüth also verblend,
Daß man was recht ist nicht erkennt.

N.
Nicht schäm dich, rath ich allermeist,
Daß man dich lehr was du nicht weißt
Wer etwas kann den hält man werth,
Den ungeschickten niemand begehrt.

O.
O merk' so einer führt ein' Klag,
Für dir, daß du sobald der Sach,
Nicht glaubest, auch nicht richtest fort,
Sondern hörst des andern Wort.

P.
Pracht und Hoffart sollst meiden sehr,
Sie bringen weder Nutz und Ehr,
Es haben beyd' Hoffart und Pracht,
Manchen zum armen Mann gemacht.

Q.
Quad (bös) von niemand gedenk noch sprech
Dann kein Mensch lebt ohn' Gebrech,
Red'st du alles nach deinem Willen,
Man wird dich gar bald wieder stillen.

R.
Ruf Gott in allen Nöthen an,
Er wird gewißlich dir beystahn,
Er hilft einem jeden aus der Noth,
Der nur nach seinem Willen thut.

S.
Sieh dich wohl für, Betrug ist groß,
Die Welt ist falsch und sehr gottlos,
Wirst du derselben hängen an,
Ohn' Schanden kommst du nicht davon.

T.
Thu' was recht und wohl ist gethan,
Ob dich schon nicht lobt jedermann,
Es kanns doch keiner machen so,
Daß Jedermann gefallen thu.

V.
Verlaß dich nicht auf irrdisch Ding,
All' zeitlich Güter acht gering,
Darum der Mensch auch weißlich thut,
Der allein sucht das ewig' Gut.

W.
Wann jemand mit dir zanken will,
So rath ich daß du schweigest still,
Und ihm nicht helfest auf die Bahn,
Dieweil er gern wollt' Ursach han.

X.
Xerxes verließ sich auf sein Heer,
Drum ward er geschlagen sehr,
So du must kriegen Gott vertrau,
Sonst allezeit den Frieden bau.

Y.
Ye länger je mehr kehr dich zu Gott,
Daß du nicht kriegst des Teufels Spott,
Der Mensch ein'n solchen Lohn wird han,
Wie er im Leben hät gethan.

Z.
Zier all' dein Thun mit Redlichkeit,
Bedenk am End den lezten Bescheid,
Dann vor gethan und nach bedacht,
Hat manchen in groß Leid gebracht.

Gewiß ist der Tod, ungewiß der Tag,
Die Stund auch niemand wissen mag,
Drum thu Guts gedenk dabey,
Daß jede Stund die lezte sey.

Im Leiden hab' einen Löwenmuth,
Traue Gott es wird bald werden gut,
Freu dich von Herzen in Schwachheit,
Das ist die höchste Vollkommenheit.

Sag nicht alles was du weist,
Thu nicht alles was du kannst.
Glaub nicht alles was du hörest,
Richte nicht alles was du siehest.

Ach Gott hilf mir erwerben,
Christlich zu leben, und selig zu sterben,
Christlich gelebt, und selig gestorben,
Ist genugsam auf Erden erworben.

Ehrlich von Geblüt,
Redlich von Gemüth,
Ist der Jugend dieser Welt
Besser als viel Gut und Geld.

Wer was weiß der schweige,
Wer wohl ist der bleibe,
Wer was hat der behalte,
Denn Unglück kommt gar balde.

Siehe hinter dich, siehe vor dich,
Die Welt ist sehr wunderlich,
Die Feindschaft ist gemein,
Die Treue ist sehr klein.

Laß dich das Glück nicht verführen,
Oder das Unglück sehr betrüben,
Und nimm dir ja nichts böses für.
Die Straf ist sonst bald vor der Thür.

Thu' Gott wie geht es immer zu!
Thu' ich unrecht so hüte dich;
Dann glückselig ist der Mann,
Der sich an andern Schaden spiegeln kan.

Junges Blut, spar dein Gut,
Denn Armuth im Alter wehe thut,
Weh' dem ist, der viel schuldig ist,
Hat kein Frist, weis nicht wo Geld ist.

Demuth hat mich lieb gemacht,
Liebe hat mir Ehr gebracht,
Ehre thät mir Reichthum geben,
Reichthum thät nach Hoffart streben,
Hoffart stürzt mich ins Elend nieder,
Elend bracht mir die Demuth wieder.

Mancher sein'n Sohn von sich sendet,
Vermeint all's sey wohl angewendet,
Verhoft er sollte Tugend lehren,
So kan er nichts als Geld verzehren,
Und kömt zu Haus ein ärg'rer Thor,
Viel ärger als er war zuvor.

Auf dich mein lieber Gott ich traue,
Ich bitt mein Gott verlaß mich nicht,
In Gnaden meine Noth anschaue,
Du weist gar wohl was mir gebricht;
Machs mit mir wiewohl wunderlich
Durch Jesum Christum seliglich.

Ach Gott wie geht es immer zu!
Daß die mich hassen, denen ich nichts thu,
Die mir nichts gönnen und nichts geben,
Die müßen doch leiden, daß ist thu leben,
Und wenn sie meynen ich sey verdorben,
So müssen sie vor sich selber sorgen.

Frisch und fröhlich,
Fromm und Ehrlich,
Treu vom Gemüth,
Ehrlich vom Geblüt,
Diese Tugend,
Ziert die Jugend.

Freund hie, Freund dort an allen Ort,
Wenn ich nichts hab, wer hilft mir fort,
Ein guter Freund versuchtes Schwerd,
Sind in der Noth viel Geldes werth.

Ein Freund in der Noth,
Ein Freund in dem Tod,
Ein Freund hinter dem Rücken,
Das sind drey starke Brücken.

Beichten ohne Reu,
Liebhaben ohne Treu,
Allmosen geben zum Gesicht,
Solche Werke taugen nicht.

Kirchengehen säumet nicht,
Allmosen geben armet nicht,
Herren Gunst erbet nicht,
Unrecht Gut fasst nicht.

Trink und iß, Gott nicht vergiß,
Bewahr dein Ehr, dir wird nicht mehr,
Von all dein Haab ein Tuch ins Grab,
Damit schab ab.

Beten und arbeiten ist die beste Kunst,
Wers fein übet der ist nicht umsonst,
Wer nicht arbeitet der soll auch nicht essen,
Merkts ihr Faulen, thuts nicht vergessen.

Mit Gott thu alles fangen an,
So wirst du Glück und Segen han,
Menschen Fleiß gar nicht gelingt,
Wo Gott nicht seinen Segen bringt.

Wohl dem der sich fein mittelmäßig nährt,
Vergnügt mit dem, was Gott bescheert,
Der hat den besten Gewinn ersehn,
Weiß nicht wie wohl sein Sach thut stehn.

Wohl dem, der sich braucht zu Gottes Ehr,
Von Gott kommt alles, was wir haben,
Der giebt einem jeden seine Gaben,
Doch einem minder dem andern mehr.

Sey bey uns auf allen Wegen,
Liebster Gott mit deinem Segen.

Reading, gedruckt bey C. A. Bruckman.

Fig. 280. The *Golden ABC*. Much of the material used in illumination of writings came from this source.

Fig. 281. Small *Fraktur* piece with verse from the *Golden ABC*.

old Schwenkfelder, George Frell, a member of the old Bohemian Brethren. It was printed as number 505 in the 1760 hymnal of the sect. The first couplet may be translated:

> At first Thou must fear God,
> Then Thou wilt become a wise man.

These pithy sayings often were committed to memory and so became copybook maxims in the schools.

The magnificent four-page ABC, dated 1808, presents both a shorter and longer ABC. The shorter one is contained in the capital letter blocks, the larger one in the related rectangular areas. Both are poetical and seem to originate with unknown seventeenth-century German religious poets.

The Vorschrift

As it developed during the period when it flourished the Pennsylvania *Vorschrift* came to be the chief form of illuminated writing among the sectarians of the piedmont. It took name from the German *Vorschriftsbuch,* or scholar's copybook, which had been a traditional part of the German educational pattern for many years. In some schools copybooks were also produced in subjects like mathematics.

Originally in teaching penmanship a single sheet of paper was folded so as to make a copybook. Soon the schoolmaster either required maturer scholars to make finished pieces to prove that they were accomplished penmen or else he himself made these sheets of specimen letters as patterns which could be used in writing. In the latter case we have another clue to why the *Vorschrift* came to such high development in early Pennsylvania. There simply were no printed textbooks on the art of penmanship at that time and the schoolmaster, possessing only a few primers, testaments, and catechisms for reading, had to make his own patterns for teaching the art of handwriting.

Consider, for example, the lovely *Vorschrift* made by Christian Strenge in 1798 (Fig. 288). Here all elements are joined. The lowest line reads: "This *Vorschrift* belongs to Daniel Maurer. Written in Springfield Township in the Month of March, 1798." The material written out consists of two Biblical passages, one from the twelfth chapter of Romans and the other from the thirty-first chapter of Sirach. Sample letters in capitals and lower case were added. Here this Lancaster County schoolmaster produced a pattern by which his pupil, Daniel Maurer, could master the calligraphic art. The decoration was added.

The *Vorschrift,* then, was a specimen of handwriting which was used by the schoolmaster to teach the art of writing. This seems to have been its original purpose. Soon, however, it came to be an independent cultural form as in the exquisitely executed piece written on February 5, 1793 (Fig. 289), either by or for Christina Biery (Beärrien) which quotes a proverbial saying: "Begin everything with God; commit thy life, deeds and works into His hands and you will prosper." At the right are the words: "This letter belongs to Christina Beärrien; God give her much fortune and blessing and, in due time, bring her to eternity." Here the original purpose of the *Vorschrift* has been expanded and a wider scope has come. Thus, under the special social and educational conditions prevailing in the Pennsylvania piedmont, the *Vorschrift* gained deeper meaning, and it came to be used for many purposes other than pedagogical.

Most *Vorschriften* present religious views for this was still the age of faith. An early piece, dated 1770, reproduced in this book, is in many ways the key for studying the meaning of the designs employed in illuminated writings. This was made by the Reverend Daniel Schuhmacher, Lutheran clergyman in what is now Lehigh County, thus showing that the *Vorschrift* was also used didactically by clerics. Here flowers are stylized and the words are from the Old Testament book, Song of Songs. In this Biblical quotation all elements which go to make up the meaning of Pennsylvania illumination are contained, for the new spiritual age which follows the deadening winter now is here and the new earth is germinating; the birds that sing in springtime, even the lonely turtledoves, are being heard.

Even the earliest Pennsylvania *Vorschriften* show a mixing of cultural traditions. Already in 1768 the English language was put on a piece. Consider the one made about this time with the interesting swan-like bird (Fig. 290). Here Scripture, hymnody and mythology join. The words illuminated are from hymn number 226 from the famous sectarian hymnal, *Die Psalterspiel,* which is Johannes Heermann's German rendering of one of St. Augustine's hymns. The lower lines are from the English Bible. The interesting bird is the goose or swan, perhaps even the *Martinsgans* associated with the Franklish Bishop Martin. The goose really is a little swan, which in folklore was the bird that bore Christ on its back. This may perhaps remind us of the Greek legend which tells that a swan bore Apollo, the Greek god of light, away from his island. Both Apollo and Diana had swans for mothers. At the right the rod of Jesse bears conventionalized flowers.

Fig. 282. Susanna Hübner's ABC.

Fig. 283. Susanna Hübner's ABC.

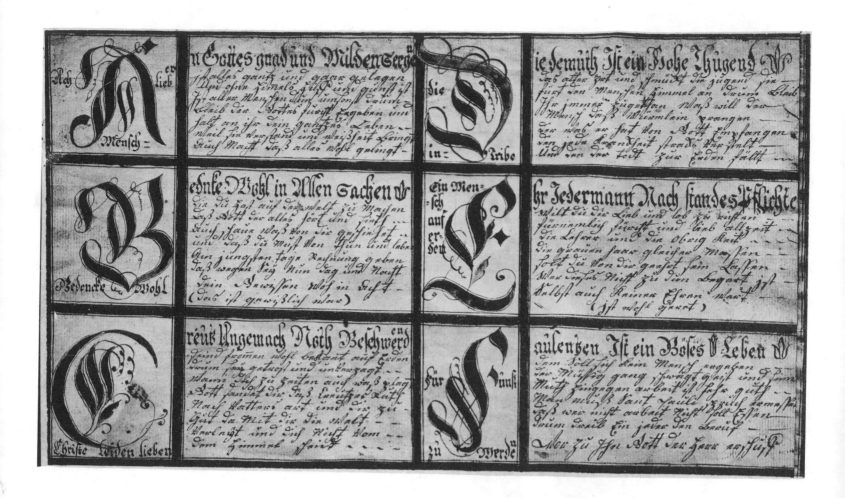

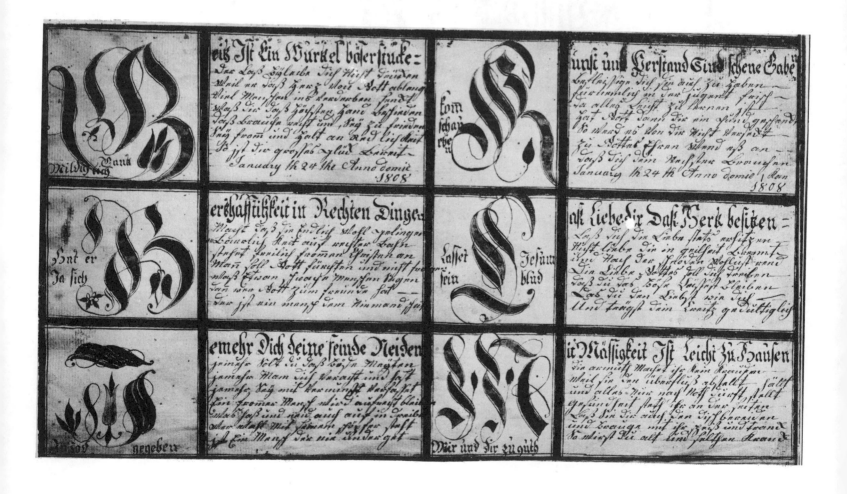

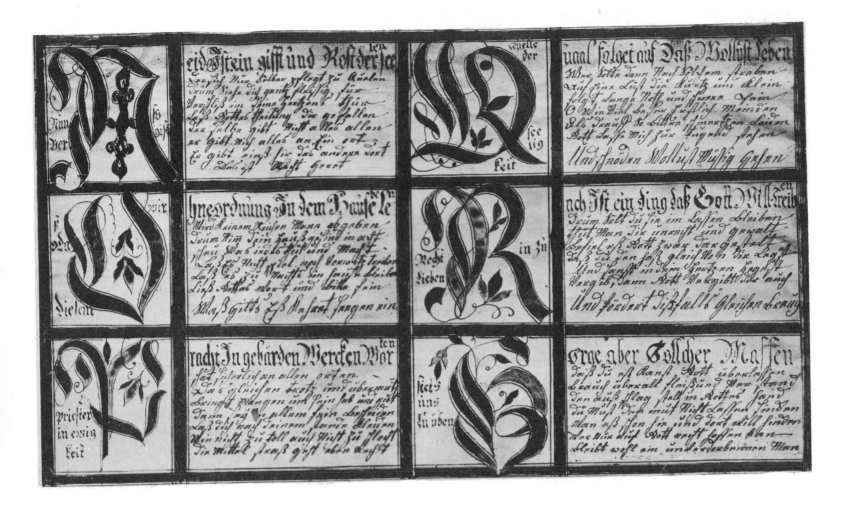

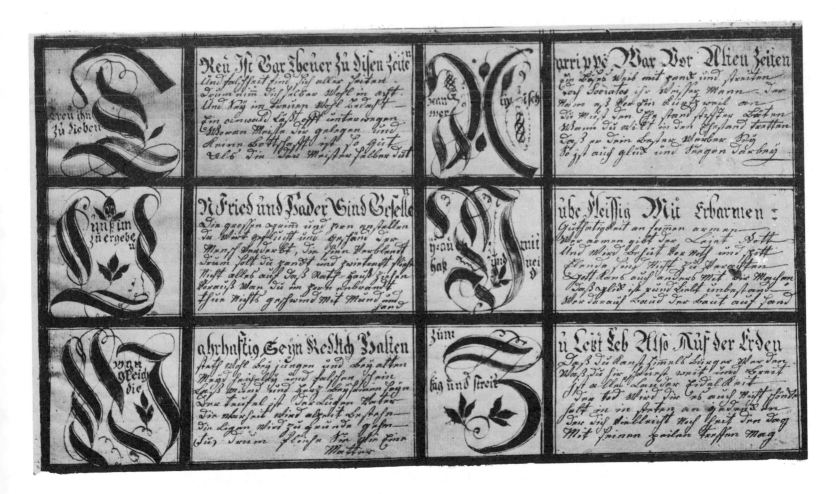

Figs. 284-287. Anonymous ABC with traditional and original verses.

Aaron's rod also appears on Huppert Cassel's letter to Abraham Heebner, dated January 24, 1773, where two languages also were used (Fig. 291). Here the Pennsylvania *Vorschrift* no longer has pedagogical purpose, and it is strictly a calligraphic form used for writing letters. The poem illuminated here has not yet been found in any of the sectarian hymnals, and there is possibility that it may even have been an original poem which Huppert Cassel was writing to his friend, Abraham Heebner, beginning

Mein Jesu Süsse Seelen-Lust	My Jesus, sweet Desire of my soul,
Mir ist nichts ausser dir bewust. . .	Nothing else but Thee do I know. . .

So, perhaps early in its American development the sectarian *Vorschrift* also became the vehicle for disseminating poetry written in Pennsylvania.

From this high degree of spirituality the *Vorschrift* ranges to the purely secular, like the tavern sign which depicts two human figures, one on the left somewhat inebriated and one on the right more prim, with a versification of the traditional tavern rules set between:

Come right in, you dear guest, if you have money in your pocket. If you have money, pray sit down; if you have none, get moving! Wife, you stay outside the door; I'll get your beer for you. Child, you be quiet until the host scratches out the check!

Here the old custom which did not permit a virtuous woman to enter a tavern but had to have her drink outside is put on the Pennsylvania *Vorschrift* which obviously hung in an early tavern.

So here is the range of the Pennsylvania *Vorschrift*—from the work of schoolmasters seeking to teach penmanship to their scholars to devout pastors preaching sermons from Biblical texts, from letters of original poetry to barroom pieces replete with the raucous fellowship of the beer mug—showing human life in all phases.

As far as decoration is concerned it can be asserted that while the *Vorschrift* was a European form it went through an elaboration of decoration here in Pennsylvania. Six *Vorschriften* are illustrated, arranged in the order of their composition (Figs. 292-297). The one on the upper left, undated, belongs to the early transitional period and may even have been made by Christopher Dock. The one on the upper right, dated 1765, was made by Martin Detweiler of Franconia Township in now Montgomery County. The one in left center, dated 1771, was made and signed by Christian Cassel, and the one in right center was probably also written by Cassel in illumination of hymn number 282 from the *Psalterspiel*

Fig. 288. *Vorschrift* signed by Christian Strenge.

Fig. 289. *Vorschrift*, 1793.

hymnal written by the celebrated mystical poet, Angelus Silesius. The piece on lower left, dated 1784, is from Salford Township, Montgomery, and the one on lower right, dated 1786, by Heinrich Landes, contains what may be an original poem beneath the lettering. Note however the gradual elaboration of style—how the *Vorschrift* becomes freer. Note too the clear division between pre-Revolutionary and post-Revolutionary pieces. All of these *Vorschriften* are from the same general region, and when viewed chronologically they demonstrate the developing traditions within the Pennsylvania *Vorschrift*.

Now, not only did the Pennsylvania *Vorschrift* thus develop in its ornamental elaboration, but, even in the pre-Revolutionary period, it began to escape from its strictly Biblical and hymn relationships. Obviously it became a fluid vehicle for the expression of original

Fig. 290. Early undated *Vorschrift*.

ideas. Thus Elizabeth's Hoch's *Vorschrift*, dated May 8, 1794 (Fig. 298), is a study in contemplation, a meditation on the fleeting transitory character of time. The theme is set by the larger letters at the top, verses which may even be original. They read in translation:

May the lamps of my soul, loveliest Bridegroom of Heaven, burn with the oil of faith when Thou comest, O Lamb of God, in the last midnight, when we shall hear the trumpets. Blessed is he who watches attentively, when everything shall be changed.

The rest of the verses deal with the prudent employment of time. Some appear to be proverbial, others have the flavor of originality. In any event, whoever wrote them, they reminded Elizabeth Hoch that she should not be a foolish but a wise virgin and that she should stay awake for the midnight crowning of the Heavenly Bridegroom. Here we have a mood similar to that of Ephrata where the congregations arose at midnight to await His coming.

Original poetry also comes forward on the *Vorschrift* with thirteen hearts, each containing a stanza. This poem is in imitation of one by the celebrated German religious poet, Paul Gerhard, entitled, "Ist Ephraim nicht meiner Kron?" (Fig. 299). The first stanza of this American poem, reads in translation: "Ephraim, art thou saddened that thou hast inherited evil? Do thy misdeeds oppress thee? Then let not the thought of all-highest grace depart from thee. Rather heed the following advice. . . ." Twelve moralizing stanzas follow on various moral and spiritual themes along with some plainer counsel of a proverbial nature. Here religion, folklore and proverb cannot be separated.

Some *Vorschriften* show how deeply-rooted this folk piety is. A piece made by Samuel Mayer (Fig. 300) illuminates a German medieval religious lyric, a passage from the *Golden ABC* and a seventeenth-century hymn.

This poetry on the *Vorschriften* was not earth-shaking, and we need not look for a Goethe, Heine, or Hölderlin to appear. This was the poetry of the folk, *Kleindichtung*, clearly imitative and at best second-rate. Its significance lies not in its literary value or in its imaginative realization but in the social and cultural significance of its ideas for it maintained connection between popular aspects of human endeavor—folklore, hymnody, proverb, and folksy humor. Yet this tradition of minor poetry kept alive a vital and even vibrant culture expressed on the *Vorschriften* of the Pennsylvania Germans.

Writing *Vorschriften* lasted from about 1765 to 1830 and it was concentrated in those areas in eastern Pennsylvania where sectarian religious schools were associated with religious meeting houses. For, as a cultural form, it could arise only where schools were established without adequate printed materials to support them.

Fig. 291. "A Letter for Abraham Heebner."

Figs. 292-297.

Fig. 298. Elisabeth Hoch's meditation.

Fig. 299. Thirteen hearts with an original poem.

Fig. 300. Samuel Mayer's *Vorschrift* with a medieval religious lyric.

The Symbolic Mood

Symbolism is a matter often hidden in ambiguity, concealed behind a veil of esoteric teaching. Arbitrarily associated meanings often are attached to designs and then symbolism becomes a matter of linking rational meaning with formal motifs.

However, if we take pains to read what the Pennsylvania illuminated writings say, if we look at the words on the pieces, we shall find that they tell us precisely what these designs mean. Then we shall not have to ask: were the artists aware of symbolism? Then we shall be able to listen to artists who were immersed in a symbolic mood far beyond our prosaic and literal point of view, and then we shall come to discover the rich and spiritually satisfying meaning of Pennsylvania folk art.

So, we need not go beyond the pieces themselves. One of the earliest illuminated writings on which words are linked with designs is Huppert Cassel's *Vorschrift,* dated December 27, 1769, an early example (Fig. 301). Like many of these earlier pieces it has both English and German materials. The English verse appears to be an original translation of the first stanza of one of the best-known German hymans, Phillip Nicolai's "Wie schön leuchtet der Morgenstern." In the spelling of the original it reads:

> How brightly shins the Morning Star
> God's gracious Light from darkness far,
> The Root of Jesse, David's Son,
> My Bridegroom, King and Wond'rous Lamb,
> My heart Thou hast possessed sweetly, friendly,
> O Thou Handsome Pretious Ransom, full of Grace,
> And set and kept in Heavenly places.

And the design which this *Vorschrift* displays at the right is a simplified rendering of the old medieval "root of Jesse," Aaron's rod, rising to bloom again from a God-possessed heart. Although this version of Jesse's rod is somewhat different from the usual use in medieval art, especially in the cathedrals, still here it is recognizable and there can be no question that Huppert Cassel knew what the design was. Nicolai's hymn is rich in "names" given to the Christ: pearl, heavenly flower, milk and honey, flame of love, trusty good, word, Psalter music, etc. Indeed, this hymn is one of the key poems, a source for the symbols which flood the Pennsylvania illuminated manuscripts.

Fig. 301. Early *Vorschrift* with English translation of Nicolai's hymn.

Moreover, Nicolai's famous hymn was one of the best-loved German religious songs in early Pennsylvania, being number 416 in the *Marburg Gesangbuch,* a work widely used in early Pennsylvania among both German Reformed and sectarian congregations. In fact it was sung as late as the third decade of the twentieth century. So there can be no question that these symbols were known.

The symbols which appear in the hymnals as "names" of Christ are really rooted in Scripture. Thus the same literary image, originally Scriptural, first appeared as a metaphor and then escaped into folk art by becoming an artistic device. However, the literary image remains constant while the style of drawing this image changes. The same metaphors were depicted in medieval art on cathedral doors, put into stained glass windows in somewhat different, and often in more ornate style, than Huppert Cassel drew them on his *Vorschrift.*

The close relationship of symbolic designs to religious imagery is further shown by Samuel Drescher's little "My Heart" *Vorschrift,* dated 1784 (Fig. 302). This piece illuminates a hymn which begins, "Mein Hertz das gute Werk bedenk"—My heart, consider the good work! The whole hymn, not copied out here, contains twelve strophes and it was written by Martin John, Jr., (1624-1707), one of the more important Schwenkfelder leaders in Europe before the sect came to Pennsylvania. It is number 216 in the 1762 Schwenkfelder hymnal, and by enclosing the words within the heart the artist joined design with verbal image.

So it is perhaps clear that Pennsylvania designs get their meanings from the literary image which is associated with them and not from what they look like. These designs really were not drawn to show us how nature looked; rather they were imaginative recreations of motifs which, while bearing some relationship o nature, really go beyond it. In matter of fact, several characteristic motifs like heart, mermaid, unicorn, and griffin also were drawn showing that something other than mere representational accuracy was being sought.

Fig. 302. "My Heart."

All this becomes clear when we make detailed analysis of three *Vorschriften* (Figs. 304, 306), made around 1810 by the queen of Pennsylvania illuminators, Susanna Hübner, also a member of the Schwenkfelder sect. Consider the question which Susanna raises on the first of these pieces:

Wie siehet man zur Frühlings Zeit	How we see in the springtime
Manch schönes Blümlein Auf der Heydt	Many lovely flowers in the field,
In Garten Wiesen komt herfür	How in garden meadows appear
Gar vielen hunten blumen zier?	Many richly colored blossoms.

Then Susanna asks:

Was will uns ferner lehren?	What more are we to be taught?

Here, perhaps, we come to the heart of it. Nature is but a steppingstone to deeper under-standing. This was then a new mood in western culture, a mood which was to come to ex-pression in Emerson's *Nature*. For many centuries western man had rejected the natural world in an ascetic denial of creation. Only with the Renaissance did nature come to be a way by which man could know spirit. The flowers in the meadow, therefore, were bridges to the spiritual world. Is this not an early transcendentalism? The poem that follows leaves no doubt that on this piece Susanna Hübner was not thinking of the natural flowers but that she was moving through them to the richly ornamented flowers which adorn a virtuous man.

Now look at her second piece! Just look at those flowers! Have you ever seen the like growing in the meadow or garden? Do they look like any flowers that nature has produced? Was Susanna trying to draw what her eyes were seeing?

This piece also contains four stanzas from a poem. Here is where we find out what these flowers are. These stanzas come from an old hymn which appeared in the manuscript hymnal of Hans Christopher Hübner, made in 1756, which Susanna's father knew as a boy and which she too may have heard used in family worship. This fine manuscript still survives in the Schwenkfelder Library. The hymn here quoted is entitled, "Ein schön altes Lied von der Himlischen Rosen und wohlriechender Lilien"—a lovely old hymn of *heavenly* roses and fragrant lilies. Note, heavenly not earthly roses and lilies! This hymn was written by the Silesian mystical poet, member of the Schwenkfelder sect, Daniel Sudermann.

Together these four verses here quoted identify the flower which Susanna Hübner drew and they also point to the source from which the literary image comes. On the upper left it says,

Mein Geliebter ist schön	My Beloved is Fair
Die Braut im Hohenlied sprach.	The Bride in Song of Songs says

So, by implication, we know that this flower is the rose of Sharon and the lily of the valley—it does not really matter how you call it—about which Solomon and the Shulamite were talking. However, between the simple Hebrew love poem from the Old Testament and the use of this image in sixteenth- and seventeenth-century poetry stood a whole millenium of allegorizing, a tradition of Scriptural interpretation in which simple literary images became descriptions of profounder spiritual experience. This tradition was cast out by the iconoclasm of the Protestant Reformation which sought exact and literal interpretation of Scripture, but it crept back through the richly imaged poetry of the religious baroque. Read the stanza which Susanna Hübner copied out:

Fig. 303. This *Vorschrift* dated 1783 presents the first verse of the twenty-ninth hymn of the *Psalterspiel* hymnal along with the unusual motif of the mermaid, the old Germanic *Wasserweib* who guards and protects children, fetching them out of the well when they have fallen in.

Ein Blum ist die Weisheit	A flower is the Wisdom
Die Ewig war bey Gott	Which ever was with God,
Ging auf in Christi Menschheit,	Arose in Christ's Humanity,
Ihr Kraft vertreibt den Todt.	Its power drives out death.
Sie ist wie zeitig Trauben	It is like ripe grapes,
Die Mein Hertz erfreut,	Which refresh my heart
Ergreift ich sie im Glauben,	When in faith I grasp them,
Es wird mir niemand rauben,	No one can take them from me,
Jetzt noch in Ewigkeit.	Now or in eternity.

The verse below on the left tells us that this flower is planted in God's holy city where it gives its fragrance to all who dwell therein.

So this flower which Susanna Hübner here drew on paper is not a picture of a flower that grows in the field. This flower, which in many forms is the chief symbol of Pennsylvania folk art—be it rose, lily, fuchsia, narcissus, or what have you—is a projection of human hope and longing. Should we then try to compare it with the flowers that we see? Or should we do what Daniel Sudermann asks us to do, "seize it in faith"?

Look at the design again. Look through it. Do not focus on it with analytical glance, but absorb it in a mood of reverie. Let it grasp you. Does it not then draw out from within you a deeply-intuited understanding of profound spiritual values? Surely these flowers on Pennsylvania illumination were not Bermuda Easter lilies, Holland tulips, or American beauty roses. For they really do not bloom in Bermuda, Holland, or Pennsylvania! They thrive in another world where eyes do not penetrate and they can only be "seen" when they come to be projected on paper through the creative spiritual imagination that comes from faith.

On her third *Vorschrift* Susanna Hübner continues her description of this heavenly flower. She tells us that by the clear and fresh waters of Paradise these young and tender flowers stand—fragrant, pleasing and clear. They bloom and foretell the spiritual summer that stands beyond the door—the time when lilies bloom, when the voice of the turtledove is heard in the land, when the rains are over and gone, and when the age of the spirit has come.

This is the symbolic mood presented to us in the designs of Pennsylvania illuminated writings and to a lesser degree in all of Pennsylvania folk art. And this is no made-up theory. We need not ask: were the artists aware of this symbolism? All we have to do is to be humble and read the pieces themselves, and they will tell us, loudly and clearly, precisely what these designs mean.

Let us now consider the greatest single piece of illuminated writing yet to appear, the *Vorschrift* drawn in 1801 by the Reverend George Geistweite (Fig. 307). Like the ancient Chalice of Antioch, which gathers early Christian symbols on one piece, so this *Vorschrift* brings together a magnificent display of the range of symbols that appear in Pennsylvania German art.

First, however, as we should always do when examining a piece of Pennsylvania German illumination, we must read the words. They come from the German metrical version of Psalm 34:

I will bless the Lord at all times; his name shall continually be in my mouth. My soul shall make her boast in the Lord; the humble shall hear thereof and be glad. O magnify the Lord with me, and let us exalt His Name together. I sought the Lord, and he heard me, and delivered me from all my fears. Keep thy tongue from evil, and thy lips from speaking guile. Depart from evil and do good.

"Let us exalt His Name together." This is precisely what George Geistweite does, for he

Fig. 307.

presents here at least fifteen, perhaps more, symbols of the Lord, images well-rooted in Scripture, medieval art, and baroque poetry. Let us now examine these symbols one by one.

At top left, standing boldly, is the rooster, ancient symbol of light and salvation who announces the coming of the new day—Christ—and who according to Gregory was the figure of the good preacher who strikes his loins with his wings, that is, does penance, before he announces the coming of the day.

At the top, in the left section of the middle block, are stag and doe. The deer (hart) is an old symbol of redemption and baptism, for in Psalm 42:2 we read of the hart that pants after the waterbrooks. The doe was typical of the soul that hungers for the waters of baptism.

At the top, in the right section of the central block, is the interesting representation of the unicorn chasing the virgin through the forest. This figure, which also appears on dower chests and birth certificates, is the wild and untamable creature of legend which can only find rest and sleep in the virgin's lap. Thus it early became a symbol of purity and ever since the thirteenth century has been a symbol of the Virgin Mary, and was thus used in medieval art as an ornament on her gown.

At the top, in the right corner block, stands the king of beasts, the "lion of the tribe of Juda" (Genesis 49:9), symbol of Christ as Almighty King and Lord of Lords. In some medieval pieces the lion, because he was supposed to wake his young on the third day, also represented the resurrected Christ. The lion also was the symbol of the evangelist Mark.

Artistically the two panels on left and right are nearly the same. They contain three main symbols, lilies, roses and turtledoves—all drawn from nature, but originally coming from the Song of Solomon. The flowers are of course the roses of Sharon and the lilies of the valley which Susanna Hübner already has described for us. The dove has many meanings. The heavenly turtledove, sometimes also called the bird of paradise, is to be distinguished from the dove which is the symbol of the Holy Spirit. In the Song of Songs we read of the earthly turtledove, forlorn and sad, which coos to heaven for its mate. This became a symbol of the longing of the soul for Christ and, by the same token, the gaudy bird of paradise then is this heavenly mate for which the earthly dove longs. In medieval art when two doves were standing by a beaker of water it signified baptism.

Within the large central block gather a group of fascinating symbols. Within the letter *I*, above, are the joined birds, a symbol the exact nature of which is not yet clear. It may possibly be the united turtledoves, the heavenly joining of the earthly bird which has cooed for and found her heavenly mate, but the heraldic device of the double eagle also comes into the picture. Certain it is that in early Christian art the double eagle device is unknown. Below, protected by the lily, is the pelican, one of the earliest symbols of Christ who, it was believed, tore open His breast to feed His young, thus becoming symbol of the self-giving Lord in His atonement. At the top, among the lilies towards the right, is the crowned bird or phoenix, certainly a symbol not drawn from nature—a motif which appeared in Christian art in the catacombs already in the second century. At the bottom of the letter *I*, just to the left, is one of the oldest symbols of the Christ, the vine (John 15:1) and also the "grapes that bring the sweet new wine." To the right of the base of the letter is the curious symbol of the diamond, an old representation of Christ (Physiologus) because it shines in the darkness and the darkness comprehends it not.

In the corner box at the bottom left is the eagle, symbol of the ascending Lord who can fly higher than all other birds and who is able to look directly into the sun.

In the middle box below are two fascinating symbols. On the left is "the one who tames the bear." Like the ram, the bear was considered to be a symbol of dominion and power and in this picture He who tames the bear is the Lord who subjects natural powers to His will. He is therefore the worker of miracles. Also in this box, on the left, is "the rider on the white horse" who, according to the Book of Revelation, ruled with sharp sword and a rod of iron as King of Kings and Lord of Lords.

And finally, in the lower right corner, is the peacock, which even among the pagans was symbol of resurrection and rebirth. Already in the early Christian catacombs the peacock was a symbol of eternity and with Saint Augustine it was a symbol of the regenerated soul.

On this magnificent Vorschrift by George Geistweite at least sixteen symbols gather. Can we then believe that he knew what he was about when he wrote: "I will praise the Lord at all times." Was he not doing just that? Did he not use many symbols of His Lord's life? Perhaps he is even telling a story by arranging these symbols in some kind of order, moving from the rooster who announces His coming on upper left to the Resurrection on lower right. Surely Geistweite was aware of the meaning of these symbols or he could not have joined them all together, not allowing a foreign symbol to creep onto his *Vorschrift*. All the symbols here point to the same spiritual reality.

Rich as it is, this *Vorschrift* by George Geistweite does not portray all the Christian symbols used in Pennsylvania folk art. Other pieces show other symbols. Among these are: the griffin, legendary winged lion who lives on both earth and air and so is symbol of the heavenly and earthly being, Christ; also the fish that lives in the water, element of baptism; and the dragon likewise appears on several pieces for he is the ancient symbol of Satan and so is the antagonist of the lion who is the prototype of divine might and of the unicorn who is the image of purity.

Although these many symbols of the Christ thus gather on this one truly magnificent piece, other designs appear elsewhere on other pieces of Pennsylvania folk art which do not seem to be symbolic. The kangaroo, ant-eater, and other exotic animals were drawn by our illuminators and their significance has not yet been discovered. Moreover, symbols like the mermaid and seahorse were taken from mythology and folklore.

The several symbols employed in Pennsylvania illuminated writing are related to traditional Christian imagery because they come from the same basic source—holy Scripture. Yet Pennsylvania symbolism was not imitative; it was neither copied nor repeated from memory. It was created, made afresh by people who were reading their Bible in old ways and who saw meanings in it which even the mania for literalness which the Protestant Reformation fostered could not eliminate. Certain it is that the Pennsylvania illuminators shared a symbolic mood capable of making these symbols live again, clothing them with the warm rich fabric of new faith. Ardent students of Scripture, they were able to re-create traditional Christian symbols, sometimes with new emphases, out of the wealth of spiritual imagination with which they came to look at the natural world.

Sermon in Pictures

The Pennsylvania *Vorschrift* soon outgrew its narrow pedagogical purpose. After the schoolmasters had employed it to teach the art of writing, preachers used it to present moral and spiritual teaching, and soon it came to be a general folk instrument for the conveying of pious admonitions and even a means of preserving original poetry.

The earliest and in many ways one of the most interesting illuminators to work in Pennsylvania was the Reverend Johann Daniel Schuhmacher. He had been born in Hamburg, Germany, son of Georg and Maria Elizabeth Schuhmacher. In April, 1752, with seven hundred Germans, he came to Nova Scotia; in April, 1754, he was in Pennsylvania where he settled on Schweitzer Creek, Weisenberg Township, in what is now Lehigh County. Here he married Maria Elizabeth Steigerwalt and they raised six children.

Daniel Schuhmacher became a prominent itinerating minister serving scattered Lutheran congregations in eastern Berks County and what was then the western end of Northampton County. Among his literary legacy is his *Diary*, now in the Library of the Lutheran Seminary in Mount Airy, a choice, unpublished bit of early Pennsylvania literature. He died in 1787 and was buried in an unmarked grave in the Weisenberg church. His will was probated in Easton.

The calligraphic art of Daniel Schuhmacher was noteworthy for its sharp clear iconography, for its contemporaneous character, and for the bold vigor of its presentation.

The first piece known to have been illuminated by him is the double title page of the church record book of the Albany Lutheran congregation in Allemängel Township (Fig. 308).

Fig. 308. Daniel Schuhmacher's illumination of the Albany Church record book.

With this piece, dated 1768, we stand at the beginning of the post-Ephrata period of Pennsylvania illumination and the patterns and forms which were to undergo considerable expansion during later years were already clear. The right page of this dedication contains this verse:

Komt her und fallt auf eure knie,   Come here and fall down on your knees
Vor Gottes Majestät allhie,   Before the majesty of God herein.
Es ist sein Heiligthum und Haus,   This is His sanctuary and house;
Wer Sünde liebt gehört hinaus.   He who loves sin belongs without.
    Hallelujah 1768   Hallelujah 1768.

Even the log church on the frontier was a holy sanctuary, a church which was shared by Lutheran and Reformed congregations.

In the year 1769 all Pennsylvania was stirred by the comet which passed across the heavens. Pastor Schuhmacher, like so many others, saw a chance to draw, rather than preach, a sermon (Fig. 309). So he pictured this crude comet passing from east to west with angel announcing what he felt was the holy will with the words:

Auf zum Gericht! Auf! Säumet nicht!   Arise to Judgment! Arise! Do not delay!

Below is a terse statement that a comet-star of sallow color had appeared in the Pennsylvania heavens in August, 1769; then the Pastor added:

Ihr Menschen fragt euch doch   You people are asking yourselves
was dieser Stern thut deuten;   What this star means,
Ob Gott euch straffen will!   Whether God will punish you?
Ach, thu doch Busse bey zeiten!   Oh, just do timely penance!

The bold execution of this piece, the directness of its verse, show the consternation of the times.

Fig. 309. Daniel Schuhmacher's picture of the Great Comet of 1769.

I: Buch Mose Cap 49 v 21 ~ Napthali, ist ein Schneller Hirsch und gibt Schöne Rede.

Fig. 310. Daniel Schuhmacher's picture of Napthali.

Heisse dein Schifflein nur. Folgen der Wellen Spür. goft ist der Steuermann. er es schon leiten kan. Hoffnung laß für und für. Bleiben dein Schiff Panier. Sieht es heut Stürmisch drein. morgen wirds Stille Sein 1775

Fig. 311. Daniel Schuhmacher's admonition.

In similar mood is the magnificently didactic primitive done about the same time, one of the most interesting of all Pennsylvania illuminated pieces because of the richness of its meaning (Fig. 310). Here the symbolic mood has gained maturity and our folk art has found a power not known in European *Volkskunst*. This picture shows a stag pounding an erupting earth—the foundations of the earth are shaking—a rocking and undulating base for the Church. Below is a simple quotation from Genesis 59:21: "Napthali is a swift hind and gives fair words." And indeed the stag's mouth does seem to be uttering fair words, deceitful words, while his hooves rise to pound the trembling earth. The apocalypse is at hand.

Napthali was of course next to last of Jacob's sons. He was quick and decitful. According to an old idea, expressed in Jacob Boehme's mystical commentary on Genesis, *Mysterium Magnum*, the twelve sons of Jacob represented the twelve ages of history. In this Biblically-based philosophy of history Napthali signifies the age of volcanic disorder and confusion which precedes the golden age of Benjamin. In this drawing, then, the clever double-tongued Napthali pounds the earth until its foundations shake. Soon will come the end and then the peace that lasts for aye. What a picture to draw just as the American Revolution was brewing, as the Old World was in truth shaking on its foundations and as the new democratic order was about to come forth!

The third sermon-picture by Daniel Schuhmacher is his fascinating portrayal, stark in its sober simplicity, of the old mystical figure of the ship of God (Fig. 311). The verse is clearly moved by the tensions of that age:

Heisse dein Schifflein nur	Let your ship just
Folgen der Wellen Spur,	Follow the wave-course,
Gott ist der Steuermann	God is the pilot
Der es schon leiten kan.	Who can guide it.
Hoffnung lass für und für,	Let hope ever
Bleiben dein Schiff Panier,	Be your ship's banner.
Sieht es heut Sturmisch drein	If today it does seem stormy,
Morgan wirds stille seyn.	Tomorrow it will be calm.
1775	1775

Just as the American Revolution was about to break, as the militia battalions of Berks and Northampton Counties were drilling and as Pastor Schuhmacher was himself about to journey to Boston to be chaplain to some of the first troops to serve under Washington, he used this old figure of a ship as the image of a resigned soul which yields its will to the piloting of God. This is somewhat reminiscent of the medieval mystic, Johann Tauler's famous advent hymn beginning:

Es kumpt ein Schiff geladen	There comes a ship all loaded
recht uff sein höhstes Pfort,	Right up to highest hold,
es bringt uns den sunne des Vatters	It brings us the Father's Son,
das ewig ware wort.	Eternal Word and True.

In folklore the image of the ship was generally associated with sea serpents and sea spirits and Saint Peter was patron of ships and fishermen.

The spiritual hour-clock shows a German style clock without case and the verse:

Es schlägt die Stund, Gott. steh uns bey	The hour strikes, God be with us
Das diese Stund glückselig sey	That this hour be lucky for us
Komt unsre Letzte stund heran	When our last hour comes
So nehm sich Jesus unser an.	May Jesus take us to His own.

Fig. 312. Daniel Schuhmacher's spiritual clock.

Eine amsel die welt gehört uns menschen nicht
allein viel tausend vögel sollen auch drauf leben
und sich der müh gottes freun der ihnen speis und
tranf wie uns gegeben

Fig. 313. "The world belongs not only to man. Many thousand birds shall also
live upon it and enjoy God's gifts, who gives them, as us, meat and
drink."

Fig. 314. The mystical birds with poems by Rudolph Landes.

Fig. 315. Poetical *Vorschrift*.

Fig. 316. Poetical *Vorschrift*.

With Pietists generally time was a vitally significant form.

An interesting bit of direct didacticism is the little picture sermon "The Robin" (Fig. 313). Here we are no longer in the world of symbolism but in the world of analogy. Here natural objects have become the unashamed vehicles of spirit and we see a stylized bird sitting on the branch of a tree shaped like the hand of all-provident nature, with the words,

Eine Amsel	The Robin
Wie Welt gehört uns menschen nicht allein	The world belongs not only to man,
Viel tausend Vögel sollen auch drauf leben	Many thousand birds also are to live upon it.
Und sich die güte Gottes freun	And enjoy the good gifts of God,
Der ihnen speiss und trank wie uns gegeben	Who gives them, like us, meat and drink.

And the generous hand of God does indeed nourish this bird as well as man, as this homily in humility suggests.

In February, 1814, Rudolph Landis wrote down a group of metrical prayers, most likely of his own composition, adding some decoration in the form of heavenly roses and united turtledoves (Fig. 314). Here the Pennsylvania *Vorschrift* has moved out beyond its original purpose as a pattern for teaching the art of penmanship and has become the depository of original verse.

Certificates of Birth and Baptism—Taufscheine

The Taufschein, even in Europe, was a cultural form of significant meaning among peasant folk. They were drawn either by the schoolmasters or by the pastors, decorated with symbolic motifs and usually given as a present at baptism, along with a piece of money. Adolf Spamer, authority on German folk art, asserted that decorated *Taufscheine* were known in the seventeenth century even though only a few pieces from the eighteenth century survive in the European museums.

The high point of making *Taufscheine,* in Europe called *Patenbriefe,* was reached in Protestant areas, especially in Alsace where they were also called *Taufzettel.* Regional differences appeared in Europe: those from Egerland were religious miniatures; those from the Black Forest were linked with the painted clock faces made there. In northern and middle Germany baptism was recorded in carved wood and sometimes even stitched in linen—the latter custom surviving also in Pennsylvania.

The *Taufschein,* which is a certificate of birth *and* baptism, is probably the best known form of Pennsylvania illuminated writing. As only certain religious denominations practiced infant baptism the *Taufschein,* which generally records both birth and baptism on one certificate, was limited to those religious denominations which practiced baptism of infants.

Certificates of birth only have shown up, thus proving that those religious sects which did not believe in infant baptism recorded only the birth, and not the baptism, of the child. Thus the Lancaster County piece, which is clearly from a family which belonged to a denomination practicing adult baptism, presents a text which differs from that of a usual *Taufschein,* reading in translation: "Heinrich Landis / was born in the year of Our Lord, 1780, / the 19th of May, in the Sign of the Ram. / The parents were / Benjamin Landis and Susanna Landis, / Elizabeth Township, Lancaster County, / State of Pennsylvania." As expected, certicates recording birth only omit the traditional poetry associated with baptism and give no record of an event which in these religious groups took place in adult years. Moreover, these "plain" certificates of birth do not show the same rich symbolism in their decoration as do *Taufscheine* which were made for or by persons associated with churches having a richer sacramental life.

The fact that *Taufscheine* were made for or by those religious groups that believed in baptising infants restricts them to Lutheran, Reformed and possibly Moravian families. This also regionalizes the *Taufschein* and limites it to those areas in which the church people had settled, making it rarer in those areas in eastern Lancaster, upper Montgomery and upper

Fig. 317. Cut-out *Vorschrift.*

Bucks where the sects settled. So we can assert that *Taufscheine* were made for or by persons who lived in Northampton (later divided into Lehigh), Berks, Lebanon, Dauphin, and those parts of Lancaster, Montgomery, and Bucks counties where church people lived. It spread westward as far as Ohio in places settled by German church people.

So we can say further that the *Vorschrift* was sectarian while the *Taufschein* was denominational; the former came out of the sectarian school while the latter was made both by schoolmasters and itinerants. Some *Taufscheine* were made by pastors.

These though were not the only contrasts. Where the *Vorschrift* was original, individualized and flexible, the Taufschein was imitative, conventional and rigid. The *Vorschrift* could be adapted to express almost any idea from the near bawdy to the mystical; the *Taufschein* on the other hand nearly always used the same textual pattern and nearly always quoted from the same verses. This is why the *Taufschein* could be printed while the *Vorschrift*, which was by far the more interesting of the two forms, could not. The *Vorschrift* was then free while the *Taufschein* was fixed.

Only slight variants in the text of the *Taufschein* appear and there is really little change between those done wholly by hand and those with partly printed text. In fact, the printing of *Taufscheine* shows that they had become standardized. The arrangements of the several

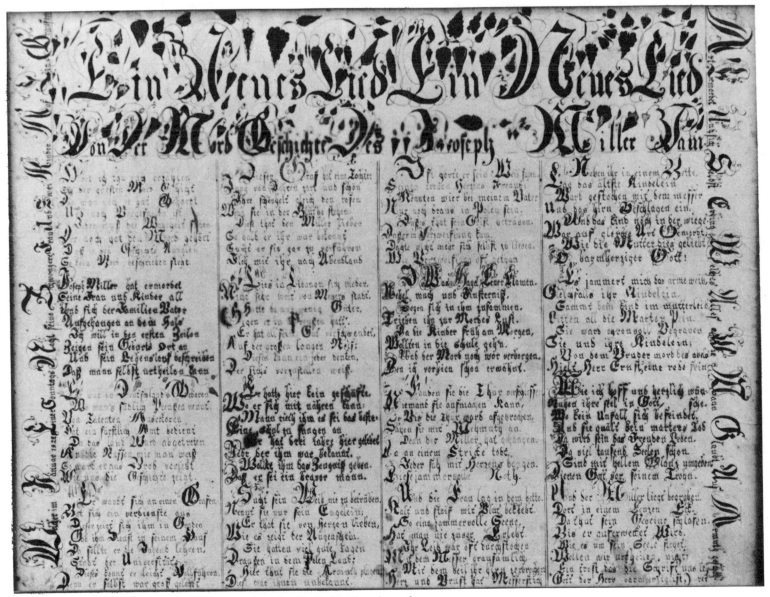

Fig. 318. The "Joseph Miller Murder Ballad" illuminated.

Fig. 319. Certificate of birth.

Fig. 320. The baptismal and wedding certificate of Philip Schafer of Richmond Township, Berks, who was born in 1770, baptized by Reformed Pastor Michael, and married Elizabeth Fetterolf on September 5, 1797. This is also remarkable in that it presents four woodcuts of obviously European origin.

elements on a *Taufschein* varied but generally their form was established and probably was important *in toto* from Europe. Generally speaking the matter inserted in script was change-able material while the printed or *fraktur* words were formal and fixed. Here is a text, the bold face letters being the standard ones:

To these spouses, as (husband's name) **and his honorable housewife** (wife's first name), **who was born a** (wife's maiden name), **a** (son or daughter) **was born into the world named** (child's first name) **in the year of our Lord, A.D.** (year date), **the** (day) **of** (month) **at** (hour) **o'clock, in the sign of the** (zodiacal sign). **This** (child's first name) **was born and baptized in America, in the State of Pennsylvania, in** (name of) **County,** (name of) **Township, and was baptized on** (date) **by the Reverend** (minister's name). **The sponsors were:** (names of god-parents).

This basic text may sometimes be altered but the information given above is generally what is contained on all *Taufscheine*.

In addition to this basic text several traditional hymns also were associated with *Tauf-scheine*, two of them with such regularity that they almost seem to be permanent fixtures on

Fig. 321. Elizabeth Fetterolf's *Taufschein*.

nearly all certificates. Usually they were enclosed in hearts or other decorative devices. The commonest of these hymns was the well-known baptismal hymn by the celebrated theologian Rambach. Its various verses were used but the following two strophes were more common. It also was customary, during the baptism ceremony, to sing these verses:

Ich bin getauft! Ich steh im Bunde	I am baptized! I am in the Covenant
Durch meine Tauf mit meinem Gott,	Through baptism with my God.
So sprech ich stets mit frohen Munde,	So ever with joyous mouth I speak
In Kreutz, in Trübsal, Angst und Noth.	In cross, in sorrow, anxiety and need.
Ich bin getauft, das freu ich mich,	I am baptized; in this I rejoice—
Die Freude bleibt mir ewiglich.	This joy stays with me evermore.
Ich bin getauft ob ich gleich sterbe,	I am baptized! Though directly I die,
Was schadet mir das kühle Grab?	How can the cool grave hurt me?
Ich weiss mein Vaterland und Erbe,	I know my fatherland and heritage
Dass ich bei Gott im Himmel hab:	Which I have received from heaven.
Nach meinem Tod ist mir bereit	There is prepared for me at death
Das Himmels Freud und feiner Kleid.	The joys of heaven and a fine cloak.

The second of these verses associated with the *Taufscheine* is of more popular origin and its last four lines are metrical versions of proverbial wisdom. Perhaps these verses were even composed by Heinrich Otto, one of the roaming *Lohnschreiber* who travelled over eastern Pennsylvania making *Taufscheine:*

Wann wir kaum gebohren werden	From the time of our birth
Ist vom ersten Lebenstritt	And our first step of life
Bis ins kühle Grab der Erden	To the cool grave of earth
Nur ein kurtz gemessner Schritt.	Is but a short measured step.
Ach mit jedem Augenblick	Yes, with every moment
Gehet unsre Kraft zurück,	Our vitality decreases
Und wir sind mit jedem Jahre,	And with every passing year
Allzu reiff zur Toden hahre.	We grow ripe for death's tomb.
Und wer weiss in welcher Stund	Who knows at what hour
Uns die letzte Stimme weckt;	The last call shall awaken us?
Dann Gott hat's mit seinem Munde	For the mouth of God
Keinem Menschen noch entdeckt.	Has not yet revealed it to anyone.
Wer sein Haus nun wohl bestellt	He who rightly orders his house
Geht mit Freude aus der Welt.	Leaves the world with joy.
Da die Sicherheit hingegen	For security, on the contrary,
Ewige Sterben kan erregen.	Stirs up eternal death.

Here the proverbial occupation with death and the brevity of mortal existence is clear, the usual theme that baptism yields eternal life.

The designs on the *Taufscheine,* like those on the *Vorschift,* can be broken down into individual styles, and it is rather easy to identify the work of itinerants like Heinrich Otto and the artist who illuminated the pulpit Bible in the Easton Reformed Church. To stress the individualistic character of this art is to miss the social nature of the *Taufschein.* The existence of itinerant artists who went from farm to farm making these pieces suggests a somewhat stable life where sacramental practices were well-established. On the frontier, where there were no churches and few resident clergy, where there were no established farms and few schools, few *Taufscheine* show. This further suggests that *Taufscheine* arose in the

Fig. 322. Catharina Schup's *Taufschein.*

Fig. 323. Michael Fackenthal's *Taufschein.*

Fig. 324. Catharina Seiffert's *Taufschein*.

interim period between the amorphic culture of the frontier and the time when printing became prevalent in the piedmont areas. Thus the *Taufschein* was a characteristic product of the piedmont during the period just before provincial printshops appeared. In matter of fact, sometimes the illumination was done quite a few years after the event being memorialized, thus showing some cultural stability. It is a mistake to date the *Taufschein* from the date of baptism.

Sometimes other memorable events were recorded on the same document. Thus the strange product made by Friedrich Krebs who travelled in eastern Berks County which contains records of birth and baptism as well as of the marriage of Phillip Schaeffer to Elizabeth Fetterolf (Fig. 320). The date of the baptism was 1770 and of his marriage in 1797. Moreover, this certificate also records the birth and baptism of Elizabeth Fetherolf whose own *Taufschein* also is reproduced here (Fig. 321), and shows a different mood from Phillip's. Phillip's father was Georg Schaeffer who had been a Major in Pulaski's Corps in the Continental Army under Washington and saw service in the battles of Long Island and Trenton and was present in the Valley Forge encampment. The most unusual feature of Phillip Schaeffer's *Taufschein* is the four woodcuts with their Latin inscriptions. Other pieces with similar designs from woodcuts have been found. These were taken from blank copy books used in the schools and there are in in the Schwenkfelder Library copybooks with these designs on them. However, while these woodcuts on Phillip's *Taufschein* have Latin inscriptions on them, they seem hardly suitable for the staunchly Protestant Schaeffer family, whose descendent, Nathan C. Schaeffer, was Superintendent of Public Instruction for the Commonwealth of Pennsylvania.

A similar use of woodcuts taken from school copybooks printed abroad appears on the certificate made to memorialize the baptism of Catherina Schup of Chestnut Hill in what is

Fig. 325. Johannes Schaffer's *Taufschein* with mermaids and seahorses.

Fig. 326. Elisabeth Bender's *Taufschein* by Heinrich Otto.

Fig. 327. Johannes Stumpf's *Taufschein*.

Fig. 328. Michael Wohlfarth's *Taufschein.*

Fig. 329. Carl Hertzell's *Taufschein* made by his brother John.

Fig. 330. An interesting early *Taufwunsch,* showing the continuation in Pennsylvania of this European tradition.

now Lehigh County. These devices of pasted-on dogs, cats, hunters, and the life, suggest a mood not usually associated with Pennsylvania illumination.

The earliest *Taufschein* yet seen is fully hand-drawn and bears the date 1768. It is noteworthy for its use of three languages—German, English, and Latin. Thus, like the *Vorschrift,* the mingling of cultural traditions was apparent on the earliest pieces which were, in the main, hand-done, both text and designs. Later the text part which did not change was printed, as well as the poetry, designs being added by hand. And finally both the permanent text and the outlines of the designs were printed, with color and the recorded materials being added. These printed forms are generally called "fat angel" *Taufscheine.*

The New Years Greeting

In early Pennsylvania Christmas was not yet the commercialized spree that it has become and in spite of the fact that the Germans were more generous in celebrating it than the Puritans of New England there is little evidence that *fraktur* Greetings for Christmas were drawn. None are known. However, a series of New Year Greetings by the Reverend Daniel Schuhmacher have survived which celebrate in verses both traditional in mood and fresh in phrasing the old custom of shooting in the New Year.

As a *fraktur* genre these New Years greetings are rare. A late work on Pennsylvania German illuminated writings does not even mention them. Few survive indeed, but these are sufficient, however, to show how the tradition was maintained and what the elements were.

Fig. 331. This piece is the key that links the Pennsylvania *Taufschein* with the European *Taufwunsch*. In Europe, especially Alsace and the Palatinate, the form of the *Taufschein* as known in Pennsylvania was not much in evidence. Here a European "wish" was made in 1751 in Schoharie in New York State among the Germans there. It shows that the European tradition was in truth reproduced in America, and that the Pennsylvania *Taufschein* was a development of it.

Fig. 332. Daniel Schuhmacher's New Year's greeting, 1775.

We picture here four greetings made by Daniel Schuhmacher for the years 1775, 1784, 1785, and 1786 spanning the difficult years of the American Revolution.

The first greeting (Fig. 332) is on a single sheet of paper and presents an illuminated prayer sent by Schuhmacher to his neighbors and friends, Jacob Grimm and his wife Margaretha. The verse says:

Mit dieser gab und klein Geschenk	With this gift and small present
Seind Sie nun freundlich eingedenkt,	You are called to remembrance,
Mein Werth und leiber freund Jacob Grimm	My worthy and dear friend Jacob Grimm
Und Seiner Frau Margaretha Grim	And his wife Margaretha Grimm

He continues:

Es kommt ein Wünsch aus Hertzens Grund	A wish comes from the bottom of my heart
Zu ihnen jetzt in dieser Stund,	To you now in this hour
Beim eintritt in dem Neuen Jahr,	Upon entering into the New Year
Denn woll erfüllen der engel Schaar,	Which angelic hosts will fulfill,
Von einem freund der wohl Bekant	From your well-known friend
Und Pfarrer Schuhmacher ist genannt	Named Pastor Schuhmacher

There then follows a verse prayer, obviously composed by the pastor, containing his best wishes for the New Year, all grace, blessing and peace for everyone and the wish that these blessings be extanded to all Christendom. These words are in a traditional mood.

The greeting for 1784, of which we show the first of several pages, (Fig. 333) was written just as the American Revolution was over. The fact that none of the greetings for the war years have survived may be because during that time paper was short and Pastor Schuhmacher was busy as Chaplain to the Pennsylvania Militia. In fact, Schuhmacher was at Cambridge with the Pennsylvania Troops when General Washington took command and he left a map of the military situation around Boston. Anyway, Pastor Schuhmacher's greeting refers to the usual patterns of thought but it also brings in a mood associated with the unusual events of that period—the grim and now successful events which are clearly reflected in the text which, far from being rote repetition of folklore, was newly worked for this occasion. Here again we are in the world of *Kleindichtung*, occasional verse written not to gain literary fame but to celebrate passing events. Yet, although traditional moods are evident, how satisfying and thoughtful was the custom of composing verse greetings for specific people—something far more vital than store-bought greetings. Here is part of the translation of this greeting:

Praise God! A New Year now is breaking in with its clear air and bright appearance of joy. The old is past, the new one has come; and we shall begin this new one with singing, praise and prayer! Let heaven be praised that war and war's alarms no longer are heard in our land and now have come to an end. Noble golden peace has come—a peace which holds our victory!

After opening in this way, Pastor Schuhmacher passes to the more traditional phrases of the New Year's greeting, praying that his friends shall be protected from wars, pestilence, earthquage, and other dangers, that the coming year be blessed, that he prosper, receiving God's grace and spirit, good health, fortune and again peace, that whatever he do he completed with blessing, according to God's will and pleasure.

Comparing these two greetings with the first page of the one for 1785, show not only that the text was changed in that the pastor rewrote it in fresh verse, but the illumination comes to be more accurate (Fig. 334). Likewise, the greeting for 1786 (Fig. 335) was a fresh writing, although the ideas tended to remain well within the folk tradition.

Fig. 333. New Year's greeting for 1784.

Fig. 334. New Year's greeting for 1785.

The Bookplate

The blank pages in the front of books and manuscripts offered the early Pennsylvania illuminator opportunity to ply his craft. After the Colonial period this genre of *fraktur* developed into a somewhat traditional pattern, and by the time the Federal period was over it had become fixed. One of the earliest bits of illumination is a Schwenkfelder manuscript hymnal of 1753, quite simple in illumination, and a few hymnals with imprints of German printing houses have been found with illuminated flyleafs. Also, surprisingly, several copies of the Amish hymnal, *Die Ausbundt,* like Fronica Schneider's, have been found with no clues as to when they were illuminated.

The earliest dated illumination of a bookplate so far found is the one already illustrated (Fig. 308) made by Daniel Schuhmacher. It is the two-page illumination of the church record book for the Allemaengel Lutheran Church. Rather bold and stark in decoration, it contains suitable inscriptions. Another piece, made after the Revolution, is the double-page illumination of the pulpit Bible in the Easton Reformed Church which was given to the congregation by the Reverend Michael Schlatter who called himself "Inspector of the Free Churches of Philadelphia"—a somewhat pretentious title. The illumination was probably added several years after the gift of the Bible. Yet another Bible illumination was the work of the itinerant, Jacob Oberholtzer, who put into this work not only the *ex libris* of Hermann Rupp, the farmer gunsmith of Lehigh County, but also the record of his birth and baptism and that of his wife Susanna. A copy of a Christopher Sauer Bible with illumination by Oberholtzer, and one by another hand has been found.

One of the most interesting of eighteenth-century bookplates is that of Jacob Huppert, written by the Lancaster County schoolmaster, Christian Strenge. He quotes an interesting hymn from the Mennonite *Harfe* which repeats the old folk idea that at the twelfth hour of the day all creatures on land and sea praise their Creator and that every wild thing on this green earth entrusts himself to God.

Obviously the bookplate depends on books. While many bookplates were made for musical manuscripts used in the singing schools, the illuminated bookplate in printed works was, during the eighteenth century, limited. However during the first four decades of the nineteenth century the bookplate underwent expansion and development. This was due to two factors: first, to the rapid expansion of printing and second to the establishment of many provincial presses which turned out a considerable number of German books. The growth of church schools also aided, and the many singing schools which existed before the coming of the public schools led to rapid expansion of this form.

The book plate offered opportunity for sly versification about theft and honesty. So the bookplate of Christian Bachman, 1767, has the following: "Listen, book, to what I tell you; if someone comes and would take you away: say, let me remain in quiet rest; I belong to Christian Bachman." Jacob Hunsicker put this into his book: "Should this get lost, you can see my name here. I live in Skippack, in Perkiomen Township." Anna Stauffer quoted a more proverbial note on her verse, dated 1793: "This passes each day, who knows how near the end may be? Guide me, Thou dear Savior, and bring me into Thy Kingdom."

Three bookplates are illustrated: A signed four-part bookplate dated 1772 by Heinrich Otto with original verses (Fig. 336), the double-page illumination in two hands in the Sauer Bible (Fig. 337) and a traditional bookplate in a manuscript songbook (Fig. 338).

In diesem Jahr
werd friede Heil
der gantzen Christenheit zu Theil.

Triumph
Halleluja.
gott lässet aber
mahl ein Neues
Jahr erscheinen

Fig. 335. New Years greeting for 1786.

Fig. 336. Elisabeth Beck's bookplate, illuminated and signed by Johann Heinrich Otto. The verse appears to be an original one by the illuminator.

Fig. 337. Double-page illuminations in a copy of the Sauer Bible. The pages were done by two different people at different times.

Fig. 338. Maria Fretz's bookplate.

The House Blessing

Many house blessings, called *Haussegen,* have survived showing considerable variety and diversity both in decoration and text. Resting upon ancient folk traditions the Pennsylvania *Haussegen* is no different in mood from those of other regions and is of a piece with the Victorian wall plaques which simply said: "God Bless Our Home." However, our Pennsylvania pieces presented not only these verse prayers but illumination, and late in the period they they were printed. While varied in wording, these prayers follow well-established patterns and even traditional phraseology by which "wife and children, body and soul, property and goods, work and livestock" were commended into the divine hands. Night and darkness is; day breaks anew—so this seems to be a sort of morning prayer. All fear and fright is gone. God's angels, having protected us through the night, now will continue to guard all of His children. These folk prayers were continuously being reworked with fresh rhymes and some new ideas.

Fig. 339. Elisabeth Landes' *Haus-Segen.*

The one illustrated (Fig. 339) is signed by Elizabeth Landes. Although quite late, the illumination is fresh and shows how printed designs and handdrawn designs go together. This was printed in Lancaster.

Associated with the house blessing was a twelve hour remembrance, often done on the same sheet. As the house blessing seems to have originated as a morning prayer, so the twelve hour remembrance was a prayer for each of the hours of the waking day. Generally these prayers were arranged around a rationally allegorical order like two testaments for two o'clock, three orders (the teaching, military, and agrieulural), four last things, seven words on the Cross, Ten Commandments, eleven faithful disciples, and Twelve Apostles. Here we are taken straight back to medieval allegory when every object of the world and every idea was somehow an aspect of the life or work of Christ.

Also linked with the *Haussegen* and often enclosed in hearts was the heart clock, an inner monitor by which the more subjective processes and patterns came to be expressed— penitence, repentance, resignation, rebirth.

These forms of illumination were late and also were chiefly the product of itinerating writers, the same men who also made many of the birth certificates. Heinrich Otto had blanks printed, and he went from farm to farm with his blocks by which he stamped the designs in outline on the pieces. He was generally a welcome guest bringing news, tales, folklore, and stories often in a fantastic mood.

The Ephrata wall charts are a similar example of this genre of illuminated writings.

Labyrinths and Games

Pennsylvania Pietists, like the Quakers, were opposed to worldly amusements like card-playing and useless parlor nonsense. Rather they spent their time on more edifying pastimes. In the middle of the eighteenth century one of the more interesting of these was *Der Frommen Lotterie*, a series of one hundred and eighty-one tickets, each one with a verse written by the German religious poet, Gerhard Tersteegen. In place of wicked card games, and high-stakes gambling, devout farmers in the Pennsylvania piedmont spent their time in social gatherings on these and other pastimes. Several of these games became vehicles of *fraktur*.

One was the Labyrinth, (*Irrgarten*) the rationalization of life's pilgrimage in topsy-turvy printed broadsides. Here a long verse, of religious character, was printed first line right-side up and then topsy-turvy and sidewise so that the reader had to keep turning the piece as he read along. Colonial printers made these broadsides, perhaps on order by the roving illuminators, who illuminated them and sold them as they wandered about the rural countryside. Several hand-done labyrinths have turned up, both early and late, but for the most part they were printed. Heinrich Otto made many of them.

Another interesting phase of this religious play was the so-called metamorphoses, the folding patterns of design. As each fold is made new pictures are uncovered. Several methods of folding were used. One was to fold a square piece diagonally so that triangular areas were produced. With each fold new patterns emerged as apparently unconnected designs were integrated into the over-all pattern. Another method was to fold the paper laterally so that a division was across the middle of the piece. When closed a pattern of four related designs is shown. Also verses are included. The second design is a lion with the verse:

Der Löb vor seiner Höle brüllt	The lion roars before his den
bis das er ist mit raub erfullt,	Until he is filled with fierceness
ist bald verkehrt Ihn ein ander gesicht	Soon he changes into another form—
hebt auf und sieht wie wunderlich. . . .	Lift up and see how miraculously

Fig. 340. Printed and illuminated labyrinth by Heinrich Otto.

And then when the upper halves of each of the four sections are lifted the designs change. The second picture now shows a grifon with the verse:

Ein vogel grief möcht Ihr hier sehn	A bird griffin here you can see,
Ein halbes Thier und Vögel thier,	Half beast and bird.
So thut das blat hinunter	How fold the lower part
So wirst du sehn ein grösser wunder	And you will see a greater wonder

So, closing the upper half and opening the lower half the third sequence of pictures shows; now the griffin has become an owl. And finally, opening the lower half exposes a fourth set of designs; now the owl is an eagle, the only bird that flies into the sun and is not blinded.

There seems to be little European tradition for these pieces, and they appear to have come out of our Pennsylvania sectarian tradition.

Miscellaneous Forms of Fraktur Writing

The Pennsylvania art of illuminated writing, beginning at Ephrata in close association with religious poetry and music, and moving through many phases, finally expanded to include secular forms and themes, here coming to heights of development known in Europe. While European folk illumination never reached such heights, apart from the illuminated manuscripts made in medieval monastaries, our Pennsylvania art did achieve considerable freedom from older patterns.

By the third decade of the nineteenth century Pennsylvania illumination had reached the fullness of its development and the best examples made after that time were from outlying regions like Somerset and Juniata counties and the Mahatonga Valley. Moreover, sons of earlier illuminators continued their fathers' work, as Wilhelm Otto, who made *Taufscheine* in Snyder County. Carl Friedrich Eglemann even published a book on the art, endeavoring to continue it.

Secular pieces were made. Valentines came to be popular and some were elaborately scissored-out with delicately cut designs (Fig. 342) such as the one made in 1799, which contains a crude English verse, obviously written by some smitten swain:

Four hearts in one I do behold,
They in each other do infold,
I cut them out on such a night
And send them to my hearts delight,
On such a Night, the hour of nine,
I chuse you for my valentine,
I chuse you out from all the rest,
The reson is I liked you best,
Some draw valentines by lotts,
Some draw them that they love nott,
But I draw you which I do chuse
I hope you will not refuse,
My heart within my breast doth ake,
A tonge I have but dare not speak,
If I should speak and should not speed,
Then my poor heart would break indeed.

And finally the art of illumination came to be freed from all words and could communicate its message without them, as in the piece picturing the military wedding (Fig. 343). While traditional designs like birds and flowers appear here with the tree of life, words now are unnecessary and they have been thrust into the background. Here the Pennsylvania art of illumination has come to the end of its development.

While it thrived, however, it was a truly magnificent achievement, far and away the most distinctive form of early Pennsylvania art.

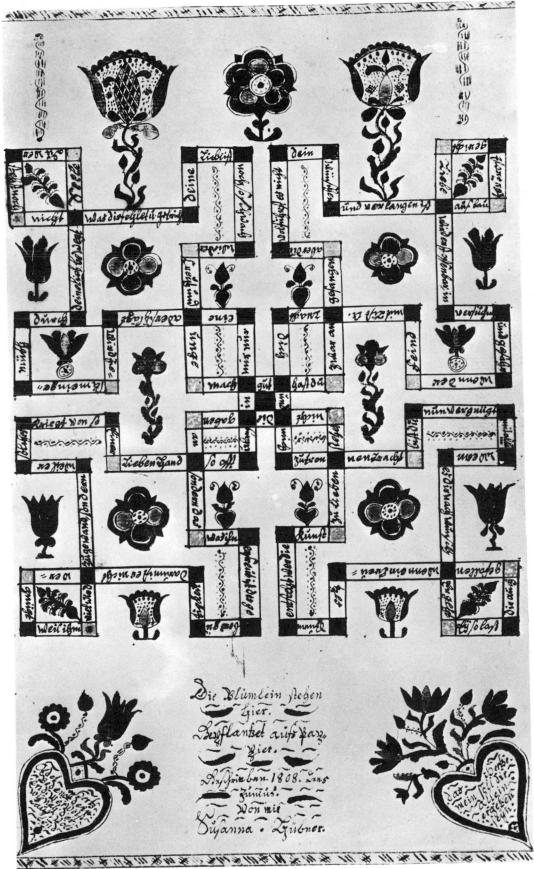

Fig. 341. Hand-drawn labyrinth by Susanna Hübner.

Fig. 342. Valentine with English inscription.

Fig. 343. The military wedding.

And finally the art of illumination came to be freed from all words and could communicate its message without them, as in the piece picturing the military wedding (Fig. 343). While traditional designs like birds and flowers appear here with the tree of life, words now are unnecessary and they have been thrust into the background. Here the Pennsylvania art of illumination has come to the end of its development.

While it thrived, however, it was a truly magnificent achievement, far and away the most distinctive form of early Pennsylvania art.

Fig. 344.

Conclusion

Imagination was in truth richly used in the arts and crafts of early Pennsylvania. For the freedom which William Penn had given us was creative, letting our forebears make many new cultural forms in which their spirits were expressed. This freedom, when joined with some of the most fertile land in America, unshackled the imagination and let our ancestors adjust quickly to their American environment.

The story of what they did with their freedom has yet to be told. But the record of what they made is clear. We can see it in the things we collect and cherish. Freedom is expressed not only in the live-and-let-live tolerance of our religious settlement but also in the common objects of our daily life. A free weaver makes more designs than one bound by strict regulations and custom. If there is one lesson that study of early Pennsylvania culture gives us it is that spiritual freedom liberates the common intelligence and lets man make new cultural forms.

Just to list the new forms which were made, or adapted, in early Pennsylvania is itself impressive evidence of the fruit of Penn's freedom. In architecture the log cabin was first introduced into America by the Swedes and Germans and became an American institution. Here too the Georgian style first was at home. Here the Greek revival began in America. In the field of furniture Pennsylvania produced many new forms. Here was created—and this seems to be the right word—the magnificent Philadelphia highboy, a form uncommon in Europe which here gained magnificence. Here too was developed, as an expression of the plain mood, the Philadelphia Windsor, a chair which was sent all over British America. Here too lived dower chest and *schank*. In the fine arts we must claim that one of our sons, Valentin Haidt, was far and away the best trained and most prolific professional painter in Colonial America who worked both as imaginative artist and limner under strong Pietist control. Another Pennsylvania son, Benjamin West, succeeded Sir Joshua Reynolds as President of the Royal Academy in London and became the father of a distinctly American school of painters. Also, there were many new craft forms: the Conestoga wagon, the long rifle, the balanced axe were some of them. And finally the whole field of illumination developed to a point where, as a German folklorist says, it is now the key which unlocks European peasant art.

What more can be said about a provincial colony, far from the cultural centers of Europe? Our freedom was building a new world.

Moreover, in Pennsylvania, as also in the other American Colonies to lesser degree, the tension between elegant and plain mounted as the eighteenth century progressed. There can be no question that the elegant taste of the Philadelphia of the 1760s was out of step with the rising plain of middle class America which was showing in the interior. The tension between aristocratic elegance and what may be called the bourgeois plain was to come to political expression in the patriot-tory conflicts of the Revolution. The Revolution killed the age of elegance. As we see it, the exquisite pieces made in Philadelphia during the immediate pre-Revolutionary period did not root themselves in the American way. Rather it was the plain tradition which, carried to interior America, became the fabric out of which our common culture emerged.

Furthermore, this American plain was in advance of Europe. Just as our revolution preceded the French, so our cultural revolution was earlier too. That which was conservative to Americans was radical to Londoners, so far ahead had the Colonial experience moved.

Indeed, it was this egalitarian spirit, linked to the plain, from which American life was to come; for it looked, not backwards to the feudal courts of Europe, but forward towards the Kentucky Hills, and even beyond, to where the new America was waiting to be born.

SOURCES OF THE ILLUSTRATIONS

1. Photograph by Wiliam B. Daub.
2-3. Courtesy of the Pennsylvania Historical and Museum Commission.
4. Photograph by Wiliam B. Daub.
5-8. Photograph by Karl F. Lutz.
9. Photograph courtesy of John Y. Kohl and the Allentown *Call-Chronicle*.
10. From an old photograph in the files of John Baer Stoudt.
11. Photograph by Mel Horst.
12. Photograph by W. W. Dietrich, 1905.
13. Photograph by William B. Daub.
14. Photograph by Karl F. Lutz.
15-16. Photograph courtesy of the Pennsylvania Historical and Museum Commission.
17. Photograph by Karl F. Lutz.
18-19 Photograph by John Baer Stoudt, 1912.
20. Photograph taken March 26, 1887, found in the files of John Baer Stoudt.
21. Photograph taken by John Baer Stoudt, 1914.
22. Photograph by W. W. Dietrich, 1908.
23. Photograph by John Baer Stoudt, 1914.
24. Photograph by Larry Burns.
25. Photograph by W. W. Dietrich, 1905.
26. Photograph by W. W. Dietrich, 1907.
27. Photograph courtesy of the Pennsylvania Historical and Museum Commission.
28. Photograph by William B. Daub.
29. Photograph courtesy of the Pennsylvania Historical and Museum Commission.
30. Photograph courtesy of Stuart Bolger and the Moravian Provincial Archives, Bethlehem.
31. Photograph courtesy of Stuart Bolger and the Kemmerer Museum, Bethlehem.
32. Photograph from the files of John Baer Stoudt.

33. Photograph by Karl F. Lutz.
34. Photograph Courtesy of the Pennsylvania Historical and Museum Commission.
35-39. Photographs by Karl F. Lutz.
40. Photograph by William B. Daub.
41. Photostat courtesy of the Historical Society of Pennsylvania.
42. Photograph from the collection of the Independence National Historical Park.
43. Photograph from the collection of the Independence National Historical Park.
44. Courtesy of the Historical Society of New York.
45. Photograph by John Baer Stoudt, 1915.
46. Photograph courtesy of Universal Atlas Cement, a Division of United States Steel Corporation.
47. Photograph by Guy Reinert.
48. Photograph by John Joseph Stoudt.
49-50. Photographs by Guy Reinert.
51. Photograph courtesy of the Allentown *Call-Chronicle*.
52-53. Photographs by Guy Reinert.
54. Photograph courtesy of Stuart Dewson.
55. Photograph by W. W. Dietrich, 1908.
56-57. Photographs courtesy of Philip F. Cowan.
58. Photograph courtesy of the Pennsylvania Historical and Museum Commission.
59. Courtesy of the Henry Francis duPont Winterthur Museum.
60. Courtesy of the Pennsylvania Historical and Museum Commission.
61-62. Courtesy of the Henry Francis duPont Winterthur Museum.
63. Photograph courtesy of Philip F. Cowan.
64. Courtesy of the Henry Francis duPont Winterthur Museum.
65. Courtesy of the Philadelphia Museum of Art.
66. Courtesy of the Henry Francis duPont Winterthur Museum.
67. Courtesy of the Philadelphia Museum of Art.
68. Photograph from the collection of Independence National Historical Park.
69-70. Courtesy of the Henry Francis duPont Winterthur Museum.
71. Courtesy of the Metropolitan Museum of Art.
72-73. Courtesy of the Philadelphia Museum of Art. Photographs by Karl F. Lutz.
74-76. Courtesy of the Philadelphia Museum of Art. Photographs by Karl F. Lutz.
77. Formerly in the collection of Arthur J. Sussel, who supplied this photograph.
78. Courtesy of Dr. Albert C. Barnes and the Barnes Foundation.
79. This photograph was taken in 1926 when this piece was exhibited at the Sesquicentennial Celebration as part of the Pennsylvania exhibit.
80. Courtesy of the Henry Francis duPont Winterthur Museum.
81-84. Courtesy of the Philadelphia Museum of Art.
85. Courtesy of the Henry Francis duPont Winterthur Museum.
86. From the private collection of Titus Geesey.

87. Photograph courtesy of Stuart Dewson.
88. Courtesy of Stuart Bolger and the Kemmerer Museum, Bethlehem.
89. Courtesy of the Philadelphia Museum of Art.
90. Courtesy of Philip F. Cowan.
91-92. Courtesy of the Philadelphia Museum of Art.
93. Courtesy of the *Index of American Design*.
94. Courtesy of Owen C. Stout.
95. Photograph taken by Titus Geesey while these objects, now in the Geesey collection of the Philadelphia Museum of Art, were still in his home.
96. Photograph taken when the piece was exhibited in the Pennsylvania building at the Sesquicentennial. The desk now is in the Henry Francis duPont Winterthur Museum.
97. Courtesy of the Philadelphia Museum of Art.
98. Courtesy of the Henry Francis duPont Winterthur Museum.
99. Formerly in the collection of George Horace Lorimer.
100-101. Courtesy of Philip F. Cowan.
102. Courtesy of Daniel M. Yost II. Photograph courtesy of Philip F. Cowan.
103-104. Courtesy of the Henry Francis duPont Winterthur Museum.
105-107. Courtesy of the Historical Society of Pennsylvania.
108. Courtesy of the Henry Francis duPont Winterthur Museum.
109. From the collection of Independence National Historical Park.
110. Courtesy of the Historical Society of Pennsylvania.
111-114. These four paintings by Johann Valentin Haidt are copyrighted by the Board of Elders of the Northern Diocese of the Church of the United Brethren in the United States of America (Moravian) and are used by their permission and the courtesy of Bishop Kenneth J. Hamilton.
115. Courtesy of the Yale University Art Gallery, the Lelia A. and John Hill Morgan Collection.
116-117. Courtesy of the Historical Society of Pennsylvania.
118. Courtesy of the Historical Society of Pennsylvania.
119. Courtesy of the New York Historical Society, New York City.
120. Photograph from the Collection of Independence National Historical Park.
121. Courtesy of the Philadelphia Museum of Art.
122-123. Courtesy of the Philadelphia Museum of Art.
124. Courtesy of John Y. Kohl.
125. Courtesy of the Fogg Art Museum, Harvard University.
126. Courtesy of the Fogg Art Museum, Harvard University.
127. Courtesy Helen B. Johnson. Photograph courtesy Philip F. Cowan.
128. Courtesy of the Henry Francis duPont Winterthur Museum.
129. Courtesy Gertrude Rittenhouse.
130. Courtesy of the Landis Valley Farm Museum and the Pennsylvania Historical and Museum Commission.
131. Courtesy of Conrad C. Miller, Jr., and the Geneological and Historical Society of Northampton County. Photograph by Richard Thorne.
137. Photograph courtesy Philip F. Cowan.
133-134. Formerly in the collection of J. Stodgell Stokes.
135. Formerly in the collection of Arthur J. Sussell.

136. Courtesy of the Yale University Art Gallery.

137-139. Courtesy of the Philadelphia Museum of Art.

140-141. Courtesy of the Landis Valley Farm Museum and the Pennsylvania Historical and Museum Commission.

142-143. Courtesy of the Bucks County Historical Society.

144. Photograph courtesy of Philip F. Cowan.

145-146. Courtesy of the Philadelphia Museum of Art.

147-151. Courtesy of the Historical Society of York County.

152-153. Courtesy of the Philadelphia Museum of Art.

154. From the author's collection.

155. Courtesy of the Philadelphia Museum of Art.

156. Courtesy of the Historical Society of Berks County.

157. Courtesy of the Bucks County Historical Society.

158. Courtesy of the Metropolitan Museum of Art.

159. Photograph by W. W. Dietrich.

160-161. Courtesy of the Historical Society of Bucks County.

162. Courtesy of Henry Chapman Mercer; found in the files of John Baer Stoudt.

163. Courtesy of the Philadelphia Museum of Art.

164. Formerly in the Collection of Arthur J. Sussel, who supplied this photograph.

165. Photograph by John A. Kubil.

166. Courtesy of the Berks County Historical Society.

167. Courtesy of Philip F. Cowan.

168. Courtesy of the Philadelphia Museum of Art.

169. Courtesy of the Henry Francis duPont Winterthur Museum.

170. Courtesy of the Philadelphia Museum of Art.

171. Courtesy of the Henry Francis duPont Winterthur Museum.

172. Courtesy of the Philadelphia Museum of Art.

173. This photograph was taken when the piece was still in the Odenwelder Collection. It is now in the Henry Francis duPont Winterthur Museum.

174-175. Courtesy of the Philadelphia Museum of Art.

176. Courtesy of the Henry Francis duPont Winterthur Museum.

177-178. Courtesy of the Philadelphia Museum of Art.

179-180. Courtesy of the Henry Francis duPont Winterthur Museum.

181. Courtesy of Mrs. Ralph Beaver Strassburger.

182. Courtesy of the Henry Francis duPont Winterthur Museum.

183. Courtesy of Mrs. Ralph Beaver Strassburger.

184-186. Courtesy of the Henry Francis duPont Winterthur Museum.

187. Formerly in the author's possession, now owned by Henry Francis duPont.

188. Courtesy of Phillip F. Cowan.

189. Courtesy of the Philadelphia Museum of Art.

190. Courtesy of William W. Swallow. Photograph by John Kubil.

191. Formerly in the Arthur J. Sussel Collection. Some of these pieces now are exhibited at Millgrove, home of John James Audubon.

192. Courtesy of William W. Swallow. Photograph by John A. Kubil.

193. Courtesy of the Metropolitan Museum of Art.

194. Formerly in the Collection of John Baer Stoudt.

195. Courtesy of the Philadelphia Museum of Art.
196. Present whereabouts of this piece is not known. Photograph taken when the piece was exhibited at the Sesquicentennial in 1926.
197. Courtesy of the Henry Francis duPont Winterthur Museum.
198. Courtesy of Joe Kindig, Jr.
199. Courtesy of the Metropolitan Museum of Art.
201-202. Courtesy of Joe Kindig, Jr.
203. Courtesy of the Metropolitan Museum of Art and the *Index of American Design*.
204-205. Courtesy of Joe Kindig, Jr.
206. Courtesy of the Landis Valley Farm Museum. Photograph by Reichmann.
207. Courtesy of the *Index of American Design*, National Gallery of Art.
208. Courtesy of the Pennsylvania Historical and Museum Commission.
209. Courtesy of the Historical Society of Bucks County.
210. Courtesy of Titus Geesey.
211. Courtesy of the Pennsylvania Historical and Museum Commission.
212. Courtesy of the Landis Valley Farm Museum. Photograph by Reichmann.
213. Source unknown.
214. In the author's collection.
215. Courtesy of the *Index of American Design*.
216. Courtesy of the Landis Valley Farm Museum.
217. Courtesy of Eric deJonge and the Pennsylvania Historical and Museum Commission.
218. From the files of John Baer Stoudt.
219. Courtesy of the Henry Francis duPont Winterthur Museum.
220. Courtesy of Paul J. deLong.
221. Courtesy of A. K. Hostetter.
222. Courtesy of Elisabeth A. Stoudt.
223. Courtesy of the Metropolitan Museum of Art.
224-227. In the author's collection.
228. Courtesy of Elisabeth A. Stoudt.
229. Courtesy of Oliver Lewis Christman.
230. Courtesy of the Pennsylvania State Library.
231. Courtesy of J. Stodgell Stokes.
232. Courtesy of Kirke Bryan.
233. In the author's collection.
234. In the author's collection. This was his grandfather's quilt.
235. Courtesy of Mrs. Vernon K. Melhado.
236-239. Courtesy of Elizabeth A. Stoudt.
240. Photograph taken by W. W. Dietrich, 1911.
241. Courtesy of the Whitman Chocolate Company.
242. Courtesy of Elisabeth A. Stoudt.
243. Courtesy of the Pennsylvania Historical and Museum Commission.
244. Courtesy of Nancy Yost Stoudt.
245. Courtesy of P. M. Vogt.
246. Formerly in the collection of Arthur J. Sussel.
247. Courtesy of the *Index of American Design*.
248. Courtesy of the American Museum in Britain and Dr. Dallas Pratt.

The photograph is by and with the courtesy of the Sport and General Press Agency, London.

249. Courtesy of the *Index of American Design*.

250. Courtesy of the Philadelphia Museum of Art.

251. Courtesy of the *Index of American Design*.

252. Courtesy William Swallow. Photograph by John A. Kukil.

253. Courtesy of Edward W. Schlechter.

254. Photograph by W. W. Dietrich.

255. From the author's collection. Photograph by William B. Daub.

256. Courtesy Eric de Jonge and the Pennsylvania Historical and Museum Commission.

257. Formerly in the Arthur J. Sussel Collection.

258. Courtesy of the Philadelphia Museum of Art.

259. From the author's collection.

260. Photograph by W. W. Dietrich, 1905.

261. Photograph by Robert L. Schaeffer, Jr.

262. Courtesy of Robert L. Schaeffer, Jr.

263. From the files of John Baer Stoudt.

264. Photograph by Guy Reinert.

265. From the files of John Baer Stoudt.

266. Photograph courtesy of Arthur.D. Graeff.

267. Photograph by William B. Daub.

268. From the files of John Baer Stoudt.

269. Photograph courtesy of the Allentown *Call-Chronicle*.

270. Courtesy of Eric de Jonge and the Pennsylvania Historical and Museum Commission.

271-272. Courtesy of the Music Division, Library of Congress.

273-277. Courtesy of the Pennsylvania Historical and Museum Commission.

278-279. Courtesy of the Music Division, Library of Congress.

280. Courtesy of the Rare Book Room, Free Library of Philadelphia.

281. Courtesy of the Franklin and Marshall College Library.

282-283. Courtesy of the Schwenkfelder Library.

284-287. Courtesy of the Henry Francis duPont Winterthur Museum.

288-289. Courtesy of the Philadelphia Museum of Art.

290-297. Courtesy of the Schwenkfelder Library. Photographs by Daub.

298. Courtesy of the Historical Society of Montgomery County. Photograph by Daub.

299. Courtesy Joe Kindig, Jr.

300. From the author's collection. Photograph by Daub.

301-302. Courtesy of the Schwenkfelder Library. Photographs by Daub.

303. Photograph courtesy of Joe Kindig, Jr.

304-306. Courtesy of the Schwenkfelder Library. Photographs by Daub.

307. Courtesy of the Philadelphia Museum of Art.

308. Source unknown. Photograph in files of John Baer Stoudt.

309-312. Photographs from the files of John Baer Stoudt.

313. Courtesy of the Metropolitan Museum of Art.

314-316. Courtesy of the rare book room, Philadelphia Free Library.

317. Courtesy of Edward W. Schlechter.

318. Courtesy of Kirke Bryan.

319. Courtesy of the Henry Francis duPont Winterthur Museum.
320. Courtesy of the Historical Society of the Reformed Church, Lancaster.
321. Courtesy of Robert L. Schaeffer.
322. From the author's collection.
323. Courtesy of the Historical Society of Bucks County.
324. Courtesy of the Metropolitan Museum of Art.
325. From the files of John Baer Stoudt.
326. Courtesy of the Schwenkfelder Library. Photograph by Daub.
327. Courtesy of the Metropolitan Museum of Art.
328. Formerly in the collection of Arthur J. Sussel.
329. Photograph by John Kubil.
330. Formerly in the collection of Arthur J. Sussel.
331. Courtesy of Titus Geesey.
332-335. From the files of John Baer Stoudt.
326. Courtesy of the Schwenkfelder Library. Photograph by Daub.
327. Courtesy of Howard K. Fretz.
338. Courtesy of the Rare Book Room, Philadelphia Free Library.
339. Courtesy of the Philadelphia Museum of Art.
340. From the author's collection.
341. Courtesy of the Schwenkfelder Library.
342. Courtesy of the Philadelphia Museum of Art.
343. Courtesy of the Henry Francis duPont Winterthur Museum.
344. Photograph of Hope Lodge by Karl Rath.

INDEX